Jordan Swain

LINEA JOHNSON is a recent graduate from Seattle University, with a major in English and creative writing. Prior to transferring to SU, she completed three years at Columbia College, Chicago, in a musical performance program. Linea recently worked as an intern at the World Health Organization in the mental health department. She is a national speaker and writer, advocating for understanding and support for people with mental illness and the elimination of the stigma surrounding it.

Jordan Swain

CINDA JOHNSON, Ed.D., is a professor and director of the special education graduate program at Seattle University. She is a national leader in the area of transition from high school to post–high school settings for young people with disabilities. She has written articles and book chapters in the area of secondary special education and transition services, including youth with emotional and behavioral disorders and mental illnesses.

Praise for *Perfect Chaos*

"*Perfect Chaos* is as much a map as it is a memoir, a powerful resource for families and individuals navigating the confusing and painful world of bipolar and mental illness. A brave and realistic, yet life-affirming, message of hope."

—Claire Fontaine and Mia Fontaine, authors of *Come Back: A Mother and Daughter's Journey Through Hell and Back*

"A remarkable story about remarkable women! Linea and Cinda brilliantly light a path to hope, understanding, and acceptance as they smash through the stigma of brain illness. Be inspired by the strong voice they give to patients, relatives, caregivers, and especially to those unable or afraid to show their wants, needs, hope."

—Patrick J. Kennedy, former U.S. Congressman and cofounder, One Mind for Research

"I read Cinda and Linea's words with tears in my eyes. This brave and honest book will educate people who have little understanding of mental illness and allow those who live with mental illness a knowing that they are not alone."

—Jessie Close, cofounder, Bring Change 2 Mind

"*Perfect Chaos* is a memoir of a daughter and mother working together to overcome the daily challenges of living with a mental illness. Through their trials and triumphs, their story provides encouragement and hope for individuals and their families affected by these illnesses."

—Former First Lady Rosalynn Carter, founder of the Carter Center Mental Health Program and author of *Within Our Reach: Ending the Mental Health Crisis*

"This inspirational book teaches us the importance of determination, resilience, love, and HOPE. It is a testament to the human spirit that refuses to be defeated by a brain disorder—a must-read."

—Pete Earley, author of *Crazy: A Father's Search Through America's Mental Health Madness*

"About the fierce, transformative love between a mother and daughter and how they both learn to share their truths."

—Glenn Close, actress and cofounder, Bring Change 2 Mind

"A no-holds-barred 'biography of depression,' based on the alternating journal entries of a mother and daughter . . . This is a gritty account of what it is like to be down in the trenches with mental illness—fighting suicidal thoughts, battling the aftereffects of shock treatment, dealing with medication and its side effects, and resisting the temptations of alcohol and street drugs. . . . A simultaneously painful and inspiring page-turner." —*Kirkus Reviews*

"This book is a must-read for parents worried about their teen or college-aged child. It is equally compelling for teens and young adults who are struggling to understand their moods, behavior, and dark thoughts. It is a story of hope and extraordinary courage." —The Balanced Mind Foundation

"Definitely a must-read . . . A well-written, clearly told, inspiring story." —Examiner.com

"The journey for Linea and her family is a moving and hopeful one, as they better understand how she reacts to the illness, and realize that being bipolar is only a part of someone's life, not the whole." —*Publishers Weekly*

"Lyrically written with razor-sharp honesty, *Perfect Chaos* is the story of Linea's day-to-day fight with bipolar disorder and her astounding efforts to piece together her life and achieve her own stability and independence." —*She Knows*

"A grippingly honest account of Linea's debilitating emotional turmoil . . . A moving expression of both the power and limits of Cinda's love and support." —*bp Magazine*

perfect chaos

a daughter's journey to survive bipolar, a mother's struggle to save her

linea johnson and
cinda johnson

ST. MARTIN'S GRIFFIN
New York

 For information, address St. Martin's Press, 175 Fifth Avenue, New York, N.Y. 10010.

www.stmartins.com

Design by Gretchen Achilles

The Library of Congress has cataloged the hardcover edition as follows:

Johnson, Linea.
Perfect chaos : a daughter's journey to survive bipolar, a mother's struggle to save her / Linea Johnson and Cinda Johnson. — 1st ed.
p. cm.
ISBN 978-0-312-58182-4 (hardcover)
ISBN 978-1-4299-4888-3 (e-book)
1. Johnson, Linea—Health. 2. Johnson, Cinda E. 3. Manic-depressive persons—United States—Biography. 4. Mothers and daughters—Biography. I. Johnson, Cinda E. II. Title.
RC516.J64 2012
616.89'50092—dc23
[B]

2012011022

ISBN 978-1-250-02325-4 (trade paperback)

St. Martin's Griffin books may be purchased for educational, business, or promotional use. For information on bulk purchases, please contact Macmillan Corporate and Premium Sales Department at 1-800-221-7945 extension 5442 or write specialmarkets@macmillan.com.

First St. Martin's Griffin Edition: May 2013

10 9 8 7 6 5 4 3 2 1

To Charlie, for never turning away

In Loving Memory of Steve

contents

Mom and Dad, if you ever read this, then it is because I survived and published this attempt of a biography of depression. Please forgive any of the discoveries you make while reading. I love you.

—*Linea's Journal*

introduction

cinda In a memory from the not so faraway past, I am standing in the hallway outside the locked entry to psychiatric Unit C, removing the strings from my daughter's sweatpants. There is another woman waiting at the door who looks just like me. She could be a nurse, a doctor, a teacher, a professor. I remember this woman. I have seen her in the hospital hallways before; we are on a similar journey. Her daughter is the same height as mine, approaching six feet tall. Her daughter cannot walk more than twenty steps without a walker or wheelchair. Her daughter weighs a mere 105 pounds. I am pulling the strings from my daughter's sweatpants because she is on a suicide watch. The woman waiting at the door is praying that her daughter will not die of starvation in the most well-fed country in the world. I am praying that medicine, therapy, faith, and love can save my daughter from herself.

How did I get here? What signs did I miss over the last few years? Could I have saved my daughter from this pain? Could I have prevented my family this agony? Are these questions every family asks when a child or sister or mother or friend is hospitalized, in the vortex of a suicidal depression or another mental illness?

Since that day in the hospital, I have learned that love alone will not save someone from depression. You cannot simply love someone back to the safe ground of wellness (oh, that we could!). But you can love someone enough to seek, advocate, and fight for medical treatment. In fact, without that love—a love that drives you to fight for the life of your loved one—people like my daughter and the daughter of the mother in the hallway are surely lost.

I cannot read an article or story about a mother losing her son or daughter without crying, without feeling the cutting pain of fear and love that I remember so well. I came so close to losing our child. Those days and months and years, it felt as if I were hanging on to her as she dangled over the side of a cliff, as if I were holding on to her by only a piece of clothing, a very slim piece. I hoped it wouldn't tear, that she wouldn't fall from my grip. Her dad was hanging on, too, and our family and friends behind us. With all of us hanging on for her dear life, we didn't let go. She fought as well, trying her hardest to climb back up. Sometimes she was able to fight, sometimes she fought us to let go of her, and sometimes she merely dangled while we held her weight. We would not give up.

In the following pages, my daughter Linea and I tell a painful story that is only a part of the journey we took, and are still taking. It is all true. When I read Linea's words for the first time, I was filled with agony—but also with pride. She had written in journals since grade school and continued to write even during her darkest days. She is amazingly honest in her writing and in her life, and she chose to share her deepest thoughts. Hers is a voice of a young person struggling with the painful and difficult life we all share, but one that she has inhabited more deeply, more painfully, perhaps more honestly than most of us. Her words are horrific and sad and even strangely funny at times. Her honesty and willingness to share her writings and her thoughts with me moved us to a place of deeper truth with each other. It opened the door to a closer relationship that, while often painful, developed into trust and honesty that have moved beyond our family and into the world around us. This honesty changed me. I found strength I didn't know I had. I faced fears that had lurked in the back of my mind for years and, when brought into the light, healed some very old wounds. It was with the guidance of exceptional doctors and nurses, support of family, friends, and occasional angels on earth, and, mostly, the courage of my daughter that we moved from that place of horror to where we are now.

We are privileged in having the resources that allowed Linea to receive the care that she did. In our day-to-day and often minute-by-minute fight for her life, it was very clear to me that we have advantages and therefore a responsibility to add to the understanding about mental illnesses and to advocate for treatment and support for those who aren't nearly as lucky as we are. Ours is a journey through illness, but it is not only that. It is a journey steeped in love, a love that would not give up on our daughter's life. The energy and time it takes to find good treatment, continued support, and understanding for the person with a mental illness as well as his or her family are often overwhelming, but they are also often the difference between recovery and devastation.

linea I'm sitting in the living room of the home my boyfriend and I have created. I am sitting once again in my green chair (it has been through almost as much as I have) and I am crying. Pain and tears keep welling up, and I am beginning to get angry with myself for displaying these emotions. Josh is helping exactly as I've asked him to in the past. He sits and reads, pretending to pay no attention to my tears, while at the same time lending support by staying in the room with me and being aware of my pain.

I can't stand it, and I do what comes naturally in moments of pain: I head to the nearest tiled surface. I flee for the bathroom, knowing that if I can get these emotions under control within five minutes I can pretend I just had to pee. But I can't do it. I can't, and as usual I collapse on the floor, welcoming the shock of cold tile against my skin.

The bathroom is stark white. It is overwhelmingly white. I lean against the wall and try to figure out where this sudden onslaught of emotion came from. Why am I crying? What started this? Why am I crying when I am so happy with my current life? When I know that I am not experiencing any form of depression? I think and think; I try to read myself and see if there have been any overlooked emotions in the last few weeks, anything I need to examine further, that might be the source of this sadness.

Suddenly I realize where the tears and this pain came from. The book. Josh read the book. I had wanted him to. He is one of only two people who know me who have actually read these pages and heard through my own voice what I have been through.

Why is divulging my story so hard? Why do I want to expose my deepest insecurities and fears and pain to the public? Why, when I can't even show my boyfriend, a person who I can tell anything to, would I want to show more people the dirty chaos of mania, the humiliation of a drug test, the blood, pain, and starvation that accompany a suicidal depression? The pain inside is like I'm slowly being filled with a thick muddy water threatening to drown me from the inside out, and it is building and building. With my knees tight to my chest and my back to the wall, I'm swaying like I used to in the old days of wine and razor blades.

"Bear? Hey, babe? You okay?"

"I'm fine!"

"Just checking. You sure you don't want to talk about anything?"

"I'm fine! Leave me alone!"

Shit. Now I'm being mean. I hate it when I get like this. I get mean and push people away until they really don't want to help me when I really do need help. I hate myself. I hate this. I'm crazy. No one wants to read this book. No one needs to hear this sadness inside and this demented angry hate that I create for myself. Why am I doing this?

I sob on one side of the door. Josh leans with his head on the other side. I begin to hyperventilate. I begin to choke. I begin to stop breathing. Josh runs to grab a paper bag (he is trained as an EMT) and pushes the door open. He makes me sit up. I can't breathe. I'm panicking. He helps me up. He makes me stay up. He holds my head. Makes me breathe. Tries to soothe me. I yell and cry and tell him to leave me the fuck alone. This pain is all-consuming; I don't want him, I don't want anybody, it's all I can do to simply exist with this pain. My body is becoming numb. My face is tingling. My hands are tingling. I feel faint. I'm going to faint. My eyes see black spots, and I'm panting. I can't get air. Josh keeps me sitting up. Doesn't let me lie on the floor. Goddamn it! Just let me lie down! Leave me the fuck alone! I need to lie down! I can't breathe! He tells me that if I need to lie down, I need to go out to the couch. He tells me that if I need to lie down, I should lie on my left side (or is it my right?). I can't understand what he is saying. I can't breathe! I can't breathe!

I am once again alone in the bathroom. I can once again breathe, and though I know Josh is still on the other side of the door, he has left me to be alone with my thoughts. Okay, Linea. Here we are again. You on the bathroom floor. Your boyfriend tired and worried. Your mind numb. Now, given that this hasn't happened in months and months, we must figure out where it came from. It's time to use the skills that you have gained during this long and continuing journey of yours.

First: your "Am I Depressed?" checklist.

Within the last week have you been unable to read/clean/get important things done? Have you been drinking alone? Do you spend hours sitting at the computer doing nothing? Have you been unable to cry? Do you find yourself staring vacantly into space for extended lengths of time until you suddenly snap back to reality forty-five minutes later? Do you feel a need to harm yourself?

No. No. No. No. No. No.

Second: "Am I Manic?"

Within the last few days, have you been pacing, shaking, or cleaning excessively? Do you have a lot of repetitious thoughts, words, or phrases? Have you started the mantra of "I need, I need, I need . . ."? Has there been excessive spending, partying, anything?

No. No. No. No.

Third: In general, have you had an upset stomach? Been throwing up? Been cutting? Been eating excessively? Been drinking excessively? Been restricting your eating?

No. No. No. No. No. No. Everything checks out fine. This is not a bipolar episode.

Are you afraid of sharing your story with unknown and known readers? Yes. Could this be the fear of perhaps not sharing this story at all? The fear of continuing to hide your true self and feelings from the world? Yes. Could these tears mean that perhaps you haven't quite accepted all of your past feelings and memories, all of the hospitalizations and misery and sadness? Yes. That you haven't yet processed what it means to have bipolar, how to live with it, how to carry on? Yes. Why, then, if sharing all of this creates such an onslaught of pain, are you continuing on?

Ah, this is the question I am looking for. I need to show people that mental illness is real. That one in five families experiences a mental-health condition and that those who live well with this don't always talk about it. I have to show that you can live well with this big scary word "bipolar." That it takes the hardest work you will ever do, but that it is possible to live a life of joy. I need to show that there are caring doctors and loving supporters. I need to show that though some of this takes luck, there is help out there. I need to show that you can take care of yourself, as painful and terrifying and hard as it is, and that though it becomes addicting to be a mess, living a healthy, stable life has more to offer. People need to know that it is okay to feel and that we can and will survive.

I want to share my story because I want to help society see that this is a common illness. That people don't choose to get sick and don't wish to live dangerously unstable lives. I need to show that this can happen to anyone. That this is something that is normal. I need to show that the people we see as having a mental illness, those on the streets or in hospitals, are those who need the most help. That the people who we read about in the headlines, those "psycho killers," are merely people who didn't get the help they needed and that, in fact, they represent one small sliver of those living with a mental illness. I want people to know that rather than being aggressive and dangerous, people living with a mental illness are more likely to become a victim of a crime. We need to see that we are all people with the potential for feeling or thinking in a way that can be seen as unstable. That we all have varying emotions and different brains. I want people to know that one in two college students will become clinically depressed or anxious, and that a leading cause of death for teenagers is suicide. Mental instability is everywhere, and until we embrace that fact and care for our neighbors, we will never overcome the stigma and save our children.

And finally, I want to stop getting the questions "You have . . . ?" "You are . . . ?" I'm what? Crazy? Twenty-two? Six feet tall? I so often hear "You? You, an intelligent, attractive, young, middle-class American? You went through this?" I want to stop hearing "Why?" Why? Why do people get up in the morning? Why is the sky blue? Why is my brain circuitry different than yours? Why do I have bipolar? Ask a scientist.

I don't choose to act this way or that. I don't choose to have crushing depressions or extreme manias. I don't choose to need extra help from my family and friends. I don't choose to sometimes feel like killing myself. Why did I do the things that I did in my life? Did I ever have the choice? I was given a gift and a curse at the same time, and the only choice I have ever had is how to accept it. I feel because I feel, and sometimes my feelings are more extreme than most people can imagine, but I always try my best.

Even through overdoses and suicidal ideation, I tried my best. I never chose this. I want people to know that mental health is a serious thing but also one that can be humorous and even inspiring and hopeful. I want people to understand that mental illness is not something merely made up or created. It doesn't spring from a desire to be eccentric, or a need for attention, or a way to act out. It is real and it is painful and it is powerful.

This is why I am on the bathroom floor tonight. Do I have the courage to explain these things? Do I have the voice? Do I have the energy? I must find the courage and the voice and the energy. I have to demonstrate that true compassion is possible if we just learn the stories and truly listen to the people. We are all just people, after all.

Suddenly I feel lighter. I pick myself up off the bathroom floor and wash the mascara tracks off my arms and legs. I go to the living room and tell Josh I'm sorry, I'm sorry, I'm sorry. But I don't need to. He understands. He's been there too. He knows it is painful to be human, and he also knows that it is human to show compassion.

1. nostalgia

cinda I am one of those moms who worry. My job from the moment I held each of my two precious baby girls in my arms was to keep them safe. Whether from my own sense of fragility in the world or some constant premonition of danger, keeping my children safe is a guiding light of my parenting. From my earliest years I was a caretaker. My mother was often ill while I was growing up and, as the oldest child, I became watchful and learned that a girl needs to be on her toes to assure safety. My skills as a caretaker and worrier continued when I had my own two daughters. I now had two lives to protect, and I took to it with enthusiasm, often to the annoyance of my girls. Although worrying about their safety has given me many sleepless nights, it may have also given me the strength and the stamina to face the most challenging days of parenting. Worry and my basic urge to protect kept me moving forward when I wanted to quit.

I would guess that to the outside world looking in, my family seems fairly typical. We are a family of four plus one more. Curt and I have two daughters, Jordan and Linea. Cliff became our son when he and Jordan were married. We live in and around Seattle, where it doesn't rain nearly as often as most people think. We are educated but not particularly wealthy when compared to our tiny corner of the world in which we live, but vastly wealthy compared to the world as a whole. Both my husband and I chose fields of study and professions where the dollars aren't large but the work is rewarding. We are in "caring professions"—I am a professor in the field of special education and Curt is a vocational rehabilitation counselor working primarily with patients with spinal cord injuries. He works at the University of Washington Medical Center, providing support to some of the most severely injured people from all over Washington, the Northwest, the nation and, often, the world.

Sometimes I think I chose my profession to secure skills and training that would further protect my family from whatever dangers might be out there. (I do know that the experiences in the forthcoming pages solidified my commitment to my work.) I am a professor at Seattle University, six miles across the city from Curt's office. We both work in the area of disability, disease, pain, and heartache; him on a daily basis, me with a slim buffer of graduate students and professionals between my office and the field. His office is on the same floor as patients who are new to catastrophic injuries and illness or are fighting the long haul of chronic disability.

I teach graduate students in special education, school psychology, and counseling, and conduct research in the field of disability. In addition to my work with students and schools,

I often work directly with families and individuals with barriers and challenges in their lives. I get phone calls, emails, and visits from students and parents lost in the maze of disability, trying to find their way out, in search of any help they can find. I was really good at providing advice. I was "professional." I knew the resources, the connections, and the steps to take. I offered information, suggestions, and sympathy. Looking back, I realize how little I knew from a personal perspective and how different it is to be lost in the maze of finding help for my own child while overwhelmed with an intense fear that I could lose her. I didn't know nearly as much as I thought I did.

As with most couples who have been together for many years, the traits that first attract you to your mate are often the very same characteristics that irritate you after a few years of marriage and then eventually come front and center again as a focus of love and appreciation. I was attracted to Curt's great strength, loyalty, and commitment. These qualities can also present as stubbornness and tenacity, which have made the females in our household angry with him at one time or another. Yet his steadfastness is one of the reasons we all love him: He is there for us, we can count on him. And while he often tells me how strong I am, he is the strength in our family. We couldn't have made it through those difficult years without him. His stubbornness and tenacity are what held us all together.

Jordan Suzanne is our older daughter. She is seven and a

half years older than Linea, and so growing up, Linea often had one and a half mothers. Jordan has always been intensely protective of her little sister. Jordan was a fierce girl and grew into a fierce woman whose beauty is a cover for her strength. She might look fragile, but she is not. She buries her fears deeply. She uses her superpowers when necessary and her wits and guile the rest of the time.

Jordan does not particularly like the display of strong emotions, particularly if tears are involved (even though she spent the two hours before and during her wedding crying from happiness). Jordan holds her feelings inside while she projects her very competent self to the world. She is strongly caring, loving, and kind, though she'd prefer that you didn't know it. But she has never been able to fool me or anyone else who knows her.

Art and music have always been part of our lives together. Jordan earned a degree in fine arts and has her own business. A gifted artist with creativity that springs from a vivid imagination, she paints, creates murals, and teaches art.

My daughters have always been close as sisters, sharing a wild sense of humor, passion for the arts, and deep love and adoration for each other. It is my greatest joy to be part of the girl trio of Jordan, Linea, and myself. We have spent hours dancing, singing, playing, and laughing. We are very entertaining, at least to ourselves.

Jordan married a man I would have chosen as my own son if I had been given the opportunity. Cliff is confident, kind, loyal, funny, smart, and handsome. He has a wicked sense of humor that he wields deftly. He fits comfortably into our family and provides Curt the space and male camaraderie in a house of women.

Linea is a musician. She plays any instrument she can get her hands on and showed a special attraction to the piano as soon as she was tall enough to reach the keyboard. I taught her to play a few songs before she started school, and from there she moved quickly to formal piano lessons. She practiced and practiced . . . and practiced some more. We never had to bribe, threaten, or even ask her. From an early age, she learned to play the viola, the guitar, and any other instruments with strings. She began music lessons in grade school, played in orchestras in middle and high school, and attended orchestra camps during the summer, where she experimented with more instruments. Music is a passion and sheer joy for her.

Linea also has the voice of an angel. In grade school she was known for her singing; she forced her friends into productions of *Phantom of the Opera, Cats, The Wizard of Oz,* and any other musical that caught her ear. She carried around a shoe box containing recordings and programs of the selected musical-of-the-month, which she produced on the playground during recess.

When Linea was ten years old and still going by her nickname of "Mia," we moved from a school district with only four hundred students total in kindergarten through twelfth grade to Western Washington. Her new middle school had more than six hundred students in the sixth to eighth grades, but the move didn't slow Linea down at all. In the first year of middle school, Linea walked onto the stage and introduced herself to an audience larger than her entire previous grade school. Holding a cordless mike, she said, "Hi, I'm Linea," and sang a hauntingly beautiful solo. Sitting in the audience, my hands were sweating with anxiety. I would *never* have had the nerve to do that!

Afterward, Linea said to me, "I told you I wanted to be a singer. Now can I take voice lessons?" Soon she added voice, viola, and guitar lessons to the piano lessons she began in elementary school. As she got older, she concentrated more and more on piano and voice.

In addition to her music, Linea played softball and basketball from an early age and continued into high school. She was headstrong, persistent, and competitive in music, sports, and school. But she was kind and very sensitive to her friends and their needs. Her sensitivity was acute and she was easily hurt by injustice, both real and perceived, to her friends and even strangers.

My description of young Linea may sound completely unrealistic, too good to be true, and you might be asking if as her mother I am exaggerating. But my description is accurate—Linea was preternaturally talented and hardworking; she was kind, loving, and a joy to be around. Later I wondered if her tenacity and ambition in music and sports may have been a detriment, as she pushed herself to extremes so as to do everything the best. I also wondered if her unwillingness to give up may have saved her as she later fought to live. In a million years we could not have guessed what was in store for her.

Things were more difficult when Linea started high school. Competition was fierce, as in all large high schools. There were competitive spots for sports and for music, and tryouts for both were nerve-racking. Everyone was working on applications for college and counting the number of star positions they held. Even the hours of community service were competitive and seemed to be more for résumé padding than for actual service. Her freshman year was successful and she appeared able to do it all. She was consistently on the honor roll with her grades, and she sang in honor choirs and ensembles, performed in shows and musicals, and played softball.

As a sophomore, she hit a wall—it became impossible for her to continue with all of her activities. She was pitching for the varsity fast-pitch softball team and simultaneously adding more commitments in musical performances, ensembles, and music lessons. There were simply not enough hours in the day to participate in both sports and music to the degree to which she wanted. The stress was taking its toll. She wasn't sleeping well, and she had times when she couldn't stop crying. I now know these were anxiety attacks, but at the time, I was amazed at how well she managed everything most of the time.

We spent hours talking about how to simplify her life,

and I offered her all the help that I could. I wanted her to be kinder to herself. I encouraged her to let some things go and wanted her to know that all she had to do was just "be." I wanted her to know that she didn't need to have an exact goal for her future, and that her activities could be just for fun and not to assure a scholarship to a prestigious music program. I compared her anxieties to those of Jordan's at the same age and wondered and worried if I should do more . . . but more what? I questioned whether we had pushed her into overexcelling with our pride in her successes. As parents we think we are supposed to give praise for things well done. Had we given her the message that she had to achieve all of this for us to be proud of her? Did I somehow help her define "perfect"? I worried and tried to reassure myself that this was a normal progression through adolescence. My worries would escalate and then suddenly she would feel better for a while—or at least I thought she did.

I knew she was struggling with too many commitments and too much pressure. It was difficult for her to decide what activities to leave behind. The professionals in her life didn't make it any easier. When she decided to quit sports, her coach pulled her aside and tried to talk Linea into continuing. The same pressure came from her music teachers, who pushed her to hang on to everything she was doing. She had the talent to excel in many areas but simply not enough time. When Linea finally made the hard decision to let sports go, she quickly filled every hour with music. She seemed unable to leave any empty space in her schedule.

While she was trying to figure out what to do with her own young life, her friends were also struggling. Her sleepless nights were often full of worry for her them and the things they had confided in her and she had sworn to secrecy. She tried desperately to fix their problems, problems of which parents were not likely aware. One of her biggest fears was about her best friend, Chrisy.

linea Sophomore year—I am lying on the grass in the backyard, on an old cotton blanket big enough to hold me, ten books, two journals, two pillows, sunscreen, and some homework. I'm in my swimsuit even though I know that sunbathing doesn't always do well with my fair skin. I need this lake of soft green grass. This big blue sky. This cocoon of evergreens. I need them because I feel happier this way. At least a tiny bit.

Two days ago, I told my favorite schoolteacher about Chrisy's problem. I told her because I thought she would understand, because I was sure she would never jeopardize my relationship with my best friend by letting her know I was the one who told. But somehow I was the one waiting in the office when Chrisy was pulled from class in the middle of the day. I was the one blamed for the humiliation she felt when she was forced to expose the obvious scars on her arms, for having to leave the school counseling office crying in front of our classmates, when I was forced to take her to her car to get her Swiss Army knife, when I was told to take her, crying, into her classroom to gather her things. It was my fault that everyone knew. It was my fault that the unprofessional high school counselor called Chrisy's mother at work and told her that her daughter had been cutting. And it was my fault that Chrisy was never going to talk to me again.

I had to tell. I had watched through the weeks as the scars crawled farther down her arm and deeper into her wrist. I watched as she shut the door to the bathroom in front of me and told me to walk away. She told me not to worry about it. She told me it was only a phase. I watched when she told me she wasn't going to commit suicide because, well, you had to cut this way and not that way. (That will never leave my mind. I will forever know how to slit my wrists.) I had to tell.

So I sit here in my backyard, bobbing my feet to some stupid radio hit. My hair in a high tight ponytail, my red polka-dot bikini barely hanging on. I sit here and wonder. What is happening to Chrisy at this exact moment? What did her parents say? What does she do behind shut doors? Who does she talk to for support now that I no longer exist in her life?

Then the thoughts change. Could I cut myself? Where would I cut myself? I can't do it on my arm. That would be way too obvious. I can't do it anywhere people could find out because then I would be such a hypocrite and everyone already knows I was the one who told about Chrisy. But I had to. I had to because I love her. I had to because I would never forgive myself if something happened to her.

But where would I do it? On the bottom of my feet? No one would find it there. But that would hurt to walk. Under my arms? No, they would see when I play basketball. I know. Between my toes.

Wait.

No.

Yes?

The sun is shining down on me as I sit in a daze. I am utterly blank, yet my mind is racing a hundred miles a minute. I don't know what I think, or what I feel, but I have this feeling of extreme anxiety and extreme emotion. I don't know what I'm emotional about, but it is digging deeper into the depths of myself. It hurts as it overtakes me.

cinda The door to Linea's depression opened when she discovered that her best friend was cutting herself. Linea was caught in a friendship in which she had promised her allegiance and confidentiality but knew that Chrisy needed adult help and support. She shared her fears with me. She was terrified of not keeping the vow she had made to her friend not to tell and yet she knew that her friend needed help. We talked about cutting and we talked about confidences and when it is necessary to help a friend who may not want it. We discussed me calling her mom or Linea and me together calling her mom with or without Chrisy involved and, finally, Linea talking to someone at school. After much discussion, Linea decided to trust a school counselor. It was not the right choice. The counselor broke Linea's trust and Chrisy's as well. She called Chrisy's mom at work and told her over the phone that her daughter was cutting her arms with a knife. Linea called me, sobbing. She never wanted to go school again.

When I teach a class of future school counselors and school psychologists, I still use this story as an example of what not to do. I was furious. I was also deeply sad for Chrisy and her family, and I was frightened at the depth of anxiety and depression I was seeing in my daughter.

Linea was a mess. She couldn't stop crying and she couldn't stop thinking about what had happened. She was terrified that Chrisy would continue to hurt herself, and she was humiliated by the scene in the counseling office. The situation had a huge and negative effect on Linea's mood, and her overwhelming schedule didn't help. Linea continued to be anxious and so very sad. We talked for hours about everything that had happened and how she was feeling, but I know now that she didn't—and couldn't—tell me everything that was going on. I did know enough to worry about her mental health, and I asked her to see a psychologist or counselor, who could assure us (I hoped) that we were doing everything we could for her and to help her build skills to deal with stress that it seemed would continue to be a part of her life as an overachiever.

But Linea didn't want to. She was angry with me and said,

"I can just talk to you. I don't need to see anyone." I needed to know that she was okay. I was afraid for her. Chrisy's cutting was a complete surprise to me, making me wonder what I didn't know about my own daughter. I pushed her to see a psychologist "for a checkup," I told her, and if not for her, for my reassurance. She finally agreed, and I drove her to her first appointment. She emerged from the inner office after less than forty minutes and asked me to come in and talk to her therapist. The psychologist had diagnosed her with depression and referred her to a psychiatrist for medication.

I was astounded and frightened. Had I missed something? The mom who should know better? The mom who was always on high alert? I knew Linea was having a very difficult time and that she was anxious about her future and worried about Chrisy. I knew she had trouble sleeping (though I didn't know how often). But clinical depression? Linea was open with me about so many of her feelings. We spent hours talking about everything going on with her, but I realize now that I didn't really know what was going on in her mind. At the time, I somehow felt that I would know if she had crossed some invisible line into an area that needed treatment. I knew that the situation with Chrisy was extremely difficult for her, but I didn't know how close to the edge Linea already was. I know now she was very close to the edge. I believe that every parent asks, "Is this typical teenage angst or something much more dangerous?" I had asked it many times during the first few years of high school, always thinking Linea struggled with the former, not the latter. I know now that the answer was that Linea was approaching something much more dangerous.

I had expected the psychologist to suggest counseling so that Linea could learn new skills to handle her stress and worries about doing everything and doing it perfectly, but I was not expecting a *psychiatrist* and *medication*. I was frightened and, to be honest, surprised.

Linea saw a psychiatrist and he prescribed an antidepressant. She took the medication for about three months and then, unbeknownst to me, decided to stop taking it, and I failed to notice a setback. I didn't see much of a change in her moods, but she told me she "felt better." I was horrified when she told me that she had just "quit taking them." I warned her of all the dire consequences of stopping medications without a doctor's supervision. At this time, reports were coming out about teenagers, antidepressants, and the correlation to suicide ideation. I talked to her about this, and she assured me that she was not suicidal. She met with the therapist a number of times and then told me that she didn't want to keep seeing her. She convinced me that she had just been worried about high school and her friend but that she was better.

In that time and place, I think we convinced ourselves that this thing now officially called depression was due to stress from school, worries about her future, and fears for her friend all wrapped up in her drive to do and be her best. Or maybe I thought that somehow, because of my knowledge, experience, and skills, I could keep whatever it was at bay. I don't know. Looking back, I can see that there were indicators of what was to come, but at the time these were merely hazy suggestions, whiffs of a more serious illness. I don't think we would have done anything differently. I certainly had no idea that this was the beginning of an illness that would almost take her from us. The question "Did you see it coming?" can be answered yes and no. In hindsight, yes, I could see it coming. But at the time, no, I couldn't. We never suspected that a severe mental illness was on its way and would try its best to destroy her.

linea Sophomore year—I just pitched at the state girls' fast-pitch tournament. I'm getting hugs and high fives everywhere I turn. Looks of approval from the stars of our high school athletic cult. I had managed to put my name on the social status A-list, a level most sophomores don't reach. I am known throughout school—senior boys and girls congratulate me and acknowledge me. Why isn't it the happiest moment of my high school career?

I am numb, a smile plastered on my face like the one I wear every day. I am completely dead to the fact that I just raised my social status by leaps and bounds. I am numb to the fact that my grandfather was the proudest he had been since my uncle was eighteen. I can't feel anything.

The pills the doctor prescribed for me kept me from the pain of sadness. They also robbed me of the euphoria of joy. I was at a painfully even keel all the time. My emotional life was bland even as my external interactions and activities should have created excitement, adventure, and pride.

What do you do when you're hurt but you stop taking your medicine? When you fall into a slump and don't know how to get out of the hole that you've dug? When you get to a point where you sit in your room thinking and listening to music for hours? When you stop sleeping because there's not enough time to think? When your mom comes in and asks you if you need "help"? When your parents are always asking how you're doing? What do you do when you realize the problem after the breakdown? What about after you think you have things figured out but still feel sad? What do you do when you feel sad even when you're smiling and giggling? When you start to feel like a complete fake because you don't really hear what anyone says but still pretend to care?

I'm so afraid not to be perfect in everyone else's eyes. I hate to think I'm self-conscious or have bad self-esteem, I just want to be the perfect one. The best. Is anyone really normal? Am I just physically or mentally tired, or do I just try too hard to be perfect?

cinda Linea's last year in high school was filled with music performances, dances, football and basketball games, church activities, and time with her friends. She sang in four choirs and traveled across the country to compete in music competitions. She played keyboards for a jazz combo while continuing with classical piano and voice lessons. She played Hodel in *Fiddler on the Roof* and was on the honor roll while taking college-prep classes. A few Sundays a month she sang the liturgy at our church. The majority of the time she appeared able to manage her many activities.

She also spent hours talking about what she was going to do after she graduated from high school. College, yes, but where? What kind? How would she know? Would she make the right decision? She wanted a career in music performance but wondered if she could make it in such a competitive field. We sat in the living room snuggled onto the couch or stretched out on one of our beds, and Linea talked and cried and laughed at herself and what she described as her "problems." "I know I don't have serious problems compared to so many people. What's wrong with me? I must be spoiled. I have a great family, great friends, and every opportunity. What is wrong with me?" Though I desperately wanted to provide her with some relief from her worries, I couldn't seem to find the right words to make it better for her.

To the outside world she appeared an organized, happy overachiever. We talked many times about her schedule and finding time to rest, but she insisted she was happiest when she was busy. Most of the time I thought that Linea was worrying too much about what she would do after high school and that once she made some decisions about her next steps she would feel calmer. I believed that what I saw as "stress" was a combination of her need to do everything perfectly and her ability to come fairly close to meeting those goals. She was happy when she was performing, and she had the energy to keep up with long days of music and academics. But interspersed were times of extreme anxiety. I didn't yet understand the level of anxiety, depression, and perfectionism that was within her and not from an outside force.

In addition to her anxieties around graduating high school, she continued to worry about her friends. She was (and is) a caretaker. Many of her friends were having crises of their own. These were the "good kids," at least in the eyes of their teachers and parents. They were leaders in the school and also deeply involved in sports and music, yet they also struggled at some level with anxiety, depression, eating disorders, cutting, and alcohol and drug use. Although the research indicates that one in five students will have a mental-health condition during the high school years, most parents are unaware of this and, anyway, don't know what to look for in their own children. Linea worried about her friends and tried not only to listen to them but to also keep everyone from harm. Linea was known for her kindness and, to her friends' parents, for her stability, her talents, and her academics. Many were shocked by how ill she became after high school.

She didn't drink or experiment with drugs in high school

but had times when she nursed the friends who did. When she was a senior, I encouraged her to get out more—in less than a year she would be in college. She went to a party one night, telling me, "There might be alcohol." The party was at the home of one of her classmates whose parents were out of the country. There were alcohol *and* drugs *and* police *and* broken windows *and* uninvited guests from an alternative high school across the city. Everything we had ever talked about that could go wrong at a party, did. Linea ended up taking a very drunk and very sick young man home, likely keeping him safe from the worst effects of alcohol poisoning. (For the rest of the school year his parents thanked Linea every time they saw her at a high school event.)

linea My mind is one big dirty room. There's a bed to sleep in and think in. There's a computer that goes as slow as it possibly can. Scattered throughout my room are my activities. Numerous jerseys are scattered and hidden on chairs and under my bed. Music books, schoolbooks, and important papers rest in random piles on shelves, chairs, and various countertops. My calendar is ripped page by page to help me organize, but it is hidden under dirty clothes and in various sports equipment and schoolbooks. Music is always playing, distracting me from the mess that is my life. Smiling pictures line the walls, reminding me that I have friends and family who care for me, while at the same time, they seem to stare down at me through the mess. I would clean my room, clean my life, if I had time. Then I wouldn't be so overwhelmed, but I don't have time. It continues to pile up, becoming even more disorganized

I think there's a point in everyone's life when it's hard to look up. When you feel you've fallen a million miles below surface and can't find a way to climb back out. It is a time when everything looks dark. It hurts to smile. You try to think of everything that could help you get out, and help you get back on your feet, but it's useless. You search for the things that will help you, but you know they really won't work. In fact, you're so tired, you don't really want them to work.

cinda Linea continued to flip between seeming content with herself and worrying about her future. She panicked whenever she thought about what she wanted to do after she graduated. She worried through her senior year about where she should go to college and if she was really talented enough to take the difficult route through a music performance program. She put off auditions for music conservatories but would not accept the offers that came from universities in the state. At the time I wasn't sure why she wouldn't or couldn't schedule auditions. Looking back, I think that like many young adults, she was not sure what she wanted to do and was too overwhelmed to take the next step. In addition, her level of anxiety (I realize now) and perfectionism froze her in her tracks, but rather than let it go or decide that she really didn't want to or wasn't ready, I think she could only worry with incredible self-criticism playing in a nonstop loop in her head.

Telling her that she could do anything she wanted and that she had it all going for her didn't help. I couldn't get through to her how talented and gorgeous and kind and smart she was. I knew that telling her that didn't make her believe it. In fact, it probably made it worse.

Finally, in February, after a cold trip to Chicago and many anguished hours of indecision, tears, anxiety, and fear before we left, she made the decision that she had been struggling with for two years. She would attend Columbia College to study music. She was awarded a scholarship and the opportunity to live in a city of nearly three million people while majoring in music performance. She was excited to push her own musical training to a higher level. She was moving to Chicago! I was ecstatic about her choice but mostly because a choice had been made.

The next few months were easier. She went to her senior prom with her boyfriend and talked to me about how strange it was to finally have a boyfriend when she was just going to leave anyway. (She had been too busy throughout high school to have a serious boyfriend.) Her graduation was a tearful ending but also a wonderful celebration. We were so proud of her as she sang during the ceremonies. The end of the school year was full of performances and awards and celebrations. I cried during most of them, thinking about what a wonderful and fun time we had with Linea during her school years.

While she waited for her name to be called for her diploma, I thought about the last few years. I believed that she had made it over the hump of whatever it was that caused her so much agony off and on. Her moods, worries, and tears were certainly much more severe than anything I had experienced with Jordan, but Linea had always been very sensitive to her own feelings and those of others, even as a young child. Having a second child made me very aware of the differences in temperaments and personalities. I was relieved that she seemed so happy about her next steps, and I was optimistic now that she had made it through the tough teenage years of "transition." Even though I knew that there would be obstacles and worries in college, I thought that the worst was over. Although I would miss her terribly, I was anticipating the "empty nest" and Linea's success in Chicago.

Toward the end of the summer, Linea, her dad, and I went to the Washington coast for a long weekend; we wanted time with her before she left for Chicago. We rented a place close to the ocean, spent the first afternoon walking on the beach, and finished the day with Dungeness crab for dinner. We had all been asleep for a while when Linea called from her room. She hadn't cried out during the night since she was a little girl. I thought she was sick and went to her. She was crying so hard that she could barely breathe. She didn't know what was wrong other than she felt "scared" and anxious. I don't know why I didn't recognize this as a full-blown anxiety attack. Her dad came in and we sat with her and tried to comfort her while she sobbed and choked, trying to catch her breath. Finally she fell asleep and we went back to bed. I thought that she was frightened about moving across the country where she knew no one and starting college in a challenging music program with other students who, according to her, might know much, much more than she did. But she was extremely well prepared, having studied with top-notch private teachers and coaches in both voice and music. I thought it was likely that every student beginning college felt insecure in the same way.

I still can't sort out which part of all of this was depression or something else and which part was anxiety of growing up, making choices, and leaving home common to all teenagers. Perhaps these years of decisions were more troublesome for someone of Linea's temperament. Curt and I both knew that her worries about her life were intense, but so were her excitement with her successes and her joys when things went well for her. She had always felt everything intensely.

After her depression and anxieties during high school, I knew that she might be susceptible to another depression in college and that her freshman year would at times be stressful as she began her life away from home. Overall her history before high school had been stable; she had mostly been happy and certainly successful in anything she wanted to accomplish. She was (and is) immensely talented in the arts. The creative mind often struggles with intense feelings, and I am familiar and comfortable with this temperament in my own family of artists. I was sensitive to her mental health, but neither Curt nor I ever considered an illness that would change all of our lives forever, almost destroying hers. It was with some sadness but much more excitement and happiness that we began to say good-bye to our daughter as she prepared to move to Chicago.

2. certainty

cinda Finally in August we all flew to Chicago and moved Linea into the nation's largest student residence, home to over seventeen hundred students—a mammoth building on South State and Congress just blocks from Michigan Avenue. We moved her things from the rental car to the queue for the elevators that would take us to her "suite" on the fifteenth floor with a view of the Sears Tower. I couldn't believe that our little girl, who lived her first ten years in an unincorporated village of fewer than three thousand people, would live in the South Loop of a city of more than three million.

That night, I prayed that this was the right decision for her and that she would be happy. She had struggled so long and hard, questioning and worrying about what she should do after high school. I wanted so much for her to settle into the music program, the city, and her dorm; to develop deep and lasting friendships; and, mostly, to enjoy the small things that she would experience every day and not to worry so much about her future.

I was excited for her, but of course I cried as we flew back to Seattle, leaving her in her new home. I felt overwhelmed and exhausted by the effort that it took to get her there and yet I was also very proud of her and hopeful that this was the right decision. She was so happy and independent while she packed and planned for her move, and she was equally happy and outgoing as she moved into her dorm, making friends with her suite mates, figuring out where her classes were, and settling into her neighborhood. So many feelings were churning inside of me as we headed home: excitement for her new life and for ours, fatigue from the physical and mental exhaustion of the move, and, of course, worry about any number of things that could go wrong. She could be hit by a car as she continued to cross streets against the lights, she could get mugged, her depression could return. Yet these emotions were all mixed together with the most potent feeling of all: hope.

We returned to Seattle and settled into our empty nest. I missed Linea terribly, of course, but there was also a sense of . . . not exactly relief but the lessening of taking care of someone. Other mothers in newly emptied nests confess a similar feeling. I had felt this initially when Jordan left for college, but it was stronger now that there were no children at home. Once your children have moved out and away, the day-to-day parenting decreases. We don't wonder if they got home on time or even if they got home at all. We don't wake up at one A.M. and check if the car is in the driveway and if they are asleep in bed. While Jordan was in college, she and I talked often and we stayed close, but I no longer knew where she was every day or when she would return from an evening out, and I didn't really think about it. I expected the same with Linea and I looked forward to her independence.

Back at home, Curt and I talked about how you feel you have been a successful parent when the child to whom you have given so much love, energy, and worry becomes independent and yet still chooses to be in your life. Linea had always been very close to us, close enough that we worried about how we would cut all those apron strings. But she was also very self-sufficient and had always made good decisions. Even though she talked to both of us about many of her feelings and worries, and we had helped her through her decisions about college and friendships, she had demonstrated the ability to take care of herself. She was responsible, she managed her schedule and her many activities while achieving high grades, and she had developed deep friendships during high school. I thought she had been honest with both her dad and me, and I believe that to the best of her ability, she was. Yes, there had been tears and anxiousness and a difficult diagnosis of depression, but I still had a strong belief that she would do very well in Chicago. She was so smart and articulate, she was a talented musician and very prepared for her field of study, and in so many ways she was mature beyond her age.

We felt so much joy for her that she was on her own. The process of growing up doesn't happen overnight, but she was moving into adulthood. She was confident and happy when we left her in Chicago, and so were we. I had been through this transition with Jordan and watched her progress from a new freshman in college, sometimes stumbling but mostly moving steadily forward, to independence. I expected the same for Linea.

In the first month of school, we talked every other day or so while she filled me in on her classes, activities, and new friends. As she got busier, I talked to her less and less. But one day in October, she didn't sound quite right to me. She sounded anxious and unhappy, complaining about feeling behind in her schoolwork and practice sessions. I tried to understand what was going on with her. Was this another depression? Her dad talked to her and we would ask each other, "Do you think she's okay?" I continued to worry as she was either anxious or sounded flat when she talked with us on the phone. Curt and I were concerned, but we didn't want to intervene in her life more than necessary.

We remembered how Jordan wasn't always happy and upbeat her first year in college, and we convinced each other that Linea was just working through the newness of her freshman year living so far away from home. Jordan had called many times her freshman year, crying and even wanting to come home at one point, complaining about difficulties with roommates and feeling very stressed because of the lack of privacy and her inability to find any time for herself. I remembered nights that Jordan called and I would be awake much of the night worrying about her and wondering if I needed to see her in person. The next morning I would call her and she would barely remember what had been so difficult the night before. She needed her mom as a place to vent, and then she moved on even if I was still a little behind worrying about her. Jordan made it through her college years with a broken rib, a severe ankle sprain, various colds and flu, and upheavals with friends and roommates, but she also acquired a degree, good friends, and a great boyfriend (Cliff!), and she remained emotionally intact.

At this point there wasn't much more we could do except check in with Linea and, of course, worry (which wasn't very effective!). But by early December, a feeling of trepidation was beginning to follow me around. Linea was never far from my thoughts. I never knew what to expect when I talked to her. She was either having a great and wonderful adventure or she was feeling anxious and down. I became less confident each time we spoke. Her happiness and excitement about her classes would last for only a short time before she moved into a darker place. She would call, full of enthusiasm and anticipation of upcoming events, telling me about an audition that went well, a paper she aced, and a new friend she had made while attending some amazing cultural event. The next call would be full of anxiety about too much work or even anxiousness about her anxiety. "I am so anxious I don't know what's wrong with me," she would tell me. But just when I was ready to head to Chicago, she would seem so much calmer and convince me she was doing okay. Yet I continued to worry.

linea I am in Chicago. Finally. A city so big you could fit almost four Seattles into it, suburbs included. Everything is big here, big and flat. I miss the trees and the mountains, but I'm here. And I'm here on my own. Alone. Now my mom can't call me if I'm out at night and she hears an ambulance. Now I can be out late with boys without my dad knowing. Now I can drink and not feel paranoid all the time. I'm free and I can do what *I* want. It's my life. My own life. Away from them. My parents. My friends. People who know me. People who think I'm good and perfect and innocent. I can do whatever the fuck I want. I can swear. I can drink. I can stay over with boys. Hell, I can even do drugs.

cinda Linea came home for the holiday break, and we were excited and happy to spend time with her. I wanted to see her and assure myself that she was okay. During her visit, she seemed happy with college life and Chicago, but she worried about her studies and all the music pieces she needed to learn. Yet she didn't practice or appear to do any work on assignments while she was home. She was certainly in a better mood than Jordan had been during her first holiday break. Jordan had come home with a bad cold and exhausted from her social life and schoolwork. She was not always easy to get along with as we all readjusted to a having a college freshman in the house. With Linea, I convinced myself it would take a few days for us all to get back into a family routine, and then things would settle down.

Linea was tired but overall in a good mood, and I was reassured that she was "okay." How do you know the difference between typical behaviors of a college freshman and a young adult in the onset of a mental illness? I know now that you can only stay calm, pay attention, and wait.

linea January—I'm home for college break and I feel as if I am drunk. I have a permanent smile on my face and I can't help but dance naked in my room while I brush my wet hair. I apply my makeup with a new ease and look at my clothes as if it will never again matter what I wear.

I know this is the year. I have a feeling of complete hope and optimism that I had lost these past four years of high school depression. Suddenly, I'm over it. I break my new makeup, and instead of being completely devastated, as I would have been a day earlier, I simply pick it up and throw away the broken pieces. I continue dancing and joyously await the impending New Year. Only five hours until I get to celebrate with my favorite friends at a concert with my favorite band. I am finally all right with myself. I am beautiful and happy and free, and for some reason I feel it is suddenly all right to show it.

cinda In the New Year, I was once again feeling optimistic that the new semester would be a good one for Linea. She was happy during the break and she left rested and seemingly calm. It didn't last long. Shortly after she returned to school in January, I received a phone call from her. I was in a meeting and left the room to take what I thought would be a quick call, just long enough to tell her I would call her back. I didn't return to my meeting for more than thirty minutes while Linea cried from over two thousand miles away.

She didn't know what was wrong with her. We talked and she cried and I listened, trying to figure out what was going on with her. She told me she was just "overwhelmed" and felt terrible but she didn't know why. Once again I was hearing, "I don't know what's wrong with me, Mom. I don't have any reason to feel this way." She said that this made her feel even worse. She had everything she had ever wanted and she was doing well in school. What *was* wrong with her? And again, her concern about others was there as well. She kept thanking me for taking the time to listen to her and told me to go back to my meeting; she reassured me that she would be all right. I told her I would talk as long as she wanted to and she kept apologizing for taking me out of my meeting. We agreed to talk later in the day and I finally hung up with a heavy feeling in my chest.

By then the meeting was over and my friends asked me if everything was all right. I didn't know what to say. I was shaken by her call and didn't know what to do. Something didn't feel right to me, and my instincts were to race to the airport and off to Chicago. I wanted to see her. I wanted to know she was really okay.

Over the next week, Linea and I spent more time on the phone, and I persuaded her to see a college counselor. I thought she was likely struggling with depression and could use some help managing her stress. She was not enthusiastic about seeing a counselor, but she also was trying to understand why she felt the way she did.

During Linea's first visit, the counselor told her she thought she had bipolar disorder. When Linea called me, she was very upset, and my first reaction was to reassure her; she was very worked up and I just wanted to calm her. I said, "Honey, this might not be bipolar. I think you should get a second opinion." I was careful not to agree or disagree with the counselor's opinion, and although I was working to reassure Linea, I felt completely overwhelmed. I had so many mixed emotions coursing through me. I was in disbelief for many reasons. Bipolar disorder had never entered my mind. We had never seen any mania in Linea, nor had she ever described the symptoms, at least not at the level of mania I was familiar with when working with children and adolescents with bipolar disorder. I also didn't trust the counselor who had met with Linea. Of all the counselors there, she had the least experience and was not a certified mental-health provider (yes, I had spent time on the counseling Web site). It was too quick a diagnosis. I wanted a trained and experienced professional who took time to gather information, review her history, and meet with her a number of times before finalizing a diagnosis. I was frightened by the very words "bipolar disorder." It did not fit with anything I knew or thought I knew about Linea and, to be perfectly honest, my family.

I am sure now that Linea's symptoms of depression were much worse than what she had been telling me or perhaps even than she was able to describe. At the time, however, while I didn't discredit the idea that Linea might need serious help and even medication, I wasn't ready to agree to what I thought was a quick diagnosis and particularly the suggestion that she likely needed a prescription for lithium. I was beginning to see that she had depressions that hit her and then retreated, at least a little, but the diagnosis of bipolar disorder felt too sudden, too casual.

I couldn't examine my own feelings at this point because I was too concerned about Linea's. She was frightened, uncertain, and needed reassurance. She told me she was embarrassed and humiliated having to sit in the lobby of a building crowded with students she knew, waiting to see the counselor. "I feel like a total loser sitting out here in the hallway while people I know go by and look at me like I am crazy or something." She didn't want to see another counselor or doctor and particularly didn't like the idea of medication.

Linea felt the same sense of disbelief with the quick diagnosis. She said she didn't like the counselor. The counselor had asked her to "look inside all the boxes of [her] personality" and tell her what she found. According to Linea, the counselor was trying to help her find the "problem," a deep, dark secret that was causing the depression. Linea said, "I should just make something up to give her something to work on. I don't have any big secrets. I don't know why I feel this way. I am not going back." Adding to her depression, she felt even worse that she was unable to identify something that would provide a reason for her to feel so bad. She was depressed and miserable while feeling that she needed to figure out what it was that was causing her depression. Again, she said, "I have everything most kids my age would want. So what's wrong with me? There is no reason I should feel this way." I think that this particular strategy of searching for clues to her depression did little but add to her feelings of guilt and caused us all so much worry.

In retrospect, we were all playing into the idea that something concrete, something "out there," was causing Linea to feel so bad. If we could only identify what it was, then perhaps we could fix it. I thought it was stress from trying to do too much and overextending herself time and time again. I had, I thought, pinpointed many "reasons" for her depressions and anxieties while she was in high school. If only she could reduce the amount of activities she was involved with, she would feel better! If she could just make a decision about which college to go to, she would feel better! If, if, if . . . if only I could just fix it!

If it was not something outside of her, then it must be something within. What was it? Either outside of her or inside, I think the message she heard was that she should be able to fix it. Reduce outside pressures and stressors or look inside and figure out what was wrong.

It took us all considerable time to come to the realization that she had an illness and that no matter how hard she tried, she couldn't manage it on her own. Mental illness is a brain disorder, and certainly stress and exhaustion can make it worse. Yet there is a degree of guilt and blame that accompanies a mental-health condition that is not as apparent with physical illnesses. If Linea had had appendicitis, say, no one would ask her to "look inside herself" in order to determine a diagnosis and treatment. Being asked to look inside for the answers was not helpful at that point and only increased her guilt, underscored her lack of understanding, and even fueled anger.

My job was to stay calm. We talked, and she finally agreed to get a second opinion. I asked if she wanted me to help her find a psychiatrist. She did, and from that moment we stepped into a mental-health world that consisted of hours of searching for providers and treatment, fighting with the health-care system, and oftentimes suffering from overwhelming uncertainty and exhaustion. We did not know where this new diagnosis would lead us. The depressions from high school followed her to Chicago, yet something more sinister was brewing. It was pulling us along, and we were not prepared for where it would take us.

linea I am in Chicago, my second semester in, and something is happening to me. I am doing the things that most college freshmen are doing, partying a lot, kissing too many boys, staying out so late I can barely finish my schoolwork. But I have also been doing things that I know my peers are not doing. I have been extremely emotional; a conversation with my mom can move from love to sadness to anger in minutes. I stare out my window and listen to music alone for hours in the dark. I can't sleep at night unless I'm completely intoxicated. I often find myself feeling angry and left out when my roommates don't ask me fast enough to go out. I'm constantly searching for the next party, the next chance I can have to drink or get stoned. The next chance I can have to stop feeling. I oftentimes just can't stop crying. My thoughts of anxiety and depression have come back. I haven't felt this sense of suffocation and nervous fear of the world since I was a senior in high school. I feel that everything is just on the verge of collapse. Like I am standing at the edge of a cliff in a heavy wind. I need to know why. I love my life. I love the city I am in, the classes I am taking, and my roommates. My life may be crazy and wild right now, but I still love it. Why then am I feeling this way again?

I have begun seeing a counselor again. After numerous talks with my mom on the phone, she finally convinced me that I should at least try to talk to someone other than her. For the longest time I thought my mom was all I needed, but there were other things that I needed to talk about that I didn't feel comfortable telling her. I still can't talk about drinking with my mom. Not that she would judge me, but out of my own fear of not seeming perfect. Plus, I want to be an adult and I don't want to rely on her for everything.

Though I can't stand the counselor or her questions, I feel she may be the only one able to figure out why I have this constant sense of impending doom. If I want to keep living the life I love, I have to stop myself from plummeting off this cliff. She wants me to keep a journal so I can keep track of my moods. She thinks I may be bipolar. Sure. Whatever. She probably just thinks that because I thought it would be fun to test her out and play with her head. I mostly tell her about the partying and drinking. Having read the DSM since age eight, I know all about bipolar and want to see just how much I can play up the manic parts of my life. I have always known myself to be depressed, but I cannot understand the diagnosis of bipolar. I'm just a normal depressed college kid.

Given how quick she was to "diagnose" me, I feel an urge to play to her assumptions. I do this out of anger and fear more than fun. Testing to see how smart she really is, to see if she could really be telling the truth. The more I do this, however, the deeper I dig myself into a hole. I know what to tell her to make her think I'm fine, but something prevents me from doing that. As I go on with this act, I begin to realize that I may not be smart or strong or healthy enough to get myself out of this diagnosis, this label, and I am quickly realizing that my little game is only holding her back from truly helping me.

She wants me to look into whatever "boxes" are closed inside my head. She thinks that I have some deep, dark hidden secrets. She probably has nothing better to do with her time than convince poor college kids that they have suppressed fears or thoughts.

All of my worries and thoughts are those of a normal college freshman, so what makes me, of all people, bipolar? What is wrong with me?

I'm checking Facebook to see what parties are happening tonight and I'm listening to a new album I downloaded. Suddenly a song I have never heard before begins to play. My arm hairs raise, my neck hairs raise. My heart swells, and I have to concentrate on my breathing. I know something. Something important, something magical and true and the key to everything. I know it, but I can't type fast enough to explain it before the song is over. Suddenly my past depression is nothing compared to this new knowledge I have of myself. Suddenly I feel pretty and interesting and intelligent. Suddenly I feel like I can go out with my friends and be confident and impress people. I feel I have never before realized that I am worth something, but now I do. Suddenly I feel like I can do anything.

I want to dance in the park, I want to sing for an audience, I want to paint a self-portrait, I want to take pictures of strangers I think are interesting. I want to travel to foreign countries and write music the way it is meant to be felt. I don't want to write about choirs, or worry about the next year, or Juilliard, or school, or money. I want to fly away and discover a new life just my own. I want to travel, and pack few clothes, and my favorite journal, and a camera, and a voice recorder, and a computer. I want to live the way life leads me. I don't want to make decisions based on the past, I want to base decisions on the moment. I don't want to base decisions on what they will do to my future, or what they will do to my family, or what they will do for my friends, but on what they do for me in my current state of being. I want to be selfish and live the way I need to. I want to forget about due dates and money, and concentrate on the creation of something truly beautiful. I want to get away from anyone trying to create a future of wealth and pretend happiness; I want to create happiness now. I want to make the perfect movie and the perfect painting and portrait and song. I want to just be.

cinda All of this was happening a few months before a trip to Scotland that Linea had planned (and paid for) many months earlier. She had a close friend in Edinburgh, and all her plans were solidified for a trip during spring break. She had scrimped and saved and was very excited about traveling to Europe for the first time. Because Linea was feeling better, we thought that this recent bout (of what? Anxiety, depression, something?) had been another bump in the road. She was keeping up on her music and her academics, and her calls were reassuring. She sounded good and was feeling positive about her courses and program. Although she seemed much happier, to be safe, I still wanted her to follow up with a psychiatrist.

I finally found a doctor who could see her, but Linea convinced me that she could wait until after returning from Scotland. She continued to sound happier, and every conversation with her convinced me that she was better. I was hopeful that her anxieties and sadness were leaving, if not gone already. Curt and I both talked to her about the trip and to each other. We agreed that she seemed to feel much better. Her grades had not dropped and she continued to do well in all her classes. She was auditioning and performing with other students, writing brilliant papers that she would share with me, and she seemed content with her life and excited about her trip. We had no specific reason to convince her not to go, and we thought that it might provide her the opportunity to be more independent and to develop more confidence in her ability to take care of herself.

At the end of March, she flew out of O'Hare airport into Heathrow and on to Edinburgh. She loved England and Scotland, and actually told us she felt "strong and independent" after her week with her friend. Linea sounded so good when she called us from Scotland and again when she was back in Chicago.

My worries subsided somewhat, and I thought that she had weathered a depression and was continuing to feel better. She laughed when she said she had found the cure for depression—"overseas travel!" My apprehensive feelings backed off, and I began to believe that all would be okay. I thought that she was beginning to settle into her life in Chicago and into her goals for her music career. She had been a confident and independent kid throughout grade school and middle school. It wasn't until tenth grade that she had times when she was unhappy and anxious. Yet her previous years of calmness, kindness, and overall happiness steadied and reassured me that all would eventually settle down for her.

linea April—We sit on a train to the Highlands. Tyler and I. My biggest crush in high school. My best friend, the popular senior to my nerdy sophomore. It is amazing to me that somehow I am able to be on a train in Scotland with him of all people.

I've been here a week, and Tyler's tired. For some reason I have endless energy and have been running him and his roommates ragged. Somehow I am able to party until four in the morning, get on a train at six, and walk twenty miles in a complete day tour of London. Somehow I can do all that and still have energy to do it again the next day. Tyler does not have this much energy—really, no one can keep up with me. But who wouldn't have this energy and drive when visiting a foreign country for the first time? Who wouldn't be as excited flying overseas at eighteen by yourself to visit one of your favorite people in a place you always dreamed of visiting? He'll wake up. Just give him some coffee and everything will be fine.

Tyler keeps talking about the future. He keeps talking about joining the Peace Corps. It's funny how this conversation mirrors the same exact conversation I had with a friend just weeks earlier. A friend said he needed to do something bigger and better, to grow up and get away. I suddenly feel as if everyone is leaving me. I feel that everyone is slowly going to vanish out of my life to go on their own paths. I suppose I have to get used to this, but somehow I'm still stuck in the now. Why do they have to leave? Tyler says that it is time for him to grow up, time to decide where he wants to be in his life. I don't understand it. I'm still stuck here. I'm always stuck here. All I can think is why do they all want to leave me? What will I do when I lose Tyler and my friends? Who's next? Why do they need to move away? Why do they need to lose everyone who loves them to find something new?

I stare out the window blankly, and instead of enjoying the beautiful Scottish hills I watch the pale gray sky and think of how alone I am. I realize that I will no longer have the people I have always counted on. Why are they trying to lose me?

We are running through the cobblestone streets of Edinburgh in a snakelike zigzag, and I feel as if my pants will fall off. I can't see straight. The streets are wet and shiny.

Our entourage of men is chasing after us and we run faster.

But Tyler and his friends can't keep up with the excitement of two drunken girls celebrating my last night in Scotland.

My girlfriend and I reach the first club thinking it will be our last. We walk right up to the bouncer and tell him we are being followed by that crazy group of boys behind us. They have been chasing us. *Do not* let the five boys in the back in because they scare us. We get a free ticket in and a fast pass through the line of at least twenty eager twenty-somethings.

Inside the sleazy salsa club, we are met by glances and stares of hundreds of bloodthirsty men. I whisper to her to put our rings on our wedding fingers, and in our drunken splendor we both think it is a brilliant idea. I navigate around the club and happily make friends with everyone I bump into. But we find no interesting men and leave the club disappointed. Outside, we tell the boys we are moving on and take off once again into a sprint. I know that the night will only get wilder, but somehow I'm not worried about my six A.M. flight back to America.

cinda During the last quarter of the school year, we talked to Linea at least every other day. Some days she seemed to be happy and other days she was not. She'd be anxious and cranky and worried about everything, and with the next call she was happy once again.

Both Curt and I had traveled to Chicago to visit Linea and watch her performances. We met her friends and we explored Chicago together. Yet, I admit, there was underlying worry. I was not sure how much to worry and when to act. Where is the edge? When and at what point should I do more than worry? On the surface she was functioning well at school—at least her grades, performances, and friends seemed to attest to that. Her anguish seemed to come and go and maybe it was only me she was expressing this to and maybe it was my own worries that were magnifying everything. I didn't want to overreact, but I didn't want to miss something. I was concerned about her all the time and never felt completely confident that she was okay. I hoped that a summer at home would be a good rest for her and a time for me to see for myself how she was doing.

linea I want to be alone more and more. I am extremely emotional, and my moods range from depressed to anxious to angry. Today I stressed myself out over a scholarship and became extremely angry as I convulsively copied and recopied my music twenty times more than needed. Sheets of music surrounded me like an island in our dirty dorm room. I just couldn't make it perfect. I couldn't line up the sides so that nothing was cut off. I couldn't make it straight. When my suite mate shut the connecting door, I was so angry I almost threw a shoe at it.

I am going crazy. I really feel that I am. Maybe it's just crazy artist syndrome or freshman angst, but I swear to God I'm not myself. I want to go to church tomorrow. I, of all people, want to go to church. I want to find some big Catholic cathedral and escape into beauty. The art museum is only free one day a week and Scotland is too far away. So much that I see in this world is dirty and ugly and fake. I've become such a cynic. An angry, depressed, hateful person. I want to throw things and break things and cry and scream and drink and run.

I want to run away. I need to be free. Why am I still not me? I felt that if I escaped to Chicago, one of the largest cities in the country, then I would be all right. I thought I could hide. I could be free. I could be myself, but I'm not who I want to be, and every day I'm getting uglier. I'm rotting inside because of this held-in ugliness. I feel like Dorian Gray. I try to play beautiful and happy on the outside, but I'm afraid it's showing through. I'm becoming a worse person the longer I try to stay normal.

I try to be a good girl. Take care of myself. Get good grades. Be looked at as a role model. Be kind. But all I can do now is try not to fall all the way into the pit I'm looking down into. I want to lose myself in sex, in drugs, in booze, in a life of careless, disastrous behavior. But I stay in the middle, never satisfied with either side. I find myself drawn to extremes, all or nothing, good or bad. I want to be perfect or a complete disaster. I'll find myself on one side but always longing for the other. But I know that I have to stay in the middle, stay steady. Because if I don't, I know something terrible will happen. I have to keep my head on straight because these days every breath I take feels strained.

I need someone to talk to. I don't want to talk about it. I need a friend, I need someone who knows me, but all of my Seattle friends are too busy being college freshmen to care. My mom makes me want to throw my phone at the window. My counselor makes me want to puke. I am in a constant state of tension like I'm holding my breath for hours on end. My jaw is so tense it pops about four times when I open it. My body is so tense I feel like I can't even move. I can't sleep or else I sleep too much. I hate this.

cinda Linea came home to visit for Easter. I found her a cheap ticket and brought her home as a surprise for the family. No one else knew she was coming. I really did it because I wanted to see her, know that she was okay. We hardly saw her as she caught up with her friends, seeing as many of them as she could in the few short days she was home. She was home again, sleeping in her bedroom, driving her car, and living under our roof for a few days, but she was no longer a high school student. She had one foot into adulthood. It is a tricky business when a child/adult returns during the first year of living away from home. I remember well the discussions with Jordan. "When will you be home?" "I don't know. Nobody asks me that at school!" Typically, "You have a terrible cold and you are exhausted. Don't you think that bed before two A.M. would be a good thing?" I didn't see Linea nearly as much as I wanted to in those three days, and I didn't get the answer to my question, "Are you really okay?" Independence, adulthood, pulling away—all good things and exactly what I wanted for her. But what if I was missing something?

Linea returned to Chicago for the last two months of her first year in college. We were in the home stretch. I thought we had made it through the worst and that sophomore year would be better and easier for her. Everyone seems to have a difficult first year away at college. I did not expect her to carry a 4.0 or be the top student in her class, but she actually was very close. I wanted her to make decisions on her own, both good and maybe not always so good. I wanted her to become more independent and confident in herself. Even with the sadness and anxiety that had hit in February, she had traveled to Europe, returned to school, and was successfully auditioning and performing, continuing to develop the musical skills with which she wanted eventually to make a living. I was often a complicated combination of optimism and worry. In most ways I thought her first year in college was successful, yet I was very anxious for her to come home for the summer. I wanted her close for a while. I wanted assurance that she was steady, strong, and intact. It had become very clear to me how many miles were between Chicago and Seattle, and I wanted her home.

linea As I approach the Harold Washington Library, I hope for warmth. It is raining and cloudy and cold. As usual, several homeless men are standing against the wall to keep out of the rain. I realize there are several "normal" people standing there as well: Housewives, college students, and businessmen all gather against the wall. As I wait, more and more people join the crowd. We all face the door and wait for the clock to hit one. The rain gets harder and the wind blows, but everyone waits to enter the warm, bright, clean, and silent library.

The man with the red stocking cap and missing front teeth is here for the warmth. He wants to retreat to a comfy chair on the third floor and rest his troubles. The man in the beat-up tennis shoes is here for the warmth too, but he is also here to retreat into books. He is looking for a possibility of escape from the sad, harsh world. The woman beside me clutching her umbrella a little too tightly is here to get a break from the kids and possibly pick up a treat for bedtime. The young man by the garbage can, neatly dressed with a backpack, is here to find resources on deforestation in the South American rain forests.

I need a book, but why am I waiting in the rain with such anticipation, so eager to go in? I love the bright lights that force me to focus. The clean and yet musty smell. I love the endless aisles of books, endless knowledge, and endless ways to get into the heads of any kind of person. I love the rows filled purely with music. Notes on every page. And the rows filled with art, colors, and pictures.

I am here to escape from my current restless state of mind. I come here hoping to quiet my thoughts and release my clenched fists. I am the man looking for knowledge of the rain forests. I am the mom trying to get away from the kids. I am the man looking for warmth from the cold rain, and the man looking for warmth from the world. I am here for the same reasons as everyone. And I suddenly realize we are all just people. No matter how large our needs are or how complicated our problems are, we are all really the same. We all have bodies. We all have some sort of soul. And with these bodies and souls, we live our lives. People are all just people. As I awake from my thoughts, I realize there are now at least a hundred people waiting to enter the three doors in front of me.

cinda Linea returned to Seattle the summer after her freshman year. I was so happy to have her home. The end of the semester had been hard on all of us, and we spent many hours on the phone. I would listen carefully to try to gauge how she was doing. Sometimes she was angry and irritable, other times she was flat, and then she would say, "I'm sorry, Mom. I am kind of stressed, I guess." Just when I thought that she was really falling apart, she would pull it together and tell me, "Don't worry, Mom. I'm okay. I'm feeling better. I love you!"

I was anxious before, during, and often after each call. I knew something wasn't right, but I wasn't sure if it was wrong enough for me to do anything except be on my guard. I realized that something was different with her from the way it had been with Jordan as she moved into adulthood. But I attributed it to Linea's personality and temperament, so different from Jordan's. Both are sensitive, artistic, very intelligent, and emotional, but Jordan could let things go more easily than Linea. She was way more dramatic during these years, but whatever was wrong quickly faded away. Linea seemed to be holding on to churning darkness somewhere deep inside of her, but I didn't know what it was.

There were many layers in my relationship with her during the first years of her illness that I am only now beginning to understand. The first was love, that all-encompassing love for a child that will not let go and will not give up. Holding my firstborn and then my second daughter, I knew without a doubt that I wouldn't hesitate to do anything necessary to keep them safe. They were tiny and vulnerable, and my feelings of love were overwhelming. Although that fierce protective love settles down as children get older, it doesn't go away and is always at the ready if needed. The next layer was the clinical professional layer, always trying to analyze and figure out what the hell was going on, because if I could figure it out then I would have a chance to fix it. After love and clinical/professional there was the paranoid alert layer, always questioning whether I was overreacting or being too protective, worrying that I was filtering everything through my own past. And finally there was terrifying fear. It was always there, lurking down deep, panicked that I could lose a child. I didn't allow myself to acknowledge or examine this in any meaningful way. I pushed it down.

But now she was back and home, and oh, I was so happy

to finally have her close! I believed that with my care, love, and support she would be all right. I would somehow be able to fix it—whatever "it" was. I would figure out what was going on with her that caused her to fall backward into sadness and tie her up in anxiety. I would teach her how to slay the dragons, and if she couldn't do it on her own, I would do it for her. She was home. We had time to make it better for her.

Linea had a job that summer with the Seattle Center Foundation. She was working in the building next to the Space Needle with amazing and brilliant young women, women who could be mentors for her and who thought she was equally brilliant and amazing. In addition to her work at the center, she had surgery on her sinuses, tonsils, adenoids, and nose. The pain was brutal, and we were amazed by her strength and stamina during the difficult recovery. The four-hour surgery was complicated enough that I almost convinced myself that any depression she had battled was connected to a low-grade sinus and tonsil infection that was finally, after many years, treated. Her recovery was not easy and involved a couple quick trips to the emergency room, after-hour phone calls to the surgeon, and lots of ice, rest, movies, and frozen yogurt.

By the end of the summer, she was in good shape, happy, healthy, and excited to return to Chicago. She seemed confident about the job she did at the Center and had caught up with her friends from high school. Once again I believed that the worst was over. Linea was healthy and happy. I so much wanted this to be a better year than last year for her!

linea I'm home for the summer and I have landed a great internship. I work for the Seattle Center Foundation and help the people in charge of the arts and cultural events at the center. Though living at home is often frustrating, I love coming into Seattle every day for work. Working allows me to be free and independent for those eight hours.

I love being with my parents, but they always seem to watch me; whether they are just happy to see me or still worried, I'm not sure. I try to stay out with friends as much as possible, but I miss the vastness and anonymity of a large city. I miss being able to go to parties without fear of my parents worrying about me. Plus, I have to drive everywhere, so I hardly drink.

Aside from the paranoia of my parents watching me and the longing for my life in Chicago, my depression has been a lot better. I had a major surgery on my sinuses, tonsils, adenoids, and nose, so hopefully I won't be sick anymore. Part of me thought that some of my sadness in high school was the fact that I was constantly sick with a sinus infection. We will see if this clears anything up.

Only two more weeks to go and I'm back to freedom and my own life! At least in Chicago I can lie to my parents if I'm not feeling well. Here they can always tell.

3. disintegration

cinda Linea headed back to Chicago after her summer at home happy, rested, and ready to return to her studies. She seemed to be back to her former self, confident and positive about her life. I felt a sense of relief that her freshman year was over and that this would be a good year for her. It started off that way. She was more committed than ever to her music and making plans for her eventual career in performance. She changed her major from vocal performance to piano performance; her long-term plans still included singing, but she planned to use her piano skills eventually to support herself by accompanying.

"I can really study the theory that I have always wanted to and it will only help my singing. I want to really get into this," she said. She was doing gigs around Chicago, accompanying and singing. She was making money while making music! She was not only excited about her work in piano but she also had a coveted assistant teaching position in the music department.

One night she called to tell me she had been to a barbecue.

"My friend Charlie made me the most awesome salmon. The kind that you make, Mom! It was so great!" She was bubbling with excitement. I remember thinking this might be a crush or the beginning of a relationship and not merely a dinner that resonated with her Pacific Northwest upbringing.

She announced that her life was almost perfect. Phone calls from Chicago were happy and full of excitement. She and Charlie were soon dating. She liked her roommates and her new apartment. Her classes were exciting. All thoughts of talking to a counselor felt distant—everything was going so well! Her father and I would hang up the phone after her calls and laugh.

"Can you believe how well this is going for her?" we said to each other with glee. She was happy, and therefore we were happy. She would have laughed at us as we high-fived each other. We looked forward to her phone calls, and I let go of a little of my worry left over from the previous year. A wise man once told me, "Your happiness is dependent upon your least happy child's." She was happy and so were we!

The good feelings lasted through the fall. Winter break was the beginning of a downward spiral. Linea came home for the holidays. Although she was busy seeing friends and catching up on her sleep, one morning she announced to me, "Mom, I think I'm getting something." I asked her what she meant.

"Cancer, maybe, or something bad."

I asked her what hurt, what was wrong. Did she need to

see a doctor? She told me that nothing hurt and she wasn't sick, but she could feel "something coming." I asked her if she wanted to see a doctor or a psychologist. She didn't want to see either, and she really didn't want someone to write her a prescription for something.

"I'm serious, Mom. I just feel like something really bad is going to happen to me. I need to go to a retreat or something and hold this off or fix it or something."

We talked for hours. I listened, I asked questions, and I worried. I talked to my colleagues at my university, working to find someone she could talk to who wouldn't too quickly diagnose or prescribe medication.

Once again I found myself trying to figure out the cause for this, and I still was not thinking "serious mental illness." She was introspective and she shared many of her thoughts with me. She was articulate, competent, and seemingly able to accomplish everything she wanted. This didn't fit with the illnesses I had seen and worked with in my professional life. I worked with young adolescents who were completely out of control, fighting back against the world with every unhealthy tool they could find. Linea kept trying to figure out why she felt anxious and depressed, asking me, "Why?" I wanted desperately to find the answer. There could be many reasons for her anxiety. I wanted to make the fear go away for both of us.

Again, I thought about this through my experiences with Jordan as well as my friends' college-aged children. Jordan returned home with a cold or the flu, exhausted after finals or midterms and staying up all night with friends. She would be cranky and irritated about living with us again after being free and on her own. I told myself that this must be part of Linea's problem. She was tired, she was cranky, she had a stress fracture in her foot and a cast, she had a cold, maybe it was another sinus infection, maybe she was anemic, maybe she was . . . I don't know, I don't know. I couldn't figure it out, and if I couldn't figure it out then I couldn't fix it. Was it true that something awful was coming our way?

I had been known to worry to excess about daughters who are out late, daughters who don't answer their phones, daughters running temperatures, daughters in all kinds of troubled states. So when I told Curt about Linea's vague worries and thus my worries, he tried to reassure me just as I tried to reassure myself. I, in turn, tried to reassure Linea. I almost believed that if she didn't give these thoughts any attention, they would go away. I wanted so desperately for her to tell me that she didn't really believe in "it" and that whatever "it" was couldn't be real—that it was a figment of her imagination and therefore we could talk about it, figure it out together, vanquish it. But could we do that? *What was it?*

Linea is generally kind and happy, sometimes even giddy and silly, so, looking back, I can now see "it" creeping in over those two weeks she was at home. New Year's Eve was miserable. She spent the first part of the evening crying in her bathroom, irritable and unhappy about the night ahead with Jean, her childhood friend, and Jean's friends. When she finally left for her night out, my heart was pounding. I wanted to forbid her from going out. I wanted her to stay home and play board games with her parents. She seemed on the verge of a complete meltdown. I told myself that it must be a mammoth case of PMS. If she would only stay home with me and be safe, we could play games and toast in the New Year with the three of us in front of the fire. We would keep her safe.

But I couldn't. I couldn't keep her at home. I was walking the line between mothering a girl and a woman. Can you forbid a sophomore in college to go out with her friends? Can you ground your daughter when she is no longer a teenager? I worried and prayed and crossed my fingers that whatever was wrong was simply late-onset teenage anguish or run-of-the-mill trouble with friends or the holiday blues or a bad case of PMS. Deep down, I knew better. Linea was holding it together, but only barely.

linea The coffee table she's dancing on is blue like her dress. I'm sure it was purchased from a thrift store or found in an alley. It's short, stout, and matte blue with little black triangles on top, layers and layers of blue (perhaps even a layer of black at one point), then more blue. Blue that chips off each time she drags her pretty black heel back and forth during her knock-off Mia Wallace dance.

Like the table, Jean's dress was also found in a thrift store. The room is quite alive though somewhat dark; it's whirring with energy. Jean's on the table, I'm on the couch, other partygoers are spread throughout the room. Everyone is dancing. Dancing spinning schmoozing. This is a very schmoozy party, and I'm not in the schoomzy kind of mood. There are lots of ties, lots of heels, lots of trendy beatnik prototypes. Lots of intellectuals, musicians, artists, bohemians, rock stars, writers, and whatever far-fetched label they put next to their names. "Hi, Joe [artist/philosopher/film buff/philanthropist]. I'm Linea [musician/writer/intellect]."

I sit on the couch below, a walking cast on my foot from when a drunken college roommate stepped down on my bone with her spiked heel. I cannot dance on the table. In fact, I had a hell of a time just trying to get up the stairs of this goddamn three-story house. I sit on the dirty couch watching my drunken best friend dance obliviously above me. I am sober. I am the driver for the night, and my one-beer limit has been surpassed.

I am sitting here in my dirty jeans and wrinkled T-shirt, looking far from glamorous. Most likely my hair is dirty and out of place. Lately I have been less and less concerned with my appearance. But everyone here looks glamorous. Everyone here knew that it was a fifties-themed cocktail party. Basically, I really just shouldn't be here tonight. Just know that I am far from a place called home, too close to a place I called past, and drifting very far from a woman called Jean.

After enough you're-not-one-of-us glances from the other guests, I convince Jean to go out and have a cigarette with me when I don't even smoke. We travel down one flight of stairs, then another, me hobbling along, Jean walking elegantly, until we reach the door to the back. Behind the house we have our own little New Year's resolution ceremony. On a piece of paper we write a list of things we *don't* want to be in the new year. I write things like: too nice (I am determined to finally stick up for myself); she writes something along the lines of: too self-protective (she doesn't want to be so inwardly focused).

We have always fallen into these roles. Even when we were little, she was always protective of herself while I was too sensitive about other people's opinions and feelings. Often I wish I was more selfish. Oftentimes I think she wishes she came across as more sensitive. I once described us as sugar and salt: each different, but when combined we blend into a perfect white mess.

After we are done writing out a list of what we want to change and improve upon in the next year, we burn them. The paper is tightly clutched between her long, slender fingers, her red nails cut short and slightly chipped. Several plastic bracelets adorn her wrist. It took the red lighter multiple tries to finally light the paper, the flame slowly and silently climbing toward those red nails, that red lighter. Red and red and orange and red. Every time the paper caught fire, the wind would proceed to blow it out, and once again she would have to go through the haunting routine of relighting, relighting, relighting.

God, we used to have so much fun together. Only a year ago we would run around Seattle drunk at noon, videotaping strange people, dancing below windows to whatever garage bands might be playing, crying at foreign films, watching the cute guy in the framing store. Getting sushi and laughing laughing laughing.

Playing dress-up—just like we did when we were six—up at night and smoking too much. Drinking whiskey in the woods while listening to Lou Reed. Stealing music from the library. Climbing down Snoqualmie Falls in dresses and nice shoes.

What happened? Did anything happen? What is happening to me? I feel so off. I feel so inwardly focused. Self-centered. Me me me. Bitter. What is happening here? God, I wish I could have a fucking drink. Anything. Drugs? Are there any drugs? Fuck. What's going on?

Suddenly it's New Year's Eve and the clock just struck twelve. Trendy Seattleites pop poppers and cheer, clad in their fifties outfits. Kisses passed around by every drunken guest. I stand alone at the top of a very steep street. I stand right in the middle of the road, but no one notices me there. I am sober and alone. My friends and boyfriend are all in Chicago, and Jean is somewhere very drunk and flittering with strangers.

The fireworks reflect off the Space Needle, and instead of enjoying the beautiful night, the moon over the city, and the thought of a new beginning, I am sad. I know somewhere in my deepest being that this is not going to be a good year. I call Charlie and cry to him, wishing he were here to fix this pain. Wishing he could fix whatever *this* was. Something is going to happen, and I know it won't be good. Something is going to happen, and what scares me most is the fact that I know I will have to face it alone.

I am crying. I don't know exactly why I'm crying, but I know that somewhere out there impending doom awaits me. I think I have cancer. I have a tumor. I have some rare unknown disease. I have something, and within the new year it is going to kill me.

cinda Perhaps Charlie would cheer her up. We had not yet met him, but he was coming to Seattle to visit during the break. Linea seemed excited for his visit but also on edge and fragile. Charlie is a pianist as well, and they had played a duet together at school. I begged them to perform for our neighbors, all of whom adore Linea. We invited three couples over for dessert and piano music. We were having a soirée! She and Charlie played an achingly beautiful duet as well as a solo each. Her dad videotaped the performance for her grandparents to see and for our family archives. The video shows her laughing and talking but, when looking at it later, I see how brittle she looks and that her eyes do not match her smile. She looks haunted. I cannot watch the video now, knowing what was to come. When I remember the look on her face that day, it still brings tears to my eyes.

I hugged her often throughout the afternoon and asked how she was doing. I felt so uneasy and afraid. She told me, "Okay, I guess. I don't know what's wrong with me. I'm sorry I don't seem so happy. I am really sorry, Mom. I just don't know what it is. I still feel really strange. I know you're trying to help, but I don't think it is going to work."

"You can tell me anything, you know that. If you don't

want to go back to school, you don't have to. Do you know what you want?" I asked her.

Linea told me, "I *have* to go back to school. I want to. I'm sorry I'm worrying you. I don't want to. I'll be okay."

I didn't sleep and I continued to try to figure out what to do or what to say.

Winter break was over, and Linea left for Chicago to complete the first semester of her sophomore year. I was the mom who wouldn't quit checking and calling and looking for one more assurance that all was well. When she did not return calls for a day or two, I couldn't sleep and I couldn't stop my worry, wondering what was wrong, terrified of what was "coming." I drove Curt crazy with my fear. He asked me, "What do you want to do?" I don't know. I don't know. I don't know.

I awoke from sweaty, shaking nightmares worrying that she had been hit by a train. Or that she got on the wrong train and was torn away from us into the night. I tried to catch her, find her, save her, but I couldn't. I was exhausted by these dreams. I carried the worry with me all the time. It never left me in peace but instead hid in the back of my mind, waiting to nudge me at odd times of the day and night, waiting to shake me into a place of fear.

When we talked on the phone, I listened carefully for any nuance in her voice that would warn me that something was wrong. I knew something was desperately wrong, but I didn't know what it was and I didn't know what to do. Drawing on my profession, I tried to do an assessment over the phone. I ran through the questions to assure she was thinking straight, that she was safe, that she was taking care of herself. We had always talked about everything, but now she was quiet and flat. Too many times her response to me was, "Yeah."

As in, "You are so quiet, are you doing okay?"

"Yeah."

"Are you worried about anything?"

"Yeah, I guess."

"Do you know what it is?"

"No. Yeah. I don't know."

She ended every conversation with, "I love you, Mom. Don't worry."

I worried. There was nothing we could put our fingers on that would suggest we needed to invade her life and go to Chicago. She didn't want us to when we asked. I could only wait. Wait with the heavy companion of worry by my side.

Two weeks after returning to college, she called early in the morning. The phone rang before seven A.M. and my heart banged loudly and rapidly. I answered before the first ring finished. She was quiet and then began to cry. No, she didn't cry, she sobbed. I so wanted to reach out across the miles and hold her. My body was on high alert, my chest hurt, and I didn't even know what was wrong, but my voice stayed steady as I reassured her that it would be okay. Tell me what is wrong. I am here. I am listening. You are not alone.

She had broken up with Charlie, and her heart was breaking. She wasn't sure why she did it. She didn't know what was wrong. She couldn't understand what she was doing.

"He didn't do anything wrong. What is wrong with me? What is wrong? What?! I am hurting him so much, I am, I am really horrible but I don't know why," she sobbed.

She didn't know what to do. We weren't sure what to do. Should we go to Chicago? Was this a regular boyfriend breakup, or something worse? Was her state of mind best remedied with girlfriends, or did she need her mother? Later that week, she told me she was so depressed she didn't want to leave her room. After another week, Linea made the decision to call Charlie, her former boyfriend, now friend-who-is-a-boy, and asked him to see her again. She was in so much pain and I think he was the only one in Chicago she trusted to see that pain. He had spent many hours with her and he knew that something was very, very wrong.

My fears were beginning to be confirmed. Her behaviors were different from before. Her words described a pain that was deeper than anything I had heard from her before. She broke up with Charlie because, she told me, she just "didn't feel anything." I reached out to Charlie. His mother is a nurse, and with her help, we found a psychiatrist in Chicago. Linea traveled alone across the city to meet with him, riding the El, venturing into the Magnificent Mile and into the high-rise building by herself. I should have been there with her. It hurt so much as I thought about her traveling across the city to find an unknown address and meet with a stranger while feeling as bad as she did. I always knew that Linea was a courageous and fiercely brave girl. Her ability to take this next step for help was the first glimpse of her courage that would be tested again and again from here forward. I wished I could have held her hand all the way.

After seeing the psychiatrist, she was even more terrified. He told her that he thought she has bipolar II. This guy was a psychiatrist, not a college counselor, and now she was really worried. So was I. We researched the diagnosis on the Internet, and we were both petrified by what we read. I didn't know nearly as much as I thought I did. Yes, I had worked with children and adolescents with bipolar, and I teach about the symptoms and the treatment and support, but as I read the research, the outcomes, and the maze of medications, I began to cry. "Mom, it says that suicide is a huge risk with bipolar II. I am really sick, Mom. I'm crazy."

I learned that bipolar II is depression typically without the mania, but what a depression it is. Deep, awful, suicidal depression. I read, "Bipolar II is a version of Bipolar Disorder. Depression is obvious but mild phases of high energy ('hypomania'), which can just look like anxiety and insomnia, are also present. This doesn't look at all like 'manic-depression,' just big mood and energy swings." Here comes the scary part:

"But Bipolar II can be as severe as other forms of Bipolar Disorder, maybe even more prone to suicide" (PsychEduction.org). I was terrified. Something deep and frightening stirred inside me. I could not think about this right then.

"Are you thinking about hurting yourself, Linea?" I asked her, sitting on the floor against the wall and gripping the phone so tightly my fingers were white.

"No, not really. I don't think I am, but I just have bad thoughts. I think I'm sick. Really sick. Maybe I am crazy," she said.

I held the fear back and told her that she would be okay. She had a good doctor. The medication would start to work.

I told her, "Don't read the information on the Web right now. Don't look at it to get information. Listen to your doctor. He knows what he is doing. If he thought you were suicidal, he would hospitalize you. He will make sure you are safe. Did you tell him everything? Are you okay, baby?" I didn't want to overreact and I didn't want to underestimate what was happening to her. I had to stay calm. I was the mom. She was frightened and looking to me to keep her steady. So I stayed calm. But inside, I was crying. What *was* happening to her?

"I did, Mom. I told him everything. I can't stand this." She started to cry.

We talked for a while and she grew calmer. I had done my job for now. She said, "I'm okay. You don't have to come to Chicago. I'll be fine. Don't worry about me. I promise you I will call you every day and I will tell you if I feel like hurting myself. I promise you."

linea I broke up with Charlie. Charlie, the love of my life. The man of my dreams that I had dreamed up with my best friend Chrisy in eighth grade. Charlie, corduroy-wearing, Talking Heads–dancing, work all night, musical prodigy Charlie. He is one of the most beautiful people I have ever met, and yet this darkness doesn't seem to want me to love him anymore. Something in my soul has died and decided that I can't have the most perfect man on earth. It has decided that however hard I try, my being should not be in love with him anymore.

I have been hiding really well. I work all the time, and since I stopped eating, I never have to see my roommates in the kitchen. No one asks. Jean and my weekly phone calls stopped three weeks ago, but she hasn't noticed. Or maybe she has and I haven't noticed that she's been calling.

I stare a lot. Stare at the piano keys. Stare at the floor. Stare at the wall. I don't practice anymore. It doesn't matter. No one knows. No one sees the blood that's in my head.

The shrink prescribed me sleeping pills. He told me I needed to sleep. I'm not tired. I get rest by staring. I get rest by sitting. Plus I can't get the pills. I can't get them. I want to take them, but I can't take just one. I want them all. I want to stop seeing the blood. I can't tell my mom. Blood in my dreams. Bathtubs of dark red, *Carrie*-style blood all over my body. Plus I'm sick of my wrist throbbing. It's begging me to cut it. It starts throbbing, and it starts cutting from the inside. I can feel it. It's going to kill me. It's going to slit my wrists from the inside out.

I can't eat. I can't run. I can't think. I can't stand to be here or anywhere. I can't stand leaving my room. I can't stand. I hate myself. I can't stop hurting. I can't stop feeling crazy because I am crazy.

No one can know. I can get through this.

I need to get through this.

A few hours later and I'm feeling okay. I am extremely tense. I know I don't need a boyfriend, but I haven't acknowledged the fact that I have sent him away. He said it was a death wish for our relationship. I never intended to kill our relationship. I don't know what to do without him to take care of me. But wait, that's why I did it. I need to take care of myself. I need to be independent. I will be fine and go back to him if he is right for me. I wonder if that is the only reason I feel this anxiety. It's welling up, and I'm afraid to let it out. I'm really scared to be on my own, but I have to be okay. I have to get better. I owe it to Charlie. I'm still feeling fat. Food is all I think about. I'm always feeling hungry, but when I eat I feel as if I need to throw up. Maybe it's the anxiety. This anxiety is new for me. It goes past the depression. I think it's because I keep trying to suppress these feelings. I'm really scared that I will get to the point where I'll be beyond repair.

God, I feel like I need to throw up!

It's like how I felt yesterday breaking up with Charlie. Yesterday I sobbed so much I began hyperventilating. I freaked out. I couldn't breathe or look at him. I felt as if I was going to throw up. I know that if I let myself cry, the same thing will happen. I hurt so much. There is such a hole in my heart and a knot in my stomach. I feel tingly and dizzy. My head is swimming, and I need to close my eyes to breathe. What the fuck is wrong with me? I don't get it. Everything is perfect and yet I can't be happy because I'm not perfect enough. I don't know what to do, but I'm scared of what I'll find to fill that hole. At least I know what's coming. Maybe I can stop it.

cinda Curt and I decided that we needed to see for ourselves how Linea was doing. Curt is a guy who needs to do something rather than merely wait. In fact, he is physically incapable of waiting. He got on the next plane to Chicago.

Meanwhile, Linea gave permission for me to talk to her doctor, so while Curt was flying east I called her psychiatrist. He was kind and knowledgeable. He reassured me that my daughter is a very bright and intelligent girl and an excellent candidate for treatment. He had prescribed her Lamictal. It was found to work well for depression for those with bipolar disorder, but it can have very serious side effects, particularly a body rash. She was to move slowly to a dose that would give her relief. The medicine would likely help in five to six weeks if there were no terrible side effects that could land her in the hospital. He prescribed sleeping pills to help her through the first few weeks. She hadn't filled her prescriptions yet but promised that she would.

After talking with, him I felt panicked but knew I couldn't actually fall apart, at least not on the outside. If I let anyone know how frightened I was, they would become frightened as well and then I wouldn't be able to stand it. We needed to act as if everything WILL BE FINE, and we didn't allow ourselves to think otherwise. I realize now that it was crucially important for me to stay steady and for those around me to do the same. I couldn't let my fears come to the surface. I couldn't let myself go to a place where I thought about losing her. I wouldn't. I could remember the pain of losing someone. I wouldn't. I would not lose Linea.

Linea gave me permission to talk not only with her doctor whenever I wanted but also to anyone else who could help her. Curt and I talked with everyone we knew in the field. Once again I found out I didn't know as much about bipolar disorder as I thought I did. The more research I did, the more completely frightened I became. Yes, the rate of suicide is very high with this diagnosis. Cycles are tricky; they can be over long periods of time or, worse, "rapid cycling." These are swings between mania and anxiety and depression that happen as a quick and violent attack, often lasting until the person has no more strength to fight it off. Had we seen any mania? This could not be. It didn't fit with anything that I thought I knew about her, about the illness, or about our place in the world.

Everything was tipping. Not my child. Not Linea, of all kids. No. No. I kept telling myself that the medications would work and work quickly.

Curt soon reached Linea. She told him she was "okay and don't worry . . . I love you, Daddy." We talked about what to do. Linea had told her dad she was feeling better, she had a doctor, and she was taking her medication. We were on the edge. There was a part of us that was in disbelief that the correct diagnosis was bipolar. There was another part that knew it was an explanation for what was going on with her. But what could we do? She wanted to continue with her life in Chicago. We had to be as strong as she was. Would the path forward be uphill? What did this all mean? We said we would wait and see. We said, "We can deal with anything." We were calm, cool, collected, but only on the outside. On the inside, my heart didn't slow down, my mind did not stop worrying. I felt as if I was waiting, worrying, praying, waiting, worrying, praying. My sleep was always on alert, preparing for whatever was coming.

Curt spent four days with her while she seemed to get on with her life. But he returned without the reassurance we both needed. He should not have unpacked his bag so quickly. She had warned us. She knew.

linea My dad flew out to see me. He's worried that I need help. We found a shrink so that we can fix this before it starts.

I know I will be okay. I just need to ease my mom's mind. Nothing bad is going to happen. It will be fine. They're just too cautious. Maybe now my mom will leave me alone. Maybe he can convince her. Maybe she will be like every other mom and call me once a week. I just have to convince them I'm fine. I will be fine. I will play fine. It's easy. I've done it before.

I am supposed to begin school and work tomorrow, and due to a "family emergency" I am unable to. I am staying and talking all day tomorrow with my dad. The talking is getting me nowhere. It's all the same. I just don't know what will make it better at this point because everything makes me want to puke. There is no point in talking anymore because I have no new answers for the same old questions. I am so frustrated that I want to run away, or just die. I don't want to deal with it anymore, or deal with them. I am merely cooperating because I love them and I'm scared I will sink beyond any level of faking this. I feel I need to be better so I can continue to be a perfectionist, but there is no point because there is nothing I can be perfect at. I need to know what is going on and kill it before it gets me first. I just can't stand this bullshit that everyone keeps dishing out. "Talk nice to yourself." "Live in the moment." The worst are the questions. "Well, what makes you happy?" I don't know! If I knew I would do it! "If you knew where it was, where would it be?" I am just about to give up. Fuck this. Just let me rot.

4. devastation

linea Charlie comes into the lab, where I sit, staring out the window as usual. He wants to talk. I go with him into a private practice room and he corners me. He wants to know what is happening. He wants to know if I am okay. He demands it. I'm fine. He doesn't believe me.

"What is going on?"

"I'm fine."

"Your roommates are worried."

"I'm fine."

"They say you don't eat. They say you're always in your room."

"I eat. I had a Snickers bar. I had rice."

"Linea, what is going on? How did your doctor's appointment go?"

"Fine. He gave me sleeping pills."

"Did you pick them up?"

"No. I don't need them."

"Why don't you want them?"

"I don't need them."

"Linea."

"I want to take them all."

"Why?"

"I can't stop seeing blood. I can't stop seeing blood when I close my eyes, and I'm sick of my wrists tearing themselves apart from the inside. I don't want to be here anymore. I don't want to do this anymore. I don't want to try. I can't see this blood anymore. But I'm not crazy."

And then I'm shaking in the corner of the small hardly soundproof practice room and he's calling my parents. He has left the room and I can't hear their conversation, but I am shaking uncontrollably and hyperventilating. I'm panicking. I'm shaking and crying. Not breathing. I can't move.

Now he's talking to my mom. Is she okay? Is she crying on the kitchen floor? Is she freaking out? Is she booking a flight? Calling the police? Calling the hospital to come lock me up? My life is over. Everything is over. Everything that I have built and planned over this past year and a half is over. My future is ruined.

I need to run. I need to run to the Walgreens and get those pills. I need to sleep forever. I need to sleep. I need to run, but I can't move. He's back and I can't look at him. He has ruined my life.

"You're going home. Your dad is on a flight to Chicago as we speak. He'll be here around three A.M."

My life is over. I cry and shake as he picks me up off the floor and walks me out of the music building. My brain is paralyzed and I am a frozen tornado, objects floating in the air that I have picked up in my path: a broken romantic relationship, a frightened family, lost friendships. He holds my wrists and convinces me that they are not going to bleed. People look at me as if my mother just died. My life is over.

cinda My fears are finally realized. I was on the east side of Washington State presenting at a conference and visiting my father who had just had surgery, and Curt was at the airport in Seattle waiting for a flight to join me. My sister, Calla, picked me up after my presentation to take me to her home and wait for Curt. We were all going to have dinner together.

I checked my messages when we got to her house, and there was a message from Charlie. He said to call him as soon as possible. His voice told me this was it. I had hoped and prayed that Linea's initial diagnosis and medication from her psychiatrist would quickly move her back to health. But there was a constant underlying feeling that something much stronger and more forceful was trying to take over her life. Starting with Charlie's message, it seemed as if time slowed to a crawl yet everything was crystal clear. Each action was precise; each word was clear and dropped one by one into my mind. I remember every second of those next few hours.

I punched in "Charlie" on my phone.

He answered on the first ring and said to me with all the sadness a twenty-three-year-old voice can have, "You need to come and get Linea. You need to take her home. She isn't safe."

I told him that we would be there as soon as possible. Tell her that her daddy or mom is on their way. Hold on, baby. I spoke calmly, though my body was anything but calm. Pain and fear were trying to strangle me, but my voice stayed cool. Simply recalling this conversation hurts. This was it. She was really and truly very, very ill. She was not safe. I was shaking and the tears were running down my face. I am sure I was holding my breath. My voice did not give me away.

I paged Curt and our conversation was almost shorthand. We had never discussed this moment, but I think we were both prepared in some way for this call. I said, "We have to get Linea. She is with Charlie, he is keeping her safe."

"I'm already at the airport. I'll go right now."

We were efficient, we were calm. We were on a lifesaving mission. We were terrified to our very core. My sister manned one phone and I was on the other. We called airlines, Charlie, friends that work at the airlines, Charlie again and Curt, again and again. Damn it, why doesn't Curt have a cell phone? My sister kept me calm and I acted capable. I had a mission—get Curt to Linea. I couldn't stop shaking, but I kept dialing and talking and writing down more and more information. At one point I was talking to a woman in India while trying to reach the United Airlines counter in Seattle. She didn't know that my daughter needed us, that she couldn't be alone. She didn't know that "Linea wasn't safe." She kept talking and talking from around the world, telling me, no, there was no way to call Sea-Tac airport unless I wanted to call 911 and go through the police. "Is this an emergency, please?" she asked in her faraway accent. I was so irritated I hung up on her. Yes, it is a huge emergency. My daughter wants to kill herself.

We finally got Curt on a flight to Chicago. One-way and no luggage was a red flag for a full-body search, but after a sleepless red-eye flight, he finally arrived in Chicago at four A.M. Linea had spent the night at Charlie's parents' house, and Charlie had watched her all night long, keeping her safe from herself. In the early morning hours, he drove her to the airport to meet her dad.

As soon as Curt was with her, he called me from the airport. When he said, "I have her," I took a breath. I felt as if I had held my breath from the moment I first heard the words "She's not safe" come out of Charlie's mouth. Since then, I had taken only tiny sips of air, I stayed rigid; I kept myself tightly pulled together. With Curt's words—"I have her"—I finally was able to take a deep, long breath. I knew he wouldn't let her go.

They spent two nights in Chicago pulling together the bare minimum needed to bring her home. She was so very sick. Charlie asked me if he had ruined her life by calling us. I told him no, he had saved her.

Curt held her together while he and Charlie gathered all of her belongings that would fit into one suitcase. Curt explained half the truth to her roommates and friends, steadied her, propped her up, and told her anything that would get her through the next hour. I worked the phone lines and contacts at home, trying to put a plan together.

Curt called me while Charlie was with her and he had a minute alone.

"Oh, Cinda, this is so sad. She is so miserable. It hurts. She hurts."

"Is there anything else we can do? Should we stay there with her and not bring her home? I could come out and stay until she is better." The explicit act of packing up her life in Chicago and bringing her home was so extreme. A tiny part of me clinging to hope wondered if we were doing the right thing. But Curt was there with her. He knew that everything had changed.

"We have to bring her home. She is so sick and it is happening so fast."

Charlie was there those last days and hours of that cold and windy Chicago January. How could we ever thank this boy-man? He had dropped his own life to take care of Linea when she could not take care of herself. He had faced her straight on and did not turn away from this monstrous illness that hid Linea from him, that threatened to take her away from all of us. This is the kind of pain that parents are supposed to deal with. You know the first time you hold your baby you would do anything for her. Charlie could have turned away. Thank you, Charlie.

linea We're staying at a beautiful hotel in the Loop. My dad and I. A room with jewel tones and cherrywood. Large beds and lots of space in the bathroom. I held a nervous discussion with my mom on the phone. A discussion that she attempted to initiate many times until I finally gave in today. She is an apprehensive woman.

I'm terrified of some unidentifiable force, but there's something about my dad's smile and brave eyes that makes me forget. Right now it's just dad and daughter time, minus my ability to sleep.

The doctor gave me sleeping pills after weeks of my half-assed attempts to sleep. Dad gives the Lamictal and sleeping pills to me one by one between finding my pajamas and brushing my teeth. We retire to our beds exhausted after an emotional day of him playing the comforting father and me stubbornly playing the happy college girl. That is, the happy college girl covering up the fact that she was suicidal.

The beds are comfortable and warm. A bright streetlamp casts several rays of yellow light at the ceiling above the slowly climbing curtains. Wait. Climbing? They are climbing. Moving. Crawling toward the ceiling with little fingers and hands. I quickly look away, wondering if perhaps I'm a little crazier than I thought. I turn toward my dad when I notice the lamp next to his head dancing. The shade begins bobbing up and down as the little flame man underneath dances and winks at me.

I know him. He's the flame from the old Disney cartoon

shorts. The flame with a little face, arms, legs, and a flamelike cone of hair. He's the one that runs around making little baby flames until the entire house is on fire. And now he's hiding under my dad's lamp. He's under the shade and he's winking at me.

"Ummm, Da-ad? Are the blinds still crawling?"

"What, Mia?"

"The blinds. Are they . . . I mean, are they crawling up the wall?"

"No. Why? Are you okay?"

"No. Uh, I don't think so. There's a little man under your lampshade. He's gonna start our room on fire. We better move our stuff out."

"Mia? I think the Ambien's getting to you."

"I think . . . I think I'm gonna be sick."

"Mia . . . ?"

I can hear him thinking as I sit on the bathroom floor. It's cold and white. Everything in the bathroom is really white, and really clean.

"Dad! Dad! The ship is sinking!"

Suddenly I can't keep the world from tipping backward. Sinking. Tipping. My body is slowly falling backward as I try to grab on to the toilet. The entire room is sinking like the *Titanic.*

"Dad, it's sinking. It's sinking. You know like when you're on a boat and you get off and then you go to bed that night and you feel like you're rocking. Well, it's like that only it's not, 'cause the ship is sinking. It's sinking."

"Mia, we're not sinking."

I can't understand why my dad can sit up perfectly straight on the bathroom floor while the world tips to the left underneath him. He keeps pulling me upright, but I keep sinking. The toilet has the same uncanny ability to stay upright. But I truly think we're all going to burn or drown. I'm terrified.

"Mia, these are just hallucinations. They aren't real. The ship isn't sinking; in fact we aren't even on a ship. Mia, look at me. We're on dry land."

Home to Seattle. The plane takes off and my eyes are dry. My heart is numb and I have a quiet and calm feeling inside of me. I have not hurt, not felt, not thought yet, and I hope it doesn't come. Pills are no replacement for food or sleep. The pain is beyond hurting. At some point over South Dakota, or maybe Montana, I suddenly feel as though I may explode. My eyes immediately swell and I feel sick. I suddenly can't help the tears that stream down my face. This continues all the way home until I forget that I am crying.

At the airport, I shake but don't realize it. I shake more when I see that I am shaking. We travel out past security and there she is: Mom. I can't do this. I can't be here. She is holding me. I am shaking sobbing breaking. My entire body is in pain. I can't be here. I can't stand being in Seattle. My mom is holding me tight, but I don't feel her. I can't do this.

cinda, I met Linea and Curt at the airport. I will never forget the tall, beautiful woman, my child, falling into my arms with a tear-streaked face, tangled hair, and a mess of pulled-together clothing that she may have been wearing for a week. She shook violently as she cried into my neck.

"I'm sorry, Mom, I am so sorry," she whispers into my skin. My heart breaks.

"I have lost everything. My school, my friends, my boyfriend, my job, my life. I am so scared."

She wept like this when she was a baby, wet mouth and cheeks pressed into me, drenching me with her sorrow. She is not a baby now, and I couldn't pat or walk or rock her pain away. I held her. I wished I could have her pain and she could walk away, back to her life, healed. Let me have it. Please, let me have it. I am strong enough. Let me take it from her. Please, God, please. I had no idea what this pain feels like, but I would take it gladly.

We were in the middle of the concourse, passersby turning their gaze from our space, avoiding our agony. Linea hates public displays of anything, but she is unable to move out of my arms. Her pain had ranted and raved as the airplane wheels pulled up and she flew out of Chicago. She ached all the way across the country, and now she had collapsed in Seattle. I was horrified at how sick she was, and my mind was going a million miles an hour, trying to stay ahead of this—whatever this was—and figure out what to do next. What to say, what to do. But at the airport, I just held her. I didn't let go. I wouldn't let go. I would not lose this child. If she couldn't stand, I would hold her up. If she couldn't breathe, I would breathe for her. I would not let go. We moved as one to wait for her luggage, to the car, and to home.

We took her home to her bedroom, her stuffed toys, and her dependency on her parents. She constantly wondered and worried and criticized herself for being sick, for leaving school, for not being more grateful. Unimportant, all of it, but I sat with her on the bathroom floor while she sobbed her heart out and said she would never be well again. Her pain filled our house. It was in every corner. The air felt different from before, tighter and heavier.

Every minute of every day we all felt this black pain living with us. We were in charge of keeping her safe, but we weren't sure how to do it, what that meant. I watched Linea and I listened and I tried to stay one step ahead of her, to say the right words and do the right things. It was as if one part of my brain was listening to her while another was sorting through everything I had ever known, trying to grab the right words, to give the right responses. How could I lessen her agony? What words would soothe? What magic charm could I possibly do to take this all away and make her well again? Nothing I said seemed to calm the raging sadness that had overtaken her. Not quiet sadness, but raging, painful, horrifying sadness. I could only be by her side. I could sit on the bathroom floor and on her bed and be in the same room with her, but I couldn't enter that dark and terrifying place that was consuming her.

Two weeks later, her dad flew back to Chicago to pack up her life. Not wanting to intrude on her privacy but needing to close down everything in Chicago, he packed and carried and moved her most personal belongings, sorting which to bring home and which to leave. I think he was crying when he called me, "This is the hardest thing I have had to do for her. I am going through her most personal belongings."

Would she ever return to Chicago? Of course she would . . . wouldn't she? We reminded ourselves how immensely grateful we were that she was alive. We kept unsaid the fear that we could have been doing the exact same thing had she killed herself. Curt shipped boxes home, loaded suitcases, and, with some hopefulness that she would soon be well and return to Chicago, stored things with Charlie.

linea I'm home, numb, and unhappy. I hate it here. I hate this room, hate this house, and hate this city. I have no friends and I can't even talk to my parents. This is ridiculous. I want to go back. My life is over.

I can't stand it. I can't stop these panic attacks, and my parents give me pills to sleep every night. They watch me take them and watch me fall asleep. I hate this place. I have no control over any movement. A life of puppetry. A life of forced movements. The force to put the fork to my mouth. The force to open my eyes in the morning. To walk to the bathroom. To speak. I just float around, a ghost in the house. My dad brought back all of my stuff. They are working so hard to make me like it here. I'm trying really hard, too. I just can't take this numbness much longer. I set up my room so it looks somewhat like my old room in the Chicago apartment. I hung my lamp over my bed and lined the walls with books so it looks slightly like an attic. I started yoga and acupuncture. I won't let the acupuncturist use my wrists yet because the knives still come from the inside. I still have panic attacks and spend a lot of nights on the bathroom floor crying, but I am not seeing as much blood. I feel like I have nothing to write about, though, because I am so numb that nothing really matters. Nothing I am doing, not the books, the yoga, the acupuncture, the medication, the counseling. Nothing seems to help this all-consuming nothingness.

cinda While Curt worked day and night to pack up Linea's life in Chicago and return home, I stayed close to her. She cried through the three days that he was gone, knowing what was happening in Chicago. She could not be left alone. We were on a roller coaster of emotions and in agony, searching for tiny grains of hope scattered among all the tears. She told me that she hated her life and that she couldn't take it anymore. Then she cried and told me she was sorry, that she knew she was worrying me so much and didn't want me to worry about her. In her pain, she even had moments of anguish that turned to fury. This was new to her and to me; she would lash out verbally, screaming, yelling, swearing. This was nothing like the Linea I knew. She told me that she was scared when she "got mad" and felt out of control. Linea, unlike her older sister, had never yelled at me as she went through the Bermuda Triangle of ages thirteen and fourteen. Maybe this was the problem. She yelled at me now.

She locked her bathroom door and shouted, "Leave me alone, Mom! You can't fix this! Just go away and quit trying so fucking hard!" She had never said "fuck" aloud to me before. I wasn't insulted; I was terrified.

I didn't know what to do. I continually repeated to myself, "Stay calm. Stay calm." I told her that she had the right to be angry, it was okay and that anyone would feel angry about leaving a life that she loved. But these words and thoughts didn't help her and didn't give me any confidence that I could help her. There were moments that I was truly afraid that she would spin out of control, push me aside and run off into the night, never coming back. Then she would open the bathroom door and drag herself out to me.

"I'm sorry, Mom. I don't want to be mean to you. I don't

know what is wrong with me," she cried. She was depressed. She would be better soon. Five weeks at most, I told myself. Five weeks until the Lamictal worked. Her psychiatrist in Chicago had said five to six weeks until the meds would kick in, and it had been two weeks already. I would give it seven weeks in total. I didn't need to mark it on the calendar because I marked it in my brain. I could be strong for five more weeks of this. Some minutes I could barely hang on. The only thing that kept me going was that I knew it was a thousand times worse for her.

She told me she just wanted to go back to Chicago, to go back to school. I reassured her that she would. I grabbed her chin and forced her to look into my eyes.

"You will be well soon. I promise you. You will be well soon. You will have your life back." I repeated this mantra daily, hourly, and prayed that it would be true.

I didn't sleep well at night; I had the motherhood switch turned on so that I could hear her every move, so that I could keep her safe. She was taking a sleeping pill before she went to bed, but I still checked on her two or three times during the night. I watched her sleep, I touched her hair, and I sent up prayers that she would make it through this. She slept hard with the help of the sleeping pills yet she tossed and turned, and I wondered if she were able to find some peace while she slept. I could hardly stand for her to be in this much pain.

Immediately after the call from Charlie, I had started the

search for help in Seattle. I called people who knew people who knew *the* people. I found a psychologist and psychiatrist in two days because we *know people.* Even with connections, it was not easy. I made countless phone calls, calling in favors and acquaintances and close and remote links to the best professionals in the field. I felt blessed that I had the knowledge, background, and expertise to make my way through a mental-health maze of doctors with restrictions of "no one under twenty-one," "no new patients," "next available appointment is in two months," "self-pay," "we don't bill insurance companies," and "we *certainly* don't bill *your* insurance company!"

One would think that my work as a professor in special education at Seattle University and my husband's as a vocational rehabilitation counselor at a research university hospital would somehow have given us some proficiency through the maze. To some extent, it did—we had more knowledge and connections than most people. But it was extremely time-intensive, exhausting, and frustrating. I spent hours on the phone, following up leads, reading the requirements and services available, reading through our insurance policy and, something that for some reason could bring me to tears of anger, wading through long and time-consuming phone trees. My frustration would boil over when I had finally been connected after considerable time to the "right person" only to be disconnected.

Throughout the long and complicated struggle to find help for Linea, I continually had these words running in the back of my mind: "We are lucky." How do families that are single-head-of-household, poor, unable to read or speak the English language do this? How do families help their children when they struggle daily to help themselves? I had spent my professional life advocating for those who don't get the care they need, and although it was extremely difficult to find and manage Linea's treatment, I knew I should be thankful that I had some knowledge and experience and good health insurance to do this work. But this didn't help the feelings of grief and anger. The truth is that I didn't want to be "the lucky one." I didn't want the opportunity to experience any of this. I just wanted my daughter to be well.

It took two weeks to line up Linea's medical care in Seattle. Two weeks of watching Linea and waiting for something awful to happen, hoping it wouldn't, still not knowing what we were looking at, just knowing Linea was so very, very sick. When we went to her first appointment with the doctor I found, we sat in the waiting area anxiously eyeing the other patients. I was exhausted. Curt and I had held her together for more than two weeks, and we were desperate for this appointment to bring us all some relief. We needed someone to assure us that she was on the right medication and that she would be better soon. We needed someone to wave a magic wand. Finally, the nurse called Linea back for her appointment and Linea left me; the nurse would keep her safe for a minute. For the first time since that phone call from Charlie, I cried. I cried noisily and helplessly and from sheer exhaustion. My fear had worked as a strongbox, keeping all the crying inside and all the tough action and courage on the outside. Sitting in the waiting room at Virginia Mason Medical Center, it cracked. The lock broke. I cried noisily from a desperate tiredness and deep sadness.

The waiting room was shared by patients expecting babies on one side of the room and the psychiatric patients on the other. No one looked at me while I had my public breakdown. I prayed with all my heart that this doctor could help her. Once again I asked, "Give it to me, let me have it. Please, please, give me the pain."

Before I was finished with my emotional collapse, I was called back to meet Linea's doctor. He was young and handsome and brilliant. He seemed to genuinely care about Linea and was very open to me as well. He told me to call him anytime that we needed him. He assured Linea that she would be better soon and told us that he would need to monitor her closely while the new medications worked their magic. We made the next appointment and drove home. This is what we needed. This doctor obviously knew what he was doing and could make her better.

Back at home, my lockbox was back in operation. We had a plan now, we had a team, we had things to do to make Linea better. I reread the medical insurance plan for the tenth time and started files for the psychiatrist and the psychologist, the prescriptions, and the multitudes of bills. Thankfully, our mental-health coverage was good. We had twenty visits per year for her to see a psychologist. That should do it. (I had no idea what was ahead of us, how woefully short those twenty visits would fall.) I carefully read everything I could about her medication; the side effects were frightening, but by six weeks—maybe not five, as the doctor in Chicago had told us—things should turn around. We were two weeks from the prescription in Chicago and counting. Wait, I couldn't count the first two weeks because she didn't fill the prescription; she didn't take the pills. Maybe it would take her a little longer. I could hold out for a little longer. I had to.

Slowly, slowly she became a little more stable. After three months, she had few side effects and told us she felt a little better. Not completely herself, not where she wanted to be, but at least not as bad as she had been when she left Chicago. She was trying to rebuild her life and take care of herself. She was doing everything she could to get well, both mentally and physically. She wanted to try anything that could help her. She had a complete physical, she started to go to an acupuncturist to see if she could help her with her anxiety and depression, she went to yoga, she joined the YMCA, and she tried to connect with the few friends who were still around Seattle. The tears were lessening, she was no longer crying all the time, but she was certainly far from happy. There was no joy in this daughter of mine. She stepped slowly through her days without noticing life. She was trying so hard, but she could not move fully out of this low, low place that she was in.

Her family became her best friends—not that she wanted us to be and not that we wanted to be, but she didn't have anyone else. Her friends had mostly left the area or were busy with lives of their own and perhaps weren't sure how to relate to her. Jordan checked in with her regularly and tried to include her in activities and outings. She took Linea with her to paint a mural and to just hang out with her. She invited her to things that she did with her own friends, and often Linea would go along with her. She was supportive and loving and at the same time couldn't comprehend why Linea was home and sad. "I don't understand it. I just get mad, not sad. What is *wrong* with her? Can't she get over it?"

I didn't know the answers. Intellectually and clinically I did, but emotionally I didn't. I believe that if you have never suffered from a deep and relentless depression, you have no idea how painful it is. My mom has had depressions as well as serious health issues and surgeries. She told me that the depressions were the worst pain she had ever had in her life. I had experienced a short depression years before and had taken antidepressants, which were effective, but I had not experienced anything close to what Linea was going through.

We heard from friends, family, and my students about other people's "breakdowns" during the first few years of college. Everyone seemed to have a story of a kid going off the deep end for a time and then turning it around better than ever. The stories gave us hope, but we didn't hear many about kids quite as sick as Linea seemed to be. One of my students told me that she had a complete breakdown at nineteen and ended up living on the streets and doing everything she could to survive, most of which should have killed her. She recovered and went on to graduate school. I clung to her story late at night when I couldn't sleep.

The next three months slogged along. Between doctor appointments, we tried to help Linea fill her days. She had gone from a full-time student with a life packed with friends and activities to hanging out with her parents, sister and brother-in-law, and a few friends. Looking back, I see that this time was a constant struggle for her to stay in our lives. I am sure that she wanted to tell us to leave her alone and simply walk away from us, yet she continued to do her best to stay. It was a bigger struggle for her to stay in her own life. I know now that she fought every day not to walk away from her own life, not to give up and to end it all.

During those months, she didn't want to do anything on her own. I tried and tried to find something to do that would make her happy. I took her to lunch, shopping, movies, exercise and yoga classes. I bought her art supplies, music, books, clothes. I wanted so desperately to find a spark within her that I spent all of my energy trying, trying to find . . . what? Although she was no longer crying or visibly anxious or irritable, she was still flat and had little interest in doing anything. If she even vaguely suggested that she was interested in something, I would do my best to help her find that passion for life she had always had.

I began to feel that I wasn't going to be able to fix this. I believed (and still do) that she was trying as hard as she possibly could to get well. Her moods were certainly better than when she first returned from Chicago, and maybe she was getting better. Yet I couldn't sleep and I worried constantly that there was more going on with her than the tears and pain and loneliness that she shared with me. Curt and I talked constantly about what to do, how to do it, what was wrong, what was right. We analyzed whatever was wrong with Linea from every angle possible. To save ourselves, we tried to put a moratorium on talking about our own daughter after a certain number of hours or a certain amount of exhaustion. But it didn't work; we couldn't stop. We talked and talked. (How do people get through something like this alone without someone to support them in the worry?) Nothing was working. We felt like Linea wasn't coming back to us. We didn't know what to do. We couldn't find the answers. We couldn't find Linea, the Linea we knew and remembered and loved.

We talked about her constant low mood. She didn't talk about hurting herself anymore and she wasn't crying all the time, but she told us over and over again that she did not like living at home. She had everything she wanted in Chicago, and now she felt she had nothing. Could it be that she *was* better but just sad about living in Seattle and away from her friends and Chicago life? She told us that she might feel better if she were to find a job and move into an apartment. Her childhood friend was going to school in Seattle, and they plotted about finding an apartment together.

Linea wanted to make time move quickly so she could get back to Chicago and resume her life. We wanted desperately to believe she was doing better. We were walking a fine, thin line of supporting her but trying to make decisions that would keep her safe and assure her future. We were new at having a daughter with a mental illness. We didn't know the best way to proceed. We took one step forward, two back, and second-guessed ourselves constantly.

5. determination

cinda In April, Charlie flew out from Chicago to visit Linea. The family gathered to welcome him with a northwest seafood dinner. We fixed mussels and crab and salmon, and we laughed and danced and laughed some more. How fun it is to have adult children! It was the best time we had experienced since Linea came home. She was smiling! She laughed with us! I thought we must be over the worst. I was so hopeful. It was a great evening and for the next few days we saw our daughter again—not the ghost who had been living with us but the daughter we had known. She was happy! I felt light. I felt the heavy, wet, dank gray lift up and out of our home. I could breathe. I could sleep. I was grateful.

Linea and her best friend, Jean, had been talking about finding an apartment together. Linea had slowly but steadily been moving forward to a happier, calmer, and safer place. Her psychologist thought that moving into an apartment would be a good first step for her before returning to Chicago, and her psychiatrist agreed that this was a good decision. We talked long and hard about this move and asked Linea if she was safe. She said she felt a little depressed but that she was not suicidal. She said she thought most of her bad feelings right now were due to not being in Chicago for spring semester and that by working and living with her friend, she would feel better about being at home. She had always been so honest with us as well as her doctors and we wanted to support her, so we agreed.

With Charlie in tow, we went apartment hunting for the perfect place for Linea and Jean to live for six months. Six months and she could go back to Chicago. I hoped that we were over the bump in the road, although it had been a very large "bump." It was an incredibly beautiful day in Seattle in early spring. They had found an apartment on Capitol Hill they wanted all of us to see. From the roof of the apartment building with the STUDIO FOR RENT sign we could see Puget Sound, the Olympic Mountains to the west and the Cascade Mountains to the east, the Space Needle, the ferries coming in and out of Puget Sound, and Pike Place Market all by simply turning in place. What a stunning city! We were ecstatic that Linea had made it this far.

Linea, Charlie, Curt, and I went to a coffee shop across the street from the apartment. Was she ready for this? Did we all agree this was the right thing to do? After talking about it, we finally agreed that she should take the apartment. We all shook hands on the decision to support her. Her smile was blinding. She ran across the street to the apartment with such joy. Jean arrived and they held hands and jumped up and down with excitement. They had been doing this dance of triumph and excitement together for more than fifteen years, but we hadn't seen this in Linea for such a long time. I prayed that we were making the right decision.

In the next few weeks, as we waited for the apartment to become available, Linea packed and organized her room, talked to friends in Chicago, and made plans for the move. Linea, Curt, and I lugged pounds of furnishings up long flights of stairs. We didn't care. We laughed and joked and the day felt like a wonderful new beginning for her. In less than a week, she found a job one block from her apartment. The weeks and months would go quickly and she would be back in Chicago in no time. Please let this work for her!

linea April—This is Capitol Hill, where I live with my best friend, idol, and true love, Jean. Her recent disappearance into coupledom, however, has led her to completely forget our past history and allegiance, making me question our friendship and my adoration.

Jean is a willowy intellectual, clad in the very best-intended fashion. We have been best friends since the age of five, and until this last week I have thought of her as the most beautiful human being alive. But this last week, when I needed her the most, she wasn't here.

Today is Easter. Today I served selfish, rich hipsters at Urban Outfitters wearing my cutest clothes and cheesiest smile. Now I am sitting at my small kitchen table eating sushi and staring at the leftovers dropped off by my mom and grandma. I can't bear to eat the leftovers, because they remind me that I missed the celebration. They remind me I missed the warmth and fun of sitting at a table surrounded by ten of my favorite people. Easter has never really been a big religious holiday for me, more of a time to celebrate and cherish the family I love so much.

So I sit here. I sit at a table passed down through four generations of Kirkwood women, in a cluttered apartment, thinking of a cluttered friendship. I sit in emptiness, piled-up dishes, and flies.

As I sit here, my thoughts become increasingly terrifying. I start thinking about the knives in the kitchen. I start thinking about blood and my sudden obsession with its color. The juxtaposition between Easter happiness and the longing for drug-induced oblivion astounds me. I am not the person I knew myself to be. In the midst of the gory thoughts that plague my every blink, I need a way out—some sort of emotional release, or at least some sort of affection. That's how the first Charlie comes into the picture.

"Charlie One," as he is affectionately called in my family, was my high school sweetheart and is now a high-fashion model. He's pretty. Too pretty. And he's changed since high school. Since being in Milan for fashion week, he has offered less comfort and compassion and has been less aware of my needs and treacherous moods. With dangerous thoughts in my head, and knowing I have no choice but to ask for protection in these circumstances,

I call him, begging him to come over and just listen, instructing him not to initiate anything physical.

Soon, I'm sitting in my underwear on the bed, my eyes dry and longing for tears, as he puts his clothes back on and leaves to go back home for his family Easter dinner. My hair is tangled, my body yearning for more. I now don't even care enough to hurt myself. I am once again beyond tears and long for more alcohol, sex, and drugs to ease this pain. I have the option of blow, of sex, of as much alcohol as I need. I have the option of weed to completely numb me, or a blade to calm me. I try to be strong but don't know how to stop this unbelievable pain. This constant incessant pain of being alive. I didn't want this. He says "I love you" as he leaves and calls the next day to see if I'm okay. He says he'll take me out to dinner next Friday, but the damage is done. He says he loves me but still has the ability to leave me at the worst moments.

This poor decision is like someone came in and took over my body. I begin to wonder if I'm schizophrenic. Something squeezes my wrist from the inside, and I need Charlie Smith to hold it tight to keep it from bleeding, I need him to hold me tight to keep me from melting. But I have pushed him away too.

Safety takes strength, and that's when I panic. No amount of "centering" or psychiatric techniques will save me when this urge to hurt myself comes. This is when I go for the drugs. All the different types of drugs I can get my hands on. I long for Adderall or Vicodin or sleeping pills. I want. I need. I need them. I need alcohol. One night I drank all the wine in the house and took a ton of the Lamictal. Testing my limits. I need that. I need to get sleeping pills again and drink lots of wine and take them slowly, a few every fifteen minutes until the bottle is empty, and then fall asleep in the tub. Stop. These thoughts can't come back. I can't take it. I can't have them here. They need to leave or I will do it. I will if they keep coming. Make them stop. Get them out of my head.

There are two competing thoughts in my head. There is the dream of how to do it (the dream of blood that scares me into psychotic rage or fear) and there is the calm that comes before the storm (the thought of how nice it would be to sleep forever). There are the pills and there is the knife. They need to leave. They need to get out of my head. They need to leave. They need to leave.

cinda Linea was in her apartment, but things weren't going well. She would call me in frustration and anger about Jean, ants in the kitchen, Jean's boyfriend, her job, and her lack of a life that she likes, let alone loves.

We were both fighting for her life but didn't quite say the words aloud. We used other words.

Her words: "I can't do it anymore."

My words: "Are you safe?"

She promised me she was safe. I turned this promise around in my mind a million different ways, examining it for its truth. Could I believe her? Around and around we went, back and forth like a seesaw. But she wasn't all right and I knew it.

She held a mask in front of her face and kept whatever was going on deep inside. But I could tell she was not herself. I knew we had to "give the meds time" and she was seeing her doctors weekly, but it wasn't enough for me. I wanted to bring her home again so I could check on her throughout the night and watch her every minute of every day. But she told me, "I'm fine."

Linea was different from all the years of Linea I had known. She was sad and she was angry. Her emotions slammed her back and forth. She continued to talk to me, and I know she was trying as hard as she could to get rid of her depression, but she was so very unhappy, irritated with her apartment, furious with her roommate, lonesome, anxious, rude, cranky, and sad. I tried to keep steady, knowing that she was weighted down with missing her life in Chicago and that her meds weren't working yet. She wore her friends down with her anguish. Jean had been her best friend since they were in kindergarten, yet even Jean was pulling farther away from Linea as Linea fell deeper into her own pain. She was alone too often as her friends moved away from her. They deserted her, I think because they were too young, too inexperienced, too self-centered, and too afraid. I also was too afraid, but I would not desert her.

I worried night and day. In my sleep, in meetings, eating,

walking, and breathing I carried worry with me like a dank and heavy backpack. Curt and I faced this battle—a battle that didn't make sense to us and for which we had no experience and no training—together. We took turns convincing each other that everything was going to work out. He was more convincing than I. I carried my phone with me everywhere I went and it was a presence in my classrooms. When it rang, my heart would stop.

My mother and I stopped by Linea's apartment to deliver Easter dinner. Her affect was flat and she said she was tired and just wanted to go to bed. Again, I asked her, "Are you safe?"

Again, she told me, "I promise you, Mom."

We pushed through day by day, worry by worry. Finally we were offered a small break. I had an opportunity to go to Chicago to a conference, and I asked Linea if she wanted to go with me. She was ecstatic. I made flights and hotel reservations while she made phone calls to her friends, telling them she was coming home!

linea We are sitting in an apartment with no furniture, bare walls, and newly carpeted floors. I feel like I am finally happy again. I am in Chicago to visit after being gone for what seems like years. I have not felt this joy in months. I sit here with the best company, a few good records, and some whiskey, and I am perfectly content. What was it that I was trying so hard for in the past? I never realized that this is all I need.

I sit and watch as the tornado that is looming outside of Chicago causes one of the biggest lightning storms I have seen in years. Lightning hits buildings and lights up the entire block as we sit here in this dark warm room, and I am content. Tyler smokes, Stephanie dances, Brittany and Matt flirt, Chris sleeps, Jake plays the DJ, and each one of them becomes more dear and precious to me with every passing moment. It is amazing to be with my two old roommates and remember what it was like to live with people who truly cared about me. People who are there when you break up with your boyfriend or just stub your toe. Friends that are there just because they like you, not out of guilt or because they feel they should be after knowing your family for years.

Another strike hits, and as we hear the boom, the lights flicker. We watch in amazement. Jake breaks the silence and puts on Bob Dylan's "If Not for You," and I suddenly feel as though I have been shot in the chest. My eyes immediately swell and I feel sick. This song is everything I have lost. This song is the happiness of my life with Charlie. My home with my caring friends in Chicago. This song is joy. I run to the bathroom as if I am about to puke and shut the door just in time to hide my collapsing on the floor. I spend a lot of time on tile floors crying, hyperventilating. When I can't stand it anymore, it seems that the most hidden places happen to be tiled. Everyone stays in the warm dark living room as I hide in a cold fluorescent dungeon. When

I am finished crying and I'm sure that the song is over, I rejoin the group. No one has noticed.

Back to Seattle. I had asked Jean before I arrived home from Chicago to please please stay at the apartment and spend the night with me on my first night home. To please be with me. I ask the bare minimum of her, and tonight I needed a friend. I should have bribed her. But she says she tried. She is cranky and upset because she claims she is trying so hard. Well, thanks for trying. Thank you for coming home long enough to eat the dinner I made and quickly leaving again. Thanks for letting me go from ten of my closest friends across the country to this.

Jean left and I'm broken. It isn't her leaving in general—at this point I would love to not have to cohabitate with her—but it is all of my stupid visions of who I thought she was that just walked out the door. It is the vision of Jean as my one true friend, as the other half of me. I have lost all faith in her and our friendship.

I'm scared of this fear that is crawling up. It is coming and I know it. I feel it. The visions, the longing, the need to fix this pain. I'm scared because I don't have any distraction or any hand to hold when I am terrified that it will come. I am terrified because it is getting closer and I am sitting in our old Goodwill plush green chair and I am shaking and the tears are coming slowly because at this point I can't sob because I am too terrified.

I feel that it will kill me if I don't call someone, and as much as I hate to do it, I ask Jean to come back. I feel fucked-up enough that I would even call *her* and beg *her* to come back and give me a hug. I can't believe I have to beg. My eyes are so full of tears that I can barely see the numbers to dial the phone.

She comes back merely to give me a hug. I can't help but tell her how I feel and how I hurt, and she responds with words that make the pain rise higher and faster. She tells me that all I do is complain when her friends are around and that no one wants to be around a downer. She tells me that she tries so hard but she doesn't know how to deal with this. She makes up poor excuses for being a lousy friend and human being.

She said on the roof the night I finally broke up with Charlie that the reason we are living together is that she wanted to be here for me. That she felt she had been a bad friend before, by not being there for me.

Bullshit.

You say you're a bad friend. You've said this before. If you feel that way, then do a fucking thing about it. But now I realize you probably were never the person I thought you were. You have ruined my faith in all friends. You taught me that no one gives a damn. People say they care until their friend is ready to kill herself, then all of a sudden, *whoa, this isn't part of the deal. Whoa, too much friendliness.* Wouldn't any normal, caring person with a beating heart in her body stay in this house, or at least stay on the goddamn phone, and make sure that no harm is done?

So thanks, Jean. Thanks for making me realize that I have no true friends and for reminding me that this is all my fault and that I am a freak.

She says she's sorry and leaves. She leaves me with a bottle of wine, the pills, and the knives in the kitchen. I drink the wine as fast as I can. I am calmer than ever and ready to make the pain come out. I take seven Lamictal and five Advil. I wish for sleeping pills but can't walk straight enough to find any. Why can't I just let out the tears in a flood? Instead they slowly stream down my face as my mind heats up, and now I'm getting scared. I'm terrified and alone.

I want blood. I want pain, I want blood. By this point I can't breathe and I begin the mantra "I need I need I need." I go to the kitchen, and the first sight of the giant butcher knife sends me hysterical to the floor. The tears finally come, and I'm sobbing and swaying and scratching at my legs and talking to myself. "You're stronger than this, please be strong, please be strong, please be strong . . ." But the other force has come through as well, and I stand up again looking for smaller knives. Back to the floor and I am trying to battle the beat in my head while talking out loud, crying, swaying, talking, gasping, swaying. I hurt so much. I hurt so much. I have to save myself. I can't do this, and the only thing that saves me is the fact that I don't want Jean to be the one that discovers me. I don't want her to blame herself.

I call Charlie One. He doesn't know how to deal with it, but instinct tells him to stay on the phone. He tries to cheer me up. He talks me out of taking the rest of the pills and out of the kitchen. He gets me on the computer where he can keep track of my whereabouts online. He makes me talk to him on the phone and online to know that I am not doing anything bad and that I am far from the kitchen. He knows I can't handle more than two things at a time in my current state of being and talks to me until I fall asleep.

He saved my life. If Jean were to know, she'd think she caused the entire episode. She'd take it personally instead of realizing it is just me dealing with this darkness. This pain. It is just me grieving the death of my life and my friendships in Chicago. My sadness for missing the home that I was sent away from. My feelings of self-hatred for not being strong enough to stay there. It was the lack of support that topped it off. That was never the cause of the hurt. It was the lack of care or concern that made it just that much more painful.

Jean won't know what I mean when I complain of a hurt stomach tomorrow, or when she sees the scratches on my legs. She won't know. She won't know because I won't ever tell her.

I can't do it anymore. I have the "trendiest" job, on the "trendiest" street in Seattle. I get to wear the "coolest" clothes and meet the "coolest" people. Each day I greet the crowds of beautiful, trendy people. I say "Hello!" and "Welcome to Urban Outfitters," only to think about how I will end all of this pain.

"Hi, welcome to Urban!" If I can get Valium from Tim's little brother, then I can be loopy enough to not be scared. I'll call him "Hey there!" when I get off work and get it by this weekend. Then I can have time to find a good sharp razor "How ya doin' today, guys? Tell me if you need help finding your size!"

blade. I will turn off all the lights "Hello!" so I won't be scared of all the blood. I also can't forget "Hi, the dressing rooms are upstairs" to put the sign on the door telling Jean to call the police and go directly to Eric's. Then I will put on my "bath songs" playlist while I "Shoes, yeah, I can help, what size do ya need?" slit my wrists and die. No mistakes. I have to go all the way.

It makes me completely happy to think of this plan and is actually the only way I can be civil to customers. Everyone in the whole goddamn store thinks I am the peppiest person alive. All of those trendy bikers, vegans, and musical elitists see me as one of them. I have learned to morph into their vision of cool and have mastered melting even the coldest of snobs. If they only knew what I really was. How I really felt.

cinda Linea, ever the musician, made a CD with the songs appropriate for her suicide. Linea, ever the caring friend, wrote a note for the door of her apartment so that Jean would not find her body but would call 911 and not come in. Everyone knows that you are supposed to ask the depressed, "Do you have a plan?" Linea had a plan. But Linea had made a promise to her dad that night. He had picked her up at Jordan's house and driven her back across the bridge to her apartment. Curt sat with her in the car in front of her apartment and, one more time, asked her to promise to call us if she couldn't keep herself safe. He asked for a promise that she would be safe. She said she would. That night she sat on the floor in her kitchen with a knife, fighting off the demons, fighting to stay alive. Her plan involved pills, alcohol, cutting, and dying in a bathtub filled with warm water while carefully selected songs played in the background.

Somehow she made it through that long, long night. She had her standing appointment with her psychologist the very next morning. Linea finally said the magic words that will assure action from any professional: "I can't keep myself safe."

I thought I knew about depression, about mental health—I cover both in my classes with my graduate students, in lectures, and discussions. This was something vastly different. With Linea's five words to her psychologist, we were soon even further into unfamiliar territory and moved rapidly into a world about which we knew very little.

During Linea's time of darkness, these past six months, I had kept a running clock in my head: Where was she, where should she be, what was she doing, was she safe? At eleven o'clock on a sunny Tuesday morning in May I knew she was finishing her ten o'clock appointment with her psychologist. I had worried most of the night with an anxiety that gripped me and that was stronger than ever before, but I hadn't called her. I called her too much and didn't want to call her in the middle of the night. I waited until the next morning, until she finished meeting with her psychologist.

She answered on the last ring right before her phone went

to voice mail. She said she was still with Victoria. It was almost noon and I wondered if she had a breakthrough of some kind or had touched on something so deep that the appointment ran over the scheduled hour. Although it was highly unusual for her appointment to run over by even five minutes, let alone thirty, I felt calmer after just hearing her voice. She said, "I have to go. I am with Victoria. I'll call you later."

Thirty minutes later Curt called me. The first words he said were, "Honey, you have to be brave."

Brave? What the hell do you mean? Tell me, tell me, tell me now. I cannot describe my feelings. I shut the door to my office. I stood against the wall.

Everything stopped—my heart, my breath, my thoughts. I was rigid with fear.

Of course I knew it was Linea. "Was she hit by a car? Is she hurt?" Linea's appointment was in downtown Seattle and she always walked from her apartment on Capitol Hill. What else could it be? I had just talked to her less than an hour ago.

"No, she wasn't hit by a car. She is not physically hurt. I am taking her to Harborview. She told Victoria that she can't keep herself safe," he tells me. "It's going to be okay, baby." His voice wasn't as reassuring as his words. I told him I would meet them there.

"Keep her safe," I whisper.

"I will."

6. necessity

cinda Harborview is the major trauma hospital for the Pacific Northwest. It is only four blocks from my university. I was shaking too hard to walk. I knew that if I walked, I would start to run, and if I ran, I would come completely loose and run down the hill out of control, trampling pigeons and crashing onto the sidewalk. I asked a friend and colleague to drive me. She looked frightened and we took turns reassuring each other that it would be okay. All would be fine. If I kept saying those words, it would be true. I couldn't allow myself to think anything else. I sat very still in the car and held all my fear inside: I will be brave. I will be the bravest mom there ever was. I am ready to fight anything that can hurt my daughter.

When we got to the hospital, I wasn't sure where to go. Harborview Medical Center is a huge complex, and no one I knew had ever been ill enough to be there. I had been to Harborview a few times to present at conferences in the education wing, but I didn't know the campus well. We followed the signs to the emergency room, and Lisa dropped me off, telling me to call her if I needed anything at all.

The emergency room at Harborview is a fear-provoking place with some of the sickest people in Seattle. The psychiatric unit of the emergency room is even more frightening. I walked past the smokers and the street people crowded together on the sidewalk, through the swinging doors, and into the holding room. The people waiting there were very ill, very frightened, and some very agitated. Linea was one of them. She was sitting by her dad and, again, I saw that frightened little girl—the one who had met me in the airport four months prior—who needed her mom and dad to keep her safe. Her head was down and she was slumped against Curt. She looked terrible. She looked sick. As soon as she saw me, she stood up and grabbed me. I put my arms around her and she started to cry.

She clung to me and sobbed. My heart had been pounding; now it seemed to stop beating. I think it was bleeding. But then my mother heart started up again: I will keep this child of mine safe. She said, over again, "I am so sorry. I am so, so sorry." I told her how glad I was that she was alive. "Thank you for being here. I love you so. I am so thankful for your strength. You do not have one single thing to be sorry for."

Linea whispered those awful words again, "I can't do it anymore. Mom, I am so, so sorry."

Curt and I sat side by side with Linea between us. We held hands and we didn't talk. There was so much going on in the emergency waiting room that it was all we could do to stay steady on our bench as a sea of crisis pushed against us: people rushing past, crying, arguing patients carrying on loud conversations, nurses moving in and out, trying to establish some order in the room. A nurse finally called Linea's name and took her through the locked doors and into the emergency psychiatric unit. As soon as she left the waiting room, Curt and I looked at each other with the terror in our hearts. We still didn't talk. We held hands. We took a breath and waited. Neither of us could believe that we were here, in this place, with our child who wanted to kill herself.

We were finally called into the lockdown unit of the psychiatric ER to stay with Linea. There were no windows. The doors were locked. The nurses were harried. The three of us sat in a tiny room with a gurney and one chair. We didn't know what to expect and we had no information, and so we just waited. A nurse came in briefly and in response to our questions told us she had no information.

We waited. The nurses' station was across the hall from the door of our small waiting room and we watched as the staff shared a birthday cake behind the glass. We waited and watched the party. We listened to the nurses laughing with each other as patients waited, and waited, and cried and wailed up and down the halls, and I fought against the rising panic in my chest.

We waited for more than seven hours in that tiny room within the psychiatric emergency unit. As we waited, we listened to a man at the end of the hallway sob and cry and weep off and on for hours until his sedation finally kicked in and all was eerily quiet from his room. At this point in our journey I was not yet used to grown men crying like children who are hurt and want their parents, believing the pain will never stop. It was only the beginning of my education in this kind of pain. We took turns using the restroom, and on the way down the hall we walked by a shadow of a girl about Linea's age in the next room. She seemed close to dying from anorexia. She was curled up on the end of the gurney and the nurses were pleading with her to give them a urine specimen. She wouldn't. She wanted her mother. She wouldn't look at the nurse or let her draw blood. The nurse told her that she needed to help them or they would have to hold her down so that they could help her. We didn't want to listen. We didn't want to witness her very personal anguish. We soon learned that there is little that is personal in a psychiatric ward.

The waiting was excruciating, but even more agonizing was the unknown. We had no idea what to expect. I could feel Curt's anger grow as the time lengthened. My own anxiety continued to rise, but there was nothing we could do. We had to stay calm for Linea. Finally Curt walked out and questioned the nurses about what was going on, why the long and longer wait? Why were they having a birthday party complete with cake directly across the hall from us while our daughter, afraid and suffering, was waiting and waiting, growing more terrified by the moment? We were just barely holding it together but knew that we must or we would lose Linea.

linea Walking into the emergency room at Harborview, I feel everyone staring at me. It must be the short black skirt I'm wearing, or maybe the sweater tank top that cuts below my lacy black tank top that looks like a bra. Maybe it is the black nails, or the fact that I am shaking uncontrollably. Looking at me through someone else's eyes, I would have figured that I was some coke-head unable to get a fix. Maybe she is anorexic, people might think. Maybe she is a hooker.

And why is her father being so sympathetic? Why is he trying to help her when she obviously did all of this to herself? Why is she wearing those clothes? and What is she on?

I am terrified. I'm not on anything, but I am terrified enough to shake like a drug addict. My parents keep asking me if I am cold. No. I'm hot. Hot and terrified.

I sit for what seems like hours in this waiting room. The immense fluorescent waiting room that has the ability to both crush you with its claustrophobic chaos while at the same time lose you in its vastness of personalities and sadness.

I was expected. Victoria, my shrink, had called. The emergency room was ready for me. They were so ready that after the waiting room they left me sitting in a little exam room by myself for forty minutes while I contemplated how to kill myself with the few objects around me: bed with no sharp edges bolted to the floor, a chair that was smooth and rounded, white paper on the bed. Paper cuts are the only damage I could manage.

This entire trip is ridiculous. What have I gotten myself into? What happened? Did I really tell my counselor that I didn't feel safe? Did I really agree with her that I needed to come here?

They finally come in, and a meek little woman with Coke-bottle eyeglasses asks me questions: I hear you're feeling a bit low, do you feel like hurting yourself? Yes. On a scale of one to ten, how badly do you feel like hurting yourself? Ten. How could she ever understand?

In the end they tell me there are no rooms in Harborview, so they strap me to a stretcher like some nut and ship me off to the University Medical Center across town. My dad works at the University Medical Center. He will be there every day.

cinda I was numb. Somewhere deep inside of me was a completely out-of-control child screaming at the top of her lungs from sheer terror. Screaming for her momma. Screaming for someone to save her. My numbness and "professional self" kept that terrified child inside. On the outside I waited and continued to reassure Linea that all would be okay. I had no idea what the hell I was even talking about.

As we waited in the ER, we listened to the nurses as they determined that two patients would need to spend the night strapped to gurneys in the hallway because there were no mental-health beds available in the area. The patients were homeless and there was no place for them to go. Linea questioned why she, an upper-middle-class white girl with a home to go to, should be the lucky one and get a bed. She also questioned whether she should have told Victoria how sick she was.

"I shouldn't get the bed. Tell them that I can stay here tonight. Let someone else have my bed. I can go home," she said.

Of course we knew she needed help, but I ached for the people left in the hallway. As we were reeling with Linea's illness and the tangled and stressful mess of getting her treatment, I was bombarded by the limited availability of psychiatric care, particularly for the homeless and poor. Intellectually I knew this, but suddenly it was demonstrated in a very personal way. We have connections. We have insurance. Linea's dad works at the University of Washington Medical Center hospital, which is a partner with Harborview. And after many calls and more waiting, we were told there was a bed at the UWMC.

I was frightened when I heard Linea would be on 7 South, the psychiatric unit. I had thought, naïvely, that she would be in a bed for a day or two on a medical unit and then we would take her home. A bed in a psych unit was something different. We begged Harborview to let us drive her by private car to the UWMC—she would sit between us, we wouldn't let her hurt herself, we were professionals, we both worked directly with people with mental-health problems, we would get her there safely—but it was against the rules. Even Curt's UW hospital badge clipped to his shirt didn't help.

Linea was terrified and begged not to ride in the ambulance. But as we watched in disbelief, she was strapped to a gurney, loaded into the ambulance, and transferred to the very hospital where her father works, one floor below his office. He had left his office in a rush shortly after noon to pick Linea up at Victoria's. Now, at midnight, we were heading back to the UWMC where there was one bed with Linea's name on it.

We were exhausted and numb when we finally met with Linea's nurse at the UWMC. We were told that Linea would be given anti-anxiety medication and a sleep aid. Her nurse was calm and kind, and after the ER at Harborview, I felt my fear drop a very small notch. No one had reassured us at Harborview, but at UW I felt that someone cared about us, not only Linea but also our family. I had to feel this way in order to leave Linea by herself in the hospital. Before I left, I held Linea and repeated the mantra, "It will be okay."

She repeated hers, "I can't do this anymore."

I said, "You don't have to. We will do all the work now."

We assured her that she would be well soon, that "this" was for the best. We thanked her again and again for telling her psychologist the truth. We thanked her for not killing herself.

We arrived home at one A.M. and cried ourselves to sleep, each crying silently so as not to upset the other. I lay frozen in place in the dark trying not to move, and I remember thinking, Things are moving too fast. I can't get her back. I can't get her back.

Early in the morning, we were back at the hospital. In the elevator, Curt's coworkers said good morning, glancing at us as we exited the elevator one floor below his office. We checked in through the locked doors to the unit. Linea was in the small waiting room, where she had slept on the couch. Her roommate was highly agitated during the early morning hours, battling demons and addiction. The nurses told us that they were trying to get her a private room.

Linea sobbed as she told me again, "I can't do it anymore. I am so sorry, Mom, but I just can't. I have to give up. It is not because of you and I don't want to make you and Dad feel bad, but I just don't want to do this anymore."

She didn't say that "this" was "live," but we knew what she meant. I held her and I cried with her. I told her, "You can give up. Absolutely you can. Just rest. You don't need to fight it anymore. You are in a safe place. I promise you that I will fight for you. I am NOT giving up. I won't, I can't, I will not give up on you. You can rest. You can give up and just rest." I meant it. When my babies were first given into my arms, my heart told me that I would do anything in the world to keep them safe. That feeling overwhelmed then and it rushed through me again as I held Linea in my arms in the psych ward. I didn't care how frightened and exhausted I felt. I would not let her go.

Of course she didn't believe me. Her face, her voice, her body told me she had no hope of ever feeling well again. Nothing anyone could do would help her.

That afternoon, her psychiatrist, a resident, a medical student, a psychiatric nurse, a social worker, and everyone else involved in her care met with us. We all crowded into a conference room. Curt had been to many family meetings in this very hospital, and he was in disbelief that he was the family member and not one of the therapists. Linea's psychiatric team told us that she was *critically* depressed, critically as in life-threatening. Her medication was not treating the depression and they were adding antipsychotics and anti-anxiety medication to the mix. I had a question rolling around in my head that I was afraid to ask, one I didn't want to ask in front of Linea. But I couldn't talk about her treatment behind her back, so I gathered my courage and asked, "Is she psychotic?" I had accepted depression and I was in the process of accepting bipolar disorder. Did she have schizophrenia? The doctor told us that because of her depression, she was in a state that looks very much like a psychosis. Then they dropped the bombshell.

"We suggest that you consider ECT."

Electroconvulsive therapy. Electroshock. Shock treatment. Shock therapy. ECT. Call it what you will, we were horrified.

We responded with alarm and anger. "Absolutely not. This is barbaric! Like *One Flew Over the Cuckoo's Nest*? Are you kidding me? Not with my daughter. No."

We were asked to watch a video on the procedure, and we declined. We felt it was too soon. She had been in the hospital fewer than twenty-four hours. Curt was angry and defiant. He worked with this staff. He knew many of them well. His office was almost directly above her room. He could not believe that these people he knew and worked with would bring this up at our first meeting. He was terrified.

I was horrified and deeply confused. I was also beyond terrified. I began to think that perhaps I was the one suffering a breakdown and it was all an illusion or a very bad nightmare. We left finally, trying to be polite. We said we would think about it. We felt defeated, out of control. We did not know what to do.

We discussed it throughout the evening, circling back again and again, around and around as we tried to understand. I told myself not to look up ECT on the Internet, but of course I did.

I read "All about ECT Electroconvulsive Therapy" at healthyplace.com. It told me that I might be "surprised to learn that electroconvulsive therapy (ECT) is still being practiced in most, if not all, psychiatric units in general hospitals and mental institutions." "Surprised" is not a strong enough word for my emotions.

I read on and was not reassured.

"The original use of electricity as a cure for 'insanity' dates back to the beginning of the 16th century when electric fish were used to treat headaches. ECT originates from research in the 1930's into the effects of camphor-induced seizures in people with schizophrenia. In 1938, two Italian researchers, Ugo Cerletti and Lucio Bini, were the first to use an electric current to induce a seizure in a delusional, hallucinating, schizophrenic man. The man fully recovered after 11 treatments, which led to a rapid spread of the use of ECT as a way to induce therapeutic convulsions in the mentally ill."

I had no idea. Barbaric. Inhumane.

It continued, "When we think of ECT many of us recall the terrifying image of Jack Nicholson in 'One Flew Over the Cuckoo's Nest.' This is not an accurate portrayal of the present-day application of ECT. Certainly, before the development of effective muscle relaxants, it was not unusual for patients to suffer broken bones as a result of these electrically induced seizures."

I told myself I would *not* read any further.

Of course I did.

"Today, the American Psychiatric Association has very specific guidelines for the administration of ECT. It is to be used only to treat severe, debilitating mental disorders and not to control behavior. In most states, written and informed consent is required. The doctor will explain in detail to the patient and or family the reasons why ECT is being considered along with the potential side effects."

I read one more paragraph, and by then I was crying.

"ECT is generally used in severely depressed patients for whom psychotherapy and medication are proving ineffective. It may also be considered when there is an imminent risk of suicide because ECT often has much quicker results than antidepressant remedies."

"Imminent risk of suicide." This all happened too fast. I didn't understand.

We decided that there was nothing more to do about it that night. We were almost 99 percent sure that she did not need ECT, but we decided to get more information the next day. We couldn't talk about it anymore and yet we couldn't sleep. I watched mindless television and Curt stared at sports scores on the Internet. We waited until we were too tired to sit upright any longer and went to bed. Another night where I pretended to be asleep so that he wouldn't worry about me. He did the same.

The next day I brought Linea a favorite treat, sushi. When I stepped out of the elevator, Curt was waiting for me, his face strained and tired. I had been carefully holding the sushi level and I let it slide downward into the bag. What else? What now? What was wrong?

He told me that Linea now had a personal hospital assistant, known as the H.A. The H.A watches her every move. He or she follows and watches while Linea eats her meals. The H.A. watches her brush her teeth. The H.A. watches her pee. The H.A. watches and listens as she talks and cries with her parents. He/she is her shadow. Her lifeline.

I didn't understand. "Is she worse? Did she get worse during the night? What happened? Why?"

"She is suicidal. She can't be trusted to be by herself," he told me.

He was the first to say the words. We had known, but we hadn't said them aloud. We had used euphemisms like "Keep yourself safe." She had said, "I can't stand *this*." We didn't say it aloud so that it we could keep it from happening. The truth was that our daughter was suicidal. She wanted to kill herself.

It hit me again how much sicker she was than what we knew, than what we saw, than what we said. I braced myself, put on a brave face, and was buzzed into the unit. I expected to see her crying or nonresponsive. But she wasn't crying. She was on a mood stabilizer and anti-anxiety medication, and she was giddy. She looked good if a little high. She was dressed and was wearing some makeup, and her pupils were dilated. She laughed when she saw that I had brought her sushi.

"Yeah, Mom! Good job!" She giggled.

She wanted to share her sushi with her H.A. She told me she was going to ask the doctors if she could take him with her so she could go to a party on Saturday night. I wanted to grab her and pull her behind closed doors and tell her to knock it off. If she could still put her eyeliner on straight then she could by God pull it together. She sat at the table giggling and sharing her twenty-dollar sushi platter with her one-on-one hospital assistant. She could have been on a date.

I was almost in a panic mode.

I asked her doctors again if she was psychotic. They told us she was in a depressive loop of the deepest kind. She was obsessing about suicide. She was unable to stop planning, thinking, and ruminating about killing herself or, if unable to finish it, at least hurting herself badly.

She continued to eat her sushi and flirt with her H.A. Suddenly she was finished, leaving half the pieces and going to her room. She lay on the bed and stared at the ceiling. I sat with her without talking until it was time for her group session, and then I left.

When I got home, I called the psychiatrist Linea had been seeing prior to her hospitalization. He was on the faculty at Harborview and considered top in his field. He asked how she was doing and listened to the updates. I questioned him about ECT and told him that the doctors were recommending it as a treatment plan. He did not act surprised and told me that it was vastly improved from even twenty years ago. He said the "shocks" are to only one hemisphere of the brain and do not have the severity of side effects that occurred with the older treatment that hit both sides of the brain. He told me not to be afraid. ECT was only done at Harborview and the doctors were some of the best in the nation. He also told me that medication can have very serious side effects and not having the right mix can cause cognitive problems as well as physical issues. He told me that she was highly at risk for suicide and there was also the issue of time. She couldn't stay in the hospital for three months or more until the doctors landed on the right type and degree of medication. He asked how Curt and I were doing. I told him I was very, very afraid. He was so calm and reassuring that as we ended the call I told him that he could bill me for the session. He responded, "You can call me anytime. Families are most important in the process of getting people well again." Excellent and caring medical professionals are often the difference between good and bad outcomes for people with mental illness. I will be eternally grateful for Linea's team of caring doctors and therapists.

Curt and I returned to the hospital in the late afternoon. Linea asked us to take the staples from the bulletin board in her room. "I can't stop looking at them. I know they wouldn't really hurt me very much, but I keep thinking about using them to dig into my skin or under my nails . . . something that would hurt. Can you take them out?" I could hardly believe what I was hearing. This was the result of a brain that had gone into a depression and couldn't return on its own.

She told me, "I love you more than anything, Mom, and I am so sorry but I can't stand this." She told Curt, "Just let me go, please, Dad. Don't make me stay." She didn't mean the hospital.

linea Here I sit in my almost luxury hospital room. I have it all to myself and no longer have to deal with Shirley the bipolar/schizophrenic roommate from my first couple of nights in this hellhole. The H.A. is staring at me and making sure I don't do anything stupid, but I still know that I am much quicker than she is and can use my computer cord in the bathroom if I really need to. I am so sick of this place, so lonely, so heartbroken, smashed into thousands of bits impossible to ever be reassembled.

There is a nurse here named Chris. He is a musician as well. Today he showed me the unit's guitar and said that I could borrow it whenever I wanted. He showed me a few chords and let me play it in my room. Maybe this will be the thing I need to get me out of this. Maybe music can finally save me.

I have been playing the guitar nonstop and am thankfully and finally alert due to a lack of drugs, but I have become increasingly emotional and angry with all of their bullshit questions. The same ones every day. Before they ask, I should just automatically answer: "No, I haven't had a manic episode; no, I am not psychotic; no, I don't see things; no, I do not hear voices in my head; no, I haven't changed my mind about killing myself." Their questions, videos, and groups only help to increase the need to disappear completely and forever. I hate this feeling. I want to be a rock.

Imagine a medium-sized conference room. Lights off with a large TV in the front. There are around fifteen people sitting facing the TV, some shaking their heads, some rolling their eyes, some with their eyes closed breathing in deeply. On the television there is a picture of a beautiful waterfall perfectly framed by flowers on each side.

A woman's voice is saying, "Now breathe in slowly. Now

imagine your favorite place. Imagine a waterfall, maybe a beach. Now breathe out. Say to yourself, 'I am relaxed. I am relaxed. I am relaxed.' "

At this point I have to try to avoid the urge to throw the communal box of tissues at the television. I can barely keep from laughing.

"I am relaxed. I am relaxed."

Next I'm ready for her to say something like, "Find your power animal," and I can see Chuck Palahniuk writing the novel of my life. When this charade ends, I am ready to bolt to the nearest bathroom and find a lightbulb to break or some loose cord to finally end this all until my hospital assistant (or, as I like to think, bodyguard) stops me in my steps.

"Carrie has your meds."

So still feeling drugged and loopy from the last dose, I find Carrie, the nurse in charge of my part of the unit. I take the meds in the little cup and swallow as told, and just like in movies, I open my mouth and show her beneath my tongue. This is truly out of *Girl, Interrupted* or some sad movie in a mental hospital. This can't be my life.

The new meds make me even more dazed, and I wish I could use a good bottle of whiskey instead. I guess the hangover isn't nearly as bad. Now I have to wait at least a couple of hours for the appropriate time to go to bed, otherwise you are put on alert. Can't go to sleep too early and not too late. I need a distraction, so I sit and pretend to watch TV.

As the sun is setting, I realize that I have to go outside or I'll suffocate. The drugs are kicking in and my eyes begin to blur and I'm feeling drowsy. I hope that I won't pass out like they want me to. My focus is gone, words are drifting away, and I feel like my hospital assistant is staring at me. I want out of this hellhole. I just want to die. The pills take the edge off, so instead of wanting to shout how much I want to die from the top of my lungs, I can only mumble it under my breath.

I can't be this drugged up anymore. They can't drug me every time I get depressed or anxious. It'll come right back. I know I will come out of the high sooner or later.

cinda I don't know how we got through the next two days, but now we were on day three of twenty-four-hour surveillance. Linea could not continue to be medicated at this level with a twenty-four-hour guard watching her every move. The medications were changed once again, but we were told that an effect, if any, would probably take at least six weeks.

We finally agreed to watch the video on ECT. The psychiatrist explained that we "West Coasters" were much more conservative than "East Coasters" about this procedure, and if Linea were in New York City she would likely have had ECT by now. We didn't even know that ECT was done in Seattle, New York, and throughout the country. We didn't know that up until one year ago it was administered in the very hospital where Curt works. The ECT program was now entirely at Harborview and was administered daily. We didn't know that it would be administered to a twenty-year-old girl-woman with plans to finish college, travel the world, and spend holidays with her parents. To a girl with parents whom she loves and who love her. To a girl with a home to go to and a family life that was considered "normal" by most standards. I thought I was nonjudgmental. I was—and am—accepting of and caring about others, particularly those in need. My perceptions—no, my prejudices—were challenged in that psych unit. ECT is not just for poor, sick people living in alleys and sleeping on heating vents. Mental illness is for everyone. In our safe upper-echelon lives, we might call it "depression" or "anxiety," but it is mental illness. Our daughter had a mental illness and it was life-threateningly serious.

I talked to her outpatient psychiatrist again for one more opinion, and he encouraged us to go ahead, the sooner the better. He reassured us that this was really the only option we had other than to keep her hospitalized—and suffering—for months while we waited for medications to work. Linea understood the side effects of the ECT. She couldn't stand the way she felt any longer. She wanted the ECT as quickly as possible.

We had to wait for a bed to open up at Harborview and then Linea would be moved back across town. We signed the paperwork for electroconvulsive therapy with her. I did not recognize my signature.

We agonized over how to tell our family that Linea was ill and in the hospital. We had called her grandparents and aunts and uncles the first day of her hospitalization and told them that she had depression and had been hospitalized for treatment. We did not mention the word "suicidal," but they all knew. I couldn't say the word "suicide" to my parents.

We called Jordan to update her first, and she immediately began quizzing us.

"Are you sure this is the right thing? Does she really need to be in the hospital? This seems so weird. I can't believe they actually do shock therapy! Are you SURE this is the right thing to do?" Jordan's questions were the exact questions we were asking ourselves. No, we weren't SURE, but we didn't know of any options other than a long hospital stay and perhaps a move to the state psychiatric hospital.

We made the decision to tell the rest of the family about the electroconvulsive therapy. By doing so, we wanted to show that Linea's hospitalization and the ECT weren't something to hide or be ashamed of. We were proud of Linea, astounded by what she was going through, and amazed at how she was hanging on to a tiny spark of life, one that she could not see but somehow was reaching for anyway. We both knew her depression was very much out of her control and needed strong medical treatment.

Is this the time to mention my own family history? For over twenty years, I have lived with the death of my only brother by a self-inflicted gunshot. For over twenty years, my family has carried our grief and struggled to understand his death.

Although we'll never know what really happened, there have always been two stories running through my family history. The first story—and the one that I personally believe—is that he killed himself. The second story says the gun went off accidentally as he tried to hide it under the driver's seat while a police officer followed him; his car's taillight was out and he had no driver's license. The police officer, with lights flashing, followed him for eight long miles while Steve stayed at a steady sixty miles per hour. After those eight miles, his car crashed off the road. The police officer ran to his car and found that Steve was dead from a shot to the chest. He was twenty-three years old.

Steve was battered and bruised from two years of hard struggles that included witnessing the death of three of his friends, breaking a bone in his back, and finally falling from a cliff and shattering his leg. We knew he was overwhelmed by the curves that his life had thrown him, but we didn't know how deep these feelings went. He struggled with an illness that was difficult to see amid all the other carnage in his life.

The grief of his death was carried by four of us: my mother, my father, my sister, and myself. I often felt that we were dragging a blanket, each of us with a corner, with an achingly heavy weight in the middle. When one would stumble or fall, the others would need to pull harder or slow down and wait for the person falling behind, the one who hurt too much to move forward. Each of us had this huge heavy rock of pain to move, and we carried it together, never leaving it behind. People deal with grief in different ways: Some chip off little pieces of the rock as they can and others watch as large boulders shatter off and roll away, taking everyone around them in the avalanche. My father was an avalanche. He lost his only son, and his grief was terrifying. It was teeth-gnashing, bone-breaking, bloodcurdling anguish. It frightened all of us. It left my mother little room for her own sorrow. Her mourning crawled into a quiet corner of her heart and pulled a blanket over its head. It hid quietly from view for many years.

It has taken twenty years, and we will never be the same, but now we can say his name, *Steve,* aloud. Over the years, the weight we carry has lessened and the grief may not be as sharp, but the questions are always there: Why did you do this? What could I have done? Didn't you think about us? Although we can never fully get to the "why?" we are all closer and softer with each other. We say "I love you" more often.

The last time I was with my little brother, we sat at the kitchen table at our parents' house. He was staying with them while trying his best to recuperate from the injury to a leg that he almost lost for good. This six-foot-five-inch blond, beautiful, funny athlete sat there drinking a glass of milk and told me he felt like "checking out."

I, a new professional with recent psych classes that addressed suicide, asked him if he meant it.

He looked at me and grinned. "I'd never do that to you guys, Sis."

Well, he lied. All the questions will never be answered in this lifetime.

I remember minute details leading up to the night Steve died, but I can't remember what happened afterward hardly at all. Curt, Jordan, and I were living in Tucson. It was September and still hot. I had made coq au vin for dinner that night (the first and last time I made it).

The phone rang at three in the morning. Curt answered it, listened, and finally said, "I am so sorry." He took my hand and handed me the phone. I remember it being my father on the line, but years later I found out it was my uncle who told me. He said, "Steve was killed in a car accident."

Four of the five cycles of grief that are supposed to occur over time coursed through me in minutes: denial, anger, bargaining, and depression. But not acceptance. We got up and dressed and packed. We woke Jordan and headed to the airport.

When we arrived in Spokane, my sister met me at the end of the jetway. As we cried in each other's arms, she said, "Steve killed himself. I didn't want you to hear it somewhere else." I was in shock from the news that my brother was dead, but in my mind and heart a car accident made sense. This news spun me away somewhere else, a place of black, intense pain, confusion, anger, and fear. I didn't know what to do or what to think. I couldn't think.

The memorial service is still a dim and dank place in my memory. I remember very little about it except that afterward a distant relative patted my shoulder and held my hand while she asked me, "Cinda, dear, do you know why he did it?" I wanted to scream at her. I wanted to slap her. At the time I thought that if I had known why, perhaps I could have prevented it.

Now I think I am closer to knowing why Steve killed himself. Linea has let me into the dark, frightening world of depression and hopelessness. It is all-encompassing and the darkness took over her life. It wanted her life. She was at a place where she could no longer fight it on her own. Steve lost his fight.

I was so angry with my brother for the pain he caused us all and for the fork in the road for my family that his death prompted. Our youngest sibling was dead. My parents had lost their only son. Everything changed. It set into motion a sense of insecurity and fear for me. I needed to be watchful. I needed to never let my guard down, or I could lose someone I loved. I could not trust that things would be "okay." One cold morning I screamed out at him, wherever he was, "If you ever show up again I will kill you myself, you bastard."

I missed him so. My heartache caught me unawares over the years. At a high school basketball game, a blond Adonis would fly down the floor for a lay-up shot and I would feel the tears on my face. "Amazing Grace" would be noted in the bulletin at church and I would need to leave before it was sung. I don't remember hearing it when it was sung at his service, but now it haunts me in the dark places of my mind. I grappled for years with the superstitious fear that those souls that came from a suicide spent their eternity in hell. My anguish ended one night when Curt's father, dead for more than ten years and whom I had never met, appeared to me in my dreams or my thoughts, I know not which. With great kindness he looked at me and, without using words, told me not to worry. Steve was not in hell. I believed him.

My agony at Steve's death was not only as a sister but also as a daughter and a parent. My parents had lost a child. I was a mother to three-year-old Jordan and I knew mother love. I could not stand the thought of that loss. I couldn't bear the pain that I saw demolish both of my parents. I could not imagine it even though it was right in front of me. It was so raw and so painful that I didn't know what to do, where to look, or how to move forward. His death planted a seed that was always in the back of my mind. Watch out! Keep watch! Both physical and emotional health must be guarded to keep your children safe! I wondered if the grief, confusion, and mystery of Steve's death had been passed down to my daughter from one generation to the next. Was it an illness that killed him? Was it somehow my inability to keep him safe?

Although I never mentioned him to her, Steve permeated Linea's thoughts in those brutal days before and during her hospitalization. She told her medical team about him. She asked me questions about how and why he did what he did.

She said she felt very close to him, even though she had never met him. In the large world of small connections, the pastor who had officiated at my brother's memorial service twenty years earlier and three hundred miles away now lived less than five miles from us and was the pastor of our church. (We didn't make the connection until the first time my parents attended church with us and Pastor Jim greeted them. I did not remember him during the grief of those horrible days when we lost Steve.)

Pastor Jim came to visit Linea in the hospital, and her first question for him was why Steve killed himself and what was the difference between her and her uncle. Why did he die and why should she live?

Pastor Jim said, "It was a different time and a different place. Had Steve been here now with what we know about depression and the treatments that are available, he could likely still be alive. Everyone did the best with what they knew at the time. You are in a different time and different place."

She asked why God lets things like this happen. He said, "I don't know. We don't know. I think it has to do with faith." She was questioning and wondering why she should live, but she was still fighting.

There were so many people who supported Linea during those difficult days. The music director from our church came sweeping into the craziest ward in the hospital as if he were visiting Linea at her college dorm. On his third visit he brought her work to keep her busy: transcribing musical scores for the church orchestra. She did it quickly; he started coming two or three times a week to pick up work and drop off more. He confessed to me that he had to work extra hours to make work and keep up with her.

Jordan came with her husband, Cliff, and we all talked and made silly jokes and tried not to remember where we were. Jordan's best friend from elementary school was at the hospital visiting a family member and asked if she and her husband could bring their new baby to see Linea. They were buzzed in and crowded into Linea's room. The baby sat on Linea's lap, and people talked and laughed and ate candy that had been given to her by another friend. I knew how bizarre this scene was. We were not having a family get-together. We were in a psychiatric unit with a hospital attendant watching Linea from fewer than four feet away. We could not get in or out of this unit without permission. There were patients walking the hallways who didn't care if they lived or died. Having friends and family come by provided us a distraction, but it was also nerve-racking for me when I could see on Linea's face that she couldn't stand any more talk, any more people, and mostly, holding it together in front of someone else.

After everyone left, Linea said, "Mom, I have a Mother's Day gift for you. I couldn't go shopping—ha ha—but I learned this just for you. I know you love the Beatles. It is not the best and I sound like a beginner, but I have really been working on it. Don't laugh!"

Linea played "Blackbird" for me on the guitar and handed me a piece of paper folded into a card.

Dearest Mommy,

This Mother's Day is truly special and I am so glad to be here with you. I know the two of us have been through some hard times in the last few months, and I thank you for the patience and love you always have for me. We have both worked very hard to get through this and it was your love and care that kept me from giving in to my own demons. I only hope you know that I am still alive because of you and the family you created. I love you with my whole heart.

♥ Linea

The tears fell as I told her that this was the best Mother's Day I could ever have hoped for. At that moment I felt hopeful. I thought that maybe she was feeling better and she wouldn't have to go to Harborview and she wouldn't need ECT.

An hour later, everything changed. She was tired and flat. She told us to leave. We had planned to have dinner with her, but she said that she wanted to be alone.

"You need to leave." Again, the dreaded words: "I really can't do this anymore."

We left with Jordan and Cliff and forced ourselves to take a walk. I was numb and anxious and unable to even think about what the next week would hold, but it was an incredibly beautiful afternoon in Seattle, and on that walk I found a few moments of peace as we meandered through the giant cedars. I suddenly felt very small in the greater world. I recognized that this particular time was merely a speck in the universe, and that somehow comforted me. I knew that Linea was not okay, but at the same time I had a feeling of letting go and, just for a teardrop of time, I felt like it was out of my control. Maybe it was faith. Maybe it was trust. Or maybe it was acceptance. I took a breath and I felt lighter. It was a relief for the short time that it lasted.

The next morning, we got the news that Linea was to be transferred to Harborview. I was terrified by the move. The emergency room was frightening enough. What could the psych unit possibly be like? The nurses at the UWMC helped us sort through our fear. There are three units at Harborview: East, West, and Center, all on the fifth floor. Five Center is the highest security and primarily used for people who are psychotic, physically out of control, or incarcerated with a mental-health crisis. We were told that likely she would be in Five West. Linea was also terrified. Her nurse told her that she would see people who were much sicker than she was or anyone she had been with at the UWMC.

While we were trying to make sense of all of this, Linea's outpatient psychologist called the hospital to check on Linea. I talked to her on the phone and she heard the fear in my voice. She told me, "One thing I want you to remember, above all else, these are simply people. They are just sick people."

I got it. I felt my fear lessening a little. I sent up a prayer for the patients we would soon meet. They, too, were sons and daughters of people who loved them dearly. Then, as my fear came roaring back, I added an additional plea that none of them would hurt my daughter. Please, don't hurt my daughter.

linea The humming Russian lady H.A. stares at me. They have once again given me pills to numb the heart that is beating just too fast to handle. Jean came by to visit yesterday, only to give me a poem written about the loss of past happiness. Is it just my paranoia, or is the letter blaming me? She blames both of us, so why does everyone keep telling me it isn't my fault and that nothing is wrong with me?

Something is wrong with me. I want to fall out the window. I want to kill myself. This is not normal.

It's another gorgeous day outside and I haven't breathed fresh air in six days. I'm suffocating in my own misery. Tomorrow I will be taken away to a new hell. Tomorrow I will be sent to Harborview, where they will shock the sadness right out of me. Why can't they just fucking let me die?

I can't stop plotting new ways to harm myself without my H.A. noticing. All I think about is how to kill myself. The problem is that even if I did manage to hurt myself, I would quickly be swooped up and sewn shut before anything bad could happen. But I would almost rather try just to feel the pain.

I can't do this anymore. There is too much talk about the decision of ECT. Too much talk about what to do with me. Too many worried faces, worried voices. The thing I hate the most is hearing how much I have going for me and what a pretty girl I am. Don't they know that just makes me want to die more? I need to die so I can stop hearing all those ridiculous compliments.

And I am so sick of the whole bipolar talk. Maybe I am bipolar. Who knows? But I think that the partying was merely college, and the coke and drugs were merely me trying not to slit my wrists. Everyone feels happy sometimes. They make it seem like it is wrong to feel great or normal.

Everyone keeps saying I'm black or white. The nurse said that my parents told them that. Well, who the hell do they think I got it from? Uh, maybe from the people who told you? Maybe it's those two that come in every hour of every day? Really, I do love having dinner brought to me and people doting on me and bringing me presents, but it is a little much. That was always one of my problems to begin with. It's always been a problem of being perfect. A problem of them telling me how good I am at everything. They just don't understand that I'm not special, that I'm not talented. The more they compliment me, the more I realize how terrible I am and realize that I need to work harder, be better. They are the ones that make me feel like there is a black and white, a good and bad, no middle, no moderate, no mediocre. Always the best. Always special.

Now the intruding nurse from yesterday is back to watch me, and she is even worse than the Russian because she always needs to talk to me. Talk talk talk. She never stops asking me questions. She thinks that she can help this "poor beautiful artist." She thinks that she knows enough to really tell me what to live for. It's all a whole lot of bullshit right now because I am too low to be helped. Lady, you don't know the first thing that I should live for. You better pull me out of the well before you try and give me mouth-to-mouth. I'm practically already dead, so just let me die in peace.

It's Harborview day and we have made the decision to have ECT. Shock therapy. How Plathian.

I was told that Harborview is one of the largest trauma centers in the nation. This is the hospital of all hospitals, and it terrifies me. To get here they once again kidnapped me and stuffed me in an ambulance. An ambulance that smells like baby wipes. The two medics in the back are overly perky and jovial. They are actually happy.

It's funny to me to see freaks like them, and I realize that any other time in my life I would be the same as them. I was that girl who pissed people off because she was genuinely happy all the time. But look at me now. Strapped down, staring out the small window of the ambulance at the sunlight that I haven't been in in days.

cinda We were just starting lunch when the nurse told us that the ambulance was here for Linea and the room was ready for her at Harborview. We were not expecting this to happen so quickly. Linea was frantic about riding in the ambulance. She started to cry and told us she was terrified. She wanted us to drive her, but of course this was out of the question. We knew the rules now.

I followed the ambulance, parked, found my way through the maze of Harborview, and took the elevator up to the fifth floor. At the admissions office, I learned that she was not going to Five West. She was admitted to Five Center, the unit for the most severely ill, the unit where I'd wished and prayed that she would not go. My heart was pounding as I got off the elevator and reached the locked door. I picked up the phone to announce myself. The nurse told me to stand back from the door on the red line and she would let me in. I moved back six feet and waited. She opened the door and searched through my bag. I followed her to Linea's room. There was no word for my fear.

I didn't know how I could stand this.

7. misery

linea Harborview—A woman watches me through a small glass window in my door. I am in urgent care, a place they put those who are too unresponsive for group therapy. There are people screaming and running around here. People are being restrained.

The woman outside of my window is one of about twenty nurses that sit outside of the urgent care unit rooms. Up and down the hall you can see them in colorful scrubs, perched on their high stools, like prized birds kept at a fancy seaside resort.

My watcher is Ethiopian. I know this because while I was giving a urine sample she stood in front of me, watching, while talking on the phone in a foreign language. When she got off the phone, she told me her life story in fractured English, as if this would ease the awkwardness of her having had to watch me pee.

My room is private and completely bare. I have a bed and a closet with no doors. In the closet are my few clothes. On the nightstand, my piles of books. The rest of my possessions (my makeup, my computer, my music) are locked in a closet somewhere with my name on them. Everything is counted and recorded: three shirts, one pair of jeans, a short black skirt, one pair of shoes, two pairs of socks, three pairs of underwear, eight books. Everything is written on a white form. The masking tape comes out and all of my objects are labeled with my name.

There is, however, one good thing about my room: the view. If I look past the bars on the windows, I can see Puget Sound. The water is gorgeous on a sunny day, and though it reminds me of the fact that I cannot go outside, the water is calming. It is serene and free. Somehow it seems fitting that I have to look through bars to feel free.

After the head nurse and I are done counting and tagging my belongings, she takes me to the window.

She says, "Look, you see those dinosaurs out there? See, they're blue and red?"

"You mean the cranes in West Seattle?"

"No, they're dinosaurs. And you can always tell if they're a girl or boy dinosaur because they're not wearing clothes. See?"

I look and see that the cranes do indeed look like dinosaurs, and better yet, the blue ones really are boy dinosaurs with large protrusions in between their two giant dinosaur legs, which the red cranes do not have.

As I look at these naked dinosaurs, I realize that for the first time in this entire process of being crazy, I am actually laughing.

Thanks.

And she just smiles.

cinda Once I was buzzed into "Center," I was overwhelmed by what I saw. I had been in psychiatric facilities for children, but nothing like this. The unit was one long hallway with doors to patients' rooms on each side, observation windows in each door, and in front of the doors, a person sitting on a stool with a clipboard, documenting the pain and misery going on in each small room.

A common sitting area at the end of the hall had the bare minimum: a television secured to the table, plastic couches, a table and chairs. Staff were everywhere and patients shuffled down the hallway or stayed in their rooms. I could hear men and women behind the doors crying or cursing while the "watcher" patiently sat on the stool outside the room, watching and recording. I recognized some of the patients as men and women whom I had passed on street corners, under freeway overpasses, in the city parks, wandering in Pioneer Square, on Broadway, and at major intersections throughout Seattle.

It was hell. I could not, in my wildest dreams, ever have imagined that my daughter would be here. I simply couldn't think about it too much or try to process what was happening, or I would fall apart. The tears and the cries of anguish that fought to flood out of me minute by minute were swallowed whole. The world of the nameless mentally ill and the life of my beautiful daughter were one and the same. She was locked in and locked down. I cannot describe the feeling of complete panic that I fought so hard to control: Stay calm, stay calm, stay calm; reassure her; say the magic words, "It will be okay."

Her dad looked at me and said, for probably the fiftieth time, "It will be okay." I needed him to keep saying those words to me. Did any of us believe them? Was it really going to turn out all right? We couldn't give up; we had to be brave for each other. We had to be brave for her. And down deep, small and hanging on for dear, dear life, was a spark of hope, and we weren't going to let it go out.

As I walked down the hallway, I saw the girl who had been in the emergency room at Harborview the day our nightmare started. She was now sitting in a wheelchair in the hallway with a walker beside her. She couldn't walk more than a few feet. She was dying of self-inflicted starvation. Her mother was with her. I recognized her mother from our trip through security, both of us opening our bags, she taking off her belt, me removing my scarf. We made eye contact but didn't talk to each other. Like me, she was spending all her energy trying to hold on to whatever would keep her from falling completely apart.

The professionals on that floor were dealing with humanity at its sickest. The patients were all very, very ill. Some were angry, combative, and loud, threatening the nurses, other patients, and apparitions that only they could see. Some were completely silent. The nurses cared for the homeless, the violent, and the mute as gently and professionally as they did our daughter. While we were talking with Linea's nurse, two police officers brought in a patient in a wheelchair and ankle cuffs. He was screaming profanities. The nurses spoke quietly and calmly to him, with great care in their voices. They spoke gently through his loud threats of retribution and vengeance. He was wheeled into his room and the door was shut. His shouting echoed down the hallway. He screamed for weapons of revenge and drugs and alcohol to soothe him. I ached for his pain and I also wanted him to shut up. I wanted him to stay behind the door of his room. I wanted the door locked. Of all the watchers on duty, I wanted the six-foot-three-inch man who looked like a football player to keep this man in his room. I didn't want the petite woman with the flowered scrubs as his guard. Don't hurt my daughter.

Many patients were people from the streets who had no family, no insurance, and no advocates. Over the next weeks we would know most of them, learning up close and personal that they didn't have any options. Nowhere to recover, no one to help them fight the battle of long-term mental illness, and no one to pay the bills or negotiate with the insurance companies. In my personal terror of that time and place, even as I wanted Linea anywhere but there, I felt immense gratitude for the resources we had and the love and support of our friends and family.

Visiting hours came to a close, and once again I had to leave my child in a psych unit, this craziest of psych units. I did not crawl into bed with her and hang on, kicking and screaming and refusing to leave and making Curt drag me away. Instead I leaned down and I kissed her good-bye with a calmness I did not feel. I told her I loved her. In my calm voice said, "It is going to get better. I promise you."

We left that night more frightened than we had ever been. Linea's parting words to us were that it didn't really matter what they did to her because nothing was going to help; she didn't think she would ever feel any better, she would always be at the very bottom of the deepest pit. She was on the waiting list but didn't know when she would have her first treatment. We left with an overwhelming feeling of trepidation. It was one of our lowest nights.

When we arrived home, we both fell exhausted into bed. I believe we passed out more than fell asleep. We were both jerked awake when the phone rang close to midnight. Neither of us dared to breathe as I answered to hear that her first ECT was scheduled for seven the next morning. I thanked the nurse for calling us and we set the alarm for five A.M. We lay silently next to each other and waited for the alarm to ring.

linea It's five in the morning on a Tuesday. A woman I don't know wakes me. It takes a moment to register where I am and what I'm doing here. She hands me my pills and tells me it's time for the ECT. She gives me a wonderful soft white-and-blue-striped robe, which I know will be taken away immediately after the procedure because it ties with a cord. She puts me in a wheelchair, and a man I don't know pushes me out of the room and down the hall. My stomach is grumbling and very angry, and I remember I am not allowed to eat twelve hours prior to the treatment. I remember eating an old banana, some 2 percent milk, and some dirty-looking graham crackers yesterday afternoon. When I get downstairs to the treatment room I am transferred to an operating table. They stick me full of IVs and heart monitors and other wires, mimicking an alien abduction. Then they leave me. For an hour.

They leave me lying on a table connected to at least five different devices. They leave me to just think. They leave me to stew over why I am doing this. They are going to electrocute my brain until I have a seizure. They are going to reprogram my brain.

Suddenly they all file in like a funeral procession and proceed to explain the procedure. At this point I am already a little tired from my morning medication. They tell me that they have to give me oxygen because it works better if your brain has a lot of it. They explain that they will put me under and that the procedure will only take about ten minutes or less. They gave me a shot and explain that it is a muscle relaxant so when my muscles tense up I won't pull them. Oh, and by the way, can our residents watch?

They all put on their gloves and stand around me. There must be about six of them. I'm anxious and nervous. The light is shining in my eye. They are all staring at me. I start to feel numb and I can't move my arms. My heart is racing, I can hear it on the monitor, and though I still have an urge to end my own life—there must be sharp objects in these drawers—I am still wondering: What if I don't wake up? What if I'm brain damaged?

They are staring down at me. Everything is white, the light, their uniforms. They have merged into an alien group. They put an oxygen mask over my face and the anesthetic smells like my dad's old hardware store. I'm five years old again. Things are getting brighter. I'm playing with the floaty toys in the back room. Blow-up alligators and air mattresses. Staring. The aliens. I'm confused. Whiteness overtakes my vision. I'm slightly nauseous from fear. They surround me. My heart races, there are voices but I don't understand.

Just sleeeeeeeepppp.

When I wake up I can't move. I can't breathe. My body is covered in sweat. The room is a fucking sauna. My entire body has been run over by a semi and I don't remember it happening. I feel as if every bone in my body has been crushed. My head aches with the worst pain I have ever felt, like my head is in a fucking vise. My muscles are broken. I swear they are all shredded to small pieces. I have somehow managed to pull every muscle in my body. It hurts to breathe. It hurts to blink. I can't lift my arm or raise my head. A nurse comes in and tells me that it is indeed possible to pull all of my muscles. She tells me that, yes, it is possible to pull your lung muscles. I tell her about my headache, and she suggests a strong shot of something chemical in my ass.

"Your parents were here three hours ago, but you needed rest. You talked to them for a while. Do you remember?"

"They were here? No. What day is it? Saturday?"

"Tuesday. You'll remember a little more every time."

I wake up again. Still in extreme pain. The sun is no longer shining directly in on me and it is night out. I have the strangest sensation, but I can't place it. There is something very different happening in me. Then it hits me.

I don't feel like killing myself.

cinda We left the house at six A.M. so we could see Linea before she was taken away. When we got there, we were told that one of us could walk with her to the operating wing of the hospital. Curt went with her while I started a long silent litany of hope and peace for my daughter. When he returned to the waiting room near her unit, we were told to go to the surgery waiting room in the basement of the hospital. The ECT would take about forty minutes, and the doctor would meet with us when they were finished. I stumbled to follow their instructions, to continue my prayer. I couldn't think about what was happening to Linea. I couldn't stop thinking about it.

We took the elevator down and joined the other families and friends waiting for news, waiting to find out which way their lives would go, who would live and who would die. Some had set up camp, claiming space to sleep and eat and read and worry. Some had been there for hours. Some had been there for much, much longer.

We heard bits of conversations.

A doctor spoke to a family: "She is on a ventilator. She came through this first surgery well. We will keep her in an induced coma until we know if we have relieved some of the pressure."

A man talked to his mother: "We don't know, Ma, we just don't know. There is nothing we can do. He . . ."

A little girl cried and her mother snapped, "Stop, can't you help me out here? Be quiet!"

By ten A.M. I began to panic. It had been much longer than forty minutes. I was worried about the general anesthesia as well as what the shock to her brain would do to her. I flashed back eighteen years to when we waited for her to have tubes put into her ears. Everyone else's babies were returned to them within thirty minutes. We waited sixty minutes, ninety minutes, more, and we became frantic. Her dad was getting ready to barge into the OR and find her when finally she was returned to us. While the other babies were crying and struggling to move from the nurse's care to their parents, Linea was limp and groggy. The doctor told us she had "seized" during the procedure and they had had to "bag" her and put her into a deeper sleep. In all these years I had not thought of that episode, but now my mind returned to the experience and I started to worry. What if she had problems with anesthesia or some other issues unknown to us? Should we have agreed to ECT? What if . . . ?

A doctor walked through the crowded surgery waiting room calling our names. I wanted to grab him by the collar and force him to tell me, tell me quickly, was she okay? He took his time describing the procedures of ECT until I interrupted him.

"Is she okay?"

Finally he said the words I had wanted to hear immediately, "She is fine. She had a pretty hard seizure, but that is expected for the first time. Usually the first one is the worst and it gets better after that. She will likely have a headache, some nausea, temporary confusion, and muscle stiffness when she is more alert."

I took a breath.

"We will do another ECT on Thursday. I expect she will do fine with this. She is young and has a very healthy brain."

I held my breath again.

The doctor was the head of the psychiatric unit at the hospital and a top researcher in depression and bipolar disorder. He took time talking to us about the effectiveness of ECT. He described it to us as comparable to shocking a heart to return to a normal rhythm. Electrodes were placed on one side of her head and an electrical current passed through the brain, causing a seizure. Linea had been anesthetized and her muscles temporarily paralyzed to avoid the violent jerking motions of a grand mal seizure. Effective seizures generally last for about thirty seconds. There was no convulsion and she could not feel any pain.

He told us that Linea's brain's "circadian rhythms" were completely out of sync. She was not psychotic, although she was presenting that way with her "suicidal ideation." She was in a "depressive loop" that is extremely hard to change. ECT could, with a low-voltage jolt to one side of the brain, affect these rhythms much more quickly and give her relief while they figured out the right medications and dosage. Ultimately, side effects would likely be less with ECT than drugs at this point.

We were impressed by the doctor's expertise and comforted by his kindness. It was the little things that comforted me. He told us that he had talked with Linea prior to her falling asleep. They talked about Chicago and he told her that he recently had been at the Indiana Dunes on the east side of Lake Michigan. From there, he could see the great city of Chicago. When she awoke from the ECT, he said she remembered this conversation, which was an indication of how well she would do with this procedure. He said her intelligence was also a plus, but I was still terrified.

Linea was taken back to her room in Five Center. We could return in the afternoon and see her. I felt lost and exhausted. I think I had held my breath the entire hour while we waited for the doctor to tell us she had survived. Curt and I knew we could return to work since we both worked close to the hospital. Yet we were both so numb and inarticulate that instead we wandered around the hospital in a daze waiting to see her.

It was an unusually warm spring day in Seattle. Linea's room faced west and, with no air-conditioning on Five Center, it was unbearably hot in her room. She was asleep. Her hair was wet and stuck to her cheeks. She opened her eyes and smiled at us. Linea has the most beautiful smile.

"Hi, Mom and Dad. Did I sleep a long time?"

She continued to smile. Curt and I both had tears in our eyes as we sat on the edge of her cot. I had not seen her smile in so long.

The nurse came in and asked Linea how she was doing.

"I'm hot. I am really hot. Can I have some water?"

She handed Linea a plastic glass and asked, "How are the thoughts?"

"They are gone. I'm not thinking that anymore." Linea was still smiling.

For the first time in more than two weeks she was not obsessed with hurting herself. She looked relaxed. I knew ECT was not a miracle cure, but I was so grateful for her to have some relief, even if it didn't last.

Linea was woozy, so I helped her get dressed and we headed for the bathroom. As I waited for her in the hallway, a patient walked up to me. She stood there staring at me, swinging a tea bag. After studying me carefully, she finally smiled and slowly said, "You look very, very sick. I hope you do better real soon. Get some rest."

"Thanks," I told her. "I hope to."

Linea came out of the bathroom and I told her about the woman with the tea bag. She said to me, "Well, maybe you should get a room here as well. There are some good views." We both laughed. We were actually laughing together. It was not a fake or weird interchange, not a way for Linea to pretend a little and to get me to back off and leave her alone. This was real. It felt easy, this laughing like we had always done. It felt good to laugh at this strange situation that we were in together.

We left Linea to sleep, promising that we would come back soon. Outside it was still sunny. Curt and I walked and talked, almost giddy that she had come through the first ECT and that "the thoughts" were gone. We couldn't believe the change in her from one day before. We walked up and down the surrounding neighborhood and found ourselves in front of St. James Cathedral. We went inside and could feel the peace and the joy of the place. We were so deeply thankful for her smile, for the calmness, for that moment. We lit a candle and gave thanks as well as a plea. Please, please let this be the start of something better for our daughter.

When we got back to the hospital, Linea had made a sign with a piece of paper and a marker. It was taped to the wall beside her bed.

It read, YOU ARE HAPPY TODAY. DO NOT FORGET THIS. She had dated and signed it. Her doctors told us that her memory would get more and more fuzzy as she had additional ECTs. She didn't want to forget the feelings of relief. I didn't either. I still have that note tucked away in a file marked "Linea—Harborview." It was our first sign of hope.

linea The treatments are saving my life. After just one session, my improved attentiveness and responsiveness has earned me a higher office: I have been promoted to the regular wing. The place where the somewhat crazies—versus the completely crazies—of Center go. I am trusted not to throw chairs or attack fellow inmates. And my shadow is gone. I am given up to fifteen minutes of privacy. Life is beautiful. Well-earned privacy and improved gruel.

This is Five West, the psych ward where the moderate cases go. The "normal" cases. It feels like a hotel. I have a bathroom and shower in my room. I will soon have a roommate, but no one has arrived yet. I have been playing guitar nonstop and have a moderate knowledge of the chords. I can't believe how much better I feel. Aside from feeling like I got hit by a truck, I honestly feel as though I may make it out of this alive. It is such a relief, I really can't believe it. It is one week after my first session, and my mood is beginning to go back down, but nothing like before.

I have another treatment tomorrow. I am a little worried about muscle pain because I couldn't breathe after I pulled the muscles in my lungs. When I leave here I am getting a massage. I keep having memory flashbacks from the day of the procedure. I think I have to stop writing because I am actually starting to feel bad again, and I don't want to get to that point, so I have to try something else to distract me.

As I look out the window of my new unit, I can see the old ward across the way. I stare at the bars on the windows and I can't believe I made it out alive. It was terrifying.

Honestly, I'm scared here, too. My new roommate is a little crazy but nice. She tried to overdose on methadone. Killing yourself is the latest gossip in this unit. Everyone speaks of it like a new fad of clothing. But talking about it brings me back to the feelings I was running from.

cinda We developed a routine of sorts. Our rhythm revolved around the ECT schedule. The move out of Center was a huge relief. When Linea wasn't in meetings with her nurses, doctors, and therapy groups, she would call to ask me to walk over from Seattle University. I was simply keeping my head above water, barely, and not accomplishing anything else. Without my friends and colleagues, I am not sure what I would have done.

Her dad had the same support at the UWMC, but he was having different issues. He just wanted to hide in his office and do his paperwork and write reports. He didn't want to see his patients. He didn't have the energy to deal with any more pain. He felt as if he didn't have anything left to give.

Everyone handled worry and fears differently. Jordan visited Linea one beautiful early summer day and wanted to take Linea outside. Jordan felt it would do Linea good to get out of the unit. But Linea had not yet been given privileges to leave the unit, and the nurse would not let her leave the floor. Jordan became tense and angry.

"Linea, they can't keep you in here against your will. You should be able to go outside if you want to."

I told Jordan that Linea would likely get to go out in the next day or two at most, but Jordan became increasingly upset.

"The nurse is a total bitch, Mom. Linea would feel so much better if we could take her out of this place. Do you hear the way she talks to Linea? It's rude."

Linea was getting anxious about Jordan and didn't know which side to take. I led/pulled Jordan out of the unit and into the hall.

Jordan exploded. "God, Mom, how can you stand it in there? This is horrible. They are so mean to Linea. They treat her like she is a freak or something. They make her go to all those stupid meetings and tell her what to do and where to sit. It is ridiculous. We have to get her out of there. That nurse really is a bitch and you know it. I can't stand this."

I pulled her to me. I recognized her anxiety. The same

feeling had held my body together for so many weeks. I said to her, "I know you are scared."

Just like that it was over. Jordan started to cry. And cry harder. She sobbed into my shoulder. "Is she going to be okay, Mom? What is going to happen to her?"

She quickly pulled herself together and wiped her face. She looked at me and said, one last time, "Well, she *is* a bitch."

Curt and I had been in the thick of hospitals, nurses, sickness, the whole mess. Although Jordan had visited Linea at UWMC before she was moved to Harborview, and we had tried to keep Jordan up to date, I guess we also protected her from the difficult realities. With everything that had been going on, I hadn't had any time alone with her, and in front of Linea I tried to keep my updates hopeful. In just two days, a lot had happened: Harborview, ECT, therapy groups, and very sick patients sharing her unit. Jordan missed just two days of the turmoil and had fallen behind in the process. She was also frightened and didn't like to admit it. Her baby sister was sick, and Jordan was prepared to use her superpowers to break Linea out of Five West.

Most of the time, we thought—believed—that Linea was getting better. I continued to reserve my fear for every ECT. I cannot describe my dread each time she went into the OR for another round of the bizarre treatment. The doctor had told us that the danger of the anesthesia was actually more worrisome than the actual ECT procedure. If that was meant to reassure me, it didn't. Instead I worried about the law of averages; would this be the time her body reacted to the anesthesia in a deadly way? Or the next time?

Insurance and money worries also occupied our thoughts. Sorting out the medical coverage for Linea's care was complicated and time-consuming. We met with the social worker, talked with our insurance company, and filled out paperwork in case the hospitalization was not fully covered. It was all vastly confusing. We had decided on our walk back from the cathedral after her first ECT that we would gladly sell the house and our cars and live in a tiny apartment by the university if only she could be well. And needing to sell wasn't out of the realm of possibility. What in the hell do people do who don't have two incomes, good insurance coverage, and some knowledge of the system? Linea's first roommate was homeless, addicted to drugs and alcohol, and in an abusive relationship. Her and Linea's common ground was depression. Mental illness doesn't care if you are rich or poor, well connected or not, loved or deserted. But it became very clear to us that the haves have much more positive outcomes than the have-nots, particularly once they leave the hospital.

We were told that patients get better much faster with family support and that we were welcome to come as often as possible. We were usually the only family members on the unit. The other patients didn't have anyone with them: the man with the megavoice who yelled his most personal thoughts for us to hear, the woman with the wild hair who wouldn't get out of hospital pajamas but put on makeup each morning, the very tall, very muscular Eastern European man who scared me a little, and the tiny elderly woman who spent her time cleaning up after all of us and a few people that no one but she could see. Where were their families?

As the days rolled together, we learned that, yes, the other patients were all just people. Megavoice Man tried hard to control his emotions so that he could go on smoke breaks with the other patients. He knew the ropes of the unit and told us when group meetings would start, when to return from smoke breaks, which nurse was the easiest to work with and which one was most likely to strictly enforce the time limits on the breaks. When we want to know something about the way it worked on Five West, we asked Megavoice Man. The woman with the wild hair wouldn't talk to us, but she protectively kept Linea in her sights and sat between her and the more vocal patients on the floor. She provided a buffer for Linea, and for some reason I felt better leaving Linea at night while she was there.

One day I stepped into the elevator and was suddenly alone with the tall, blond man from Eastern Europe. He had reached the level where he was able to leave the unit by himself. He told me he was from Russia and asked me how my "beautiful daughter" was doing. I tensed as I told him that I hoped she would be released soon and that she was doing better.

"I have a daughter her age. It don't seem right for the young ones to have to suffer so. Me, I got the problem with alcohol and I come to get that fixed some. I pray for your girl," he told me.

"Thank you. I will pray for you as well," I whispered. Humanity. Something cracked a little bit inside of me. "I am sorry." I truly was sorry. I had so many misconceptions about the people treated in the psychiatric units.

The tiny elderly woman seemed, in her own way, as out of place as Linea. She spent all her time wiping imaginary crumbs off the tables, straightening real newspapers and magazines, and picking up microscopic pieces of fairy dust from the floor. She called Linea "honey" and always had a beautiful smile on her face. She seemed completely calm and settled but used all her energy on her compulsive obsessions. As soon as I set down a cup or a paper she would come over and ask, "Honey, are you finished with that?" As I spent days and weeks there, I met so many wonderful people struggling to be well. I wanted to know more of their stories. I wanted to know they were loved.

Linea's second roommate arrived in tears and wouldn't stop crying. Also "upper-middle-class," in the throes of depression, she had threatened to kill herself and was hospitalized against her will. At twenty-nine, she was closer in age to Linea's twenty years than anyone else on the floor. Her parents were so ashamed of her that they refused to bring her any clothing. All she had was what she was wearing when the ambulance brought her in. I offered to pick something up for her, but she said she would wash what she had, wear hospital pajamas, and wait for her sister to talk her parents into coming to see her. Her parents didn't come. Eventually I met her mother in a parking lot to pick up a change of clothes for her.

We spent one Friday night playing bingo with the patients in the "recreation hall" of Five West. A social worker was running the show with two graduate students as assistants. Everyone was in a good mood and the game was quite competitive as we all kept track of three or more bingo boards. Megavoice Man won the first round and chose the candy bars, announcing in his radio voice, "It'll probably give me DIARRHEA, but it will be WORTH it!! GLUTTONY causes DIARRHEA!"

The tiny elderly lady won the next game. She carefully picked up and looked at every single thing in the prize box. After about twenty minutes of obsessing over which prize to choose, she selected hand cream. By now there were just five of us left. We played another round because one of the men was annoyed that he wasn't able to play more games because the woman took so much time choosing her prize. I won the next game and told him he could have my prize. He then gave this opportunity to the tiny elderly lady. After another twenty minutes of debating with herself, she selected a second tube of hand cream

Game over. Another Friday night on Five West.

Many of the patients on the floor were there for mental-health issues coupled with addiction, and they attended "dependency" meetings. At first we were unsure why Linea also was required to attend these. When she finally told us she had been using drugs and self-medicating in hopes of either making herself feel better or giving herself the courage to end it all, I was not as shocked as I would have been a year earlier. My academic understanding of mental illness and drugs and alcohol was played out in front of me every day. Substance abuse to handle the pain of depression was no longer something to be noted in lecture notes. I was witnessing it up close and personal.

Every day we were the unwilling witnesses to more pain. One afternoon, Linea's first roommate was crying and begging them not to make her leave. "He will kill me! You know he will! You know it! I don't want to leave! I won't go," she cried.

The social worker explained to her that she would be going to a women's shelter and her partner wouldn't find her there and, even if he did, he wouldn't be able to get to her. A woman from the shelter was here to pick her up. The patients were either in the hall watching or they were pretending not to listen. Linea was very upset.

"Does she have to go, Mom? This doesn't seem fair at all. What are they doing to make sure she is safe?" she asked me.

The woman was crying louder as they moved her toward the door. "He is probably out there waiting for me right now. He'll kill me and you don't even care," she yelled.

Linea was crying by then and went to her room, got into

bed, and put a pillow over her head. Visitors weren't allowed in patients' rooms so I stood in the hallway and watched her and listened to the anguish continue as Penny was forced out the door. Megavoice Man yelled, "THIS IS EXACTLY WHAT HAPPENS WHEN YOU FIND YOURSELF INCARCERATED IN A NUTHOUSE. WHAT CAN YOU EXPECT? WHAT *CAN* YOU EXPECT?"

linea A meeting with my doctor:

"So, Linea, how are you doing? Are you still having suicidal thoughts?"

"Yes, and they're never going to go away."

"Where do they come from?"

"Where do they come from? I don't know. Some sick place deep down in my stomach. It's disgusting down there.

"There is a lot of hate for some reason, and I don't know why. I hate myself so much. I hate myself and I hate the world. Sometimes I even hate my family, and that's worse than anything. That really makes me want to die. That's when I really deserve to die."

"When you want to die, what comes to your mind?"

"I want to be a rock."

"A rock? Why a rock?"

"An inanimate object. I want to just be. And be nothing. I want to do nothing and think nothing. I just don't want to be anything but a blob. But this is better than before."

Last week I wanted the same thing, but wanting to be a rock alternated with the want to brutally off myself. I would sit in my room and scan it for items I could use. For example, there is a painting on the wall. It is enclosed in a plastic frame all the way around, front and sides. The plastic is probably really hard to break, let alone without a nurse noticing, but I bet it has to be wired up there somehow. I bet there is some kind of hook in the back, possibly a nail in the wall. I also notice that there is a lamp next to the bed. That's an easy one. Lightbulb. Cord. Two easy options right there. Then there is always the option of saving pills, but that one's really tricky, they are watching for it.

Anyway, those thoughts aren't there anymore, but I can sure remember them. And it's really creepy how I still can't help but study every new room I go into, everywhere I go. I don't want to kill myself anymore, but I still look.

"Do you still have a fear that you might try to do something?"

"No, well, I might sometime, but I feel like I am at a point where more often than not I don't really want to die, so I feel like I might have the strength to tell a nurse now. It's not quite as scary anymore, because I really do feel like I can count on myself to get help before I do anything stupid. And I am too tired to be sneaky anymore. I can't get away with anything because all my energy has been extinguished by the ECT."

"Well, I am glad you're feeling better. Please make a promise that you will talk to someone if those violent feelings come back."

"Well, I won't promise, because I don't feel like this kind of depression is something that you can fully understand. I mean, I don't know if I will have the control I want when that darkness takes over, but I promise I will try my hardest. At this moment, right now, I don't want to die, and I will do anything to try not to."

"Thanks, Linea. Given your eloquence and your honesty, I really think you will get through this. Thank you."

Today I reached level two and was allowed outside for a fifteen-minute "smoke" break even though I don't smoke. It was balmy outside and felt like Chicago on a warm fall night. It smelled like it, too, with smoke mixing with the warm, hazy night. Looking up, I could see the unit I used to be in. It was as if I am near my old neighborhood in Chicago, in Printers Row again, only now Printers Row represents a jail. My parents follow me like a child afraid to lose their mom in the supermarket.

I had to go to the chemical dependency meeting today with the alcoholics and meth heads. When asked what my drug of choice was, I felt like I was in *A Million Little Pieces.* They talked about treatment centers to go to when they get out of the psych ward and what they were going to change about their lifestyle.

I don't want to change anything. I was a normal college kid, drinking and smoking pot. It is ridiculous that I have to sit in this meeting. What is more ridiculous is the fact that my parents think I need to be here. That's such fucking bullshit. This is ridiculous. Thank God I have Jordan on my side to tell me what is going on behind the scenes with my parents.

I have no concept of time anymore. I'm just here.

Stuck here in this nuthouse.

I switched rooms today, and I am no longer sharing a room with a speed freak. My new room is overlooking the Sound, the freeway, and downtown Seattle. My roommate is just as good as the view. She's from Bellevue and just a little older than my sister. She's a fashion something . . . photographer? Plus, she's halfway normal. She just said the wrong thing at the wrong time and landed here. Sometimes I feel I did the same thing. I didn't mean to be here. I didn't mean for Victoria to call the hospital. I didn't want to be trapped indoors for ten days. I didn't want to possibly lose my job or my apartment. I didn't want to ruin my life.

If I had just killed myself, there couldn't have been any repercussions that I would have had to deal with. As selfish as that is, I would have just been gone, nothing to worry about. My life is fucked now. If I would have followed through I wouldn't have had to deal with it.

I sit here on a beautiful sunny afternoon. I'm able to go outside, but only if I have company to meet me. This is the first time in weeks that my family is nowhere to be found. I am very tired and cranky and have been for several days.

Do I actually feel better, or am I just anxious to be out of here? I don't know what I want. I don't know what I need. I don't have the energy to get any better than this. I feel extremely anxious and angry, but I don't know why. Do I still want to kill myself? Am I still out to die in some horrific way? I don't understand myself. It will be two weeks on Tuesday. I long to be at my counselor's on Tuesday, not here. How will I know if I'm ready? How will I know when it's time?

Today my parents and I walked to a Catholic church. It was beautiful and calm inside. Enormous stained-glass windows. A silent Mary. I loved the feeling of silence all over. I bought a necklace for Saint Dymphna. She is the patron saint of the mentally ill. The interesting part is that her birthday is May 15. That is exactly the day I got checked into Harborview the first time. It's right here on my hospital bracelet.

The nurse unlocks the door and I enter a large room with a very large bathtub. It is like some strange attempt at a sauna. Until now this door had always been a mystery to me. It was a privilege few patients get. As I walk in, she hands me the holy grail: a razor. I'm a little afraid of this object but know what must be done. I know this privilege is sacred and I must take advantage of the opportunity before it is swiftly taken away.

I enter the room, and the yellow light makes me anxious

and I think back about a conversation with my sister a few days ago.

"Eeewwww, Linea! Look at your legs. God, why don't you shave them?"

"Uh, because they won't *let* me."

"Can't you like beg them or something?"

"Nope. They think I will slit my wrists."

"Aren't you past that?"

Pause.

Pause.

Pause.

"Nope."

But now I am. Now it's time. I was given the opportunity and the confidence to shave. I could have shaved before, but someone would have had to watch me. I wasn't about to shave my legs until I could be naked in private.

And now I am. I am alone. Alone with a razor. It is a small white plastic travel razor. The kind with one somewhat dull blade. The kind the hotel gives you if you lose your suitcase. I run the water, making sure it is very hot. This is a big deal.

I have not yet conquered my fear of baths after envisioning my death so many times, but the nurse suggested this one would be good for me. This one would be different. She said it would do me good to be in a warm bath after all the ECTs so that my muscles could relax. She also said it would be good to calm my mind. I even get to use some bubble bath that my mom's co-worker brought me.

I climb in hesitantly and sit for a moment. Just me. Alone and naked. All by myself for the first time in weeks. I slowly and perfectly shave my legs, making sure to get rid of every little hair. When I'm done, I lie back and relax until the nurse pops her head in to ask if everything is going okay.

Still no privacy, but at least I had a little me time. Once I'm done and back in the hall, I hand her the razor, pleased and calm. I did it. I shaved my legs. Alone. In a bath. With a razor. I did it.

cinda Linea had graduated to thirty minutes at a time out of the unit. We sat outside in the sun, looking at the Seattle waterfront below us and relishing a beautiful day in May.

She smiled and said to me, "Hey, Mom, I can hear the space between the words."

Linea is a musician who hears background music playing wherever we go. She complains about a song playing in a store, one that I wouldn't even notice. She hears chords and majors and minors and thirds and fourths and whatever else musicians hear. I thought I knew what she meant, but I asked her because I want to hear it again.

"You know, everything just kind of ran together before. Now I hear the spaces. Things were all kind of gray. No shadows or anything. It is like things are sharper to me now."

I knew we had a long way to go, but I so loved this moment. I was very aware that thirty minutes of peace and a little happiness were not to be taken for granted.

The days slogged on. Between the ECT, her group sessions, and her breaks to go off the unit, I played game after game of Yahtzee with Linea and her roommate. We dug through the negligible arts and craft supplies in the "craft room," searching for something to create, searching for something to help pass the time. The other patients almost never had visitors, and often one or two would ask to join us. It brought back memories of playing games to pass the time, make it through a minor illness, or to keep a houseful of active children busy when they couldn't play outside. I became the room mother.

Soon Linea could leave the unit for more than thirty minutes if we called in and requested another thirty. One exceptionally warm day, Curt brought the car around and we loaded her in for a little outing. We found out later that we weren't supposed to leave the hospital campus, but before we knew, we spirited her away, ending up at a coffee shop. Linea was so happy to be away from the hospital for even thirty minutes. As we sat drinking our coffees, the two young baristas behind the counter were laughing hysterically and watching something on a cell phone.

"Jeez, dude, what a freak! Can you believe this old guy? Like *what* is he babbling about? Crazy dude." They laughed and high-fived each other as if they had just captured an award-winning funniest home video.

Linea was suddenly very tense and said, "Do you know what they did?"

We didn't.

"They took a video of that homeless guy outside at the table. I am so angry with them." She was almost in tears.

Outdoors, in the designated seating area of the coffee shop, was a very old man with long white hair. He was dressed in rags, arms and face covered in scabs and sores. All his belongings were in a dirty bag on the sidewalk. He was carrying on a very long conversation with himself, which the young man's video had captured. I was infuriated. We decided to leave, and as we did I told the baristas that I felt very sorry for the man outside and I was sorry that they had no compassion. They looked at me as if I was crazier than the old man. The guy with the video on his cell phone said, "Jeez, chill out, lady. It's just a joke."

We gave the man a cup of coffee and a roll and headed back to Harborview with a sick feeling following us. The joy of our escape had evaporated. Things were changing inside me beyond the day-to-day worry and care of Linea.

The first time someone asked me why Linea was in the hospital, I made the decision to tell the truth. I knew that by not doing so I would discredit her and diminish her illness and her fight to live. When asked about her, I said she had a very bad depression and maybe bipolar disorder. Friends and family were completely accepting and understanding and intuitively knew what to say next. But there were others who responded with an uncomfortable silence, or changed the subject. The responses that bothered me the most were lame stories that were supposed to make me feel better. Such as, "My friend's son had a bout of anxiety for a couple of weeks and had to come home. He spent about a month resting up and now he is back to school and doing great. Most kids go through this stuff." I know they do. I know that the first few years away from home can be difficult. I also think that we don't hear the whole story about many young adults who took "a break"; the reality is almost certainly much more complicated than a neatly packaged one-month "time-out." My daughter was in a psychiatric unit having shock therapy, and we had no idea how it would affect her future. I was in no mood for unrealistic fairy tale endings.

Our family and friends helped to hold us together. My parents called every day and wanted to come over from eastern Washington. I was too afraid that Linea's death wish would tear each of them apart again, and so I kept them away. I shouldn't have. I thought I was protecting them, but really I was protecting myself. My parents, sister, aunt, uncle, and cousins all called and sent cards and goodies and surrounded us with love and support. In this supportive circle there were also friends of Linea's who were wise and kind and caring beyond their years. The severity of Linea's mental illness was frightening to them and unlike anything they had experienced, but they stayed steady with Linea in her fight. Jamie was such a friend.

Jamie first entered our lives when Linea returned from Chicago in February. They were introduced through a mutual friend, and their shared interests were immediately apparent. Linea and Jamie spent hours wandering around bookstores, sitting in coffee shops, and marching for immigration rights. They had known each other less than two months when Linea was hospitalized. Soon Linea asked me to call Jamie and tell her what was happening.

I called Jamie and told her that Linea was in the hospital. The first thing she said was, "Can I come and see her?"

The day she visited, I met her in the lobby and explained the psych unit the best that I could. I told her that it was "lockdown" and that she would see some people who were obviously very mentally ill. We were buzzed in through the locked doors. Jamie and Linea hugged and headed for a room where they could talk. I read and waited until their visit ended. Jamie told Linea good-bye and we were buzzed out. Two steps beyond the door, Jamie burst into tears. I held her as she cried. She had stayed so strong throughout their time together and now she was shaking as she asked me, "She will be okay, won't she? What can I do for her?"

Although it was incredibly frightening, Jamie stayed by her side. She visited Linea, she wrote her funny and loving notes and cards, and she didn't change their friendship in any way. Jamie was another one of our angels on earth.

Charlie One was Linea's first boyfriend in high school, and they had continued to be great friends. He came to visit her in the hospital, bringing his guitar and his down-to-earth quirkiness. Not-on-purpose funny, brilliant, and handsome, he didn't miss a beat hanging out on the psych unit or on a "smoking" break, listening to Megavoice Man tell tales of smoking dope while frying burgers at the local drive-in and the one time he broke his celibacy. Charlie took it all in stride and didn't run even when one of the female patients fell madly in love with him and tried to steal his heart from Linea. He and Jamie kept coming back. They both believed that they would have their Linea back soon. I love these two friends of hers. It was amazing to me what simple acceptance and care did to support us all.

Our family meetings with Linea's team continued. The doctors couldn't positively diagnose bipolar without the manic episodes. We were asked again whether we had seen her in any manic states. We didn't think we had, but then we began to second-guess ourselves. Were the long hours of practicing music "manic"? Was she able to keep the schedule she had because of mania? No, she wasn't spending large amounts of money without second thoughts. No, she wasn't having sex with multiple partners. The most positive thing about her hospitalization, besides getting care and treatment, was that she was safe.

I was exhausted to the core of my being and I couldn't bear to think about anything beyond the next day, but once she was a little more stable I finally began to sleep. I slept because I knew exactly where she was and that someone else was watching over her. She was not hurting herself on Nurse Chris's or Carrie's or Rich's or Nina's shift. I could sleep. At least on those nights she was not having ECT the next day.

In addition to pounding headaches and muscle pain, a major side effect of ECT is memory loss. Short-term memory is the most affected and can last six to eight months but is "almost always" temporary. Long-term memory may also be affected, and this can be of a more permanent nature but is rare and, more often than not, slight. The doctor explained, "You might forget your birthday party in third grade or a few other memories from the past, and a few of these may be permanent losses."

We had talked and worried about the memory loss prior to agreeing to ECT, but Linea said, "We don't have any choice. I can't live like this now and I don't really care if I forget something from when I was eight. If I don't do this, I don't think I am going to live to remember anything."

Typically, the younger and healthier a brain is, the less significant the side effects. The first three treatments seemed to have little effect on her memory. She remembered going to the operating room, she remembered who picked her up and how she got there, she remembered which doctor administered the ECT and what happened afterward. It began to get foggier after the third ECT. By the last ECT, she had distinct problems with her short-term memory. She couldn't remember what or when she had eaten. She could pull the memory back into her conscious mind if we helped her, but it was very difficult for her. She would ask us the same thing again and again and within minutes ask again.

And then we were told she would have only six ECTs, not ten! She might need more before the summer was over, but six for now! We were ecstatic! Linea was generally positive about the treatments. "I was at the bottom, you know that. At least I know now that if things get really bad I can go to a hospital, walk in and say, *shock me*!" she said, grinning at us.

Immediately after her last ECT, she told the nurses it was time for her to leave the hospital. Her medical team wanted her to stay for four or five more days. She had been there for more than three weeks and we were all ready to leave Five West. After pleading from Linea and negotiations from us, she was told that she would likely be discharged in two days if everything went well. She had to attend group sessions while she chafed to get out of the hospital, but she did so without too much complaint. She so desperately wanted to be discharged, and finally, finally the day arrived.

Linea was going home! I believed that she was over the hurdle and that healing and recovery were next. In the back of my mind I was still frightened, but I wouldn't allow myself to go there. She had done it!

linea Tomorrow I am supposed to be able to escape. Today I had a family conference, and my parents for the first time realized that I had a problem with alcohol. They also asked if I do drugs. What am I supposed to tell them? "Why, yes, Mom! I have even tried coke!" In the end they already knew. Having to attend chemical dependency group gives a lot away. I think they are starting to get the picture, and they think the hospital has really straightened me out. I wish. I know the ECT has really helped my mood, but the little classes I was forced to take are certainly not going to make me stop drinking. I am not going to stop stressing out.

I have learned what is good for me. I have learned that I am bipolar, that I function much better with a regular light–dark schedule. I also shouldn't drink because it only makes me crazier. I especially don't need to do drugs. I wish I could talk to Steve. Maybe he was bipolar. Did he really pull the trigger? Would I be brave enough to do that? Would I have the nerve to do that to my family? I'm sitting here on my bed looking out the window at Puget Sound, and I am so ready to get out of here.

It is time for a group meeting. We are sitting in the back of the cafeteria, or the part they like to refer to as the "craft room" (even though it's only separated by a pull-out cork wall). The table is sticky and the room smells of rubber cement.

The walls are covered with cabinets full of paint, paper, board games, and Popsicle sticks. The cupboards are covered in loud, surrealist art.

We all sit in a circle. All of us, Ann, Joe, Nenette, Frank, and the rest of our fantastical unit. Jane, my overly perky nurse, is standing in front of us. In her hand is a small golden coin. As we look up at her, she glows like the Mother Mary, the bright fluorescent light bouncing off the coin, her blond hair, and her Eastery pastel uniform. She explains that the coin was to be given out today to one of the patients who was leaving tomorrow. This coin is the holy grail. This coin is freedom.

Ann is the first to speak. Ann is about four feet tall and wears pink UGGs and a blue flannel hunting hat with ear flaps. I have never seen her without the hat. We believe it may have been her husband's before he died. Whenever she walks anywhere, she holds some imaginary small person's hand. Ann goes around cleaning everything with a washcloth. She goes through the kitchen, the dining room, and the laundry room with her little wet washcloth and cleans it all. As I listen to her speak, I imagine her life outside of this prison. I see her living alone on the farm after her farmer husband dies. She has eight cats and keeps the cows and pigs in the house. I bet she is the woman that all the neighbor kids call "the crazy lady." As I dream of her life, she says in a very meek and mousy voice, "No matter what, it will always be worse, honey."

At this point Nenette, a small Filipina woman, gets down on her knees and begins rocking back and forth praising Ann with her hands together. I can't help but giggle as she keeps bowing, and Ann once again says, "No, no, honey. No, no, honey." This goes on for a few minutes until Ann convinces Nenette to sit back in her seat.

Joe, the schizophrenic Indian man with the mullet, purple tank top with cutoff sleeves, and tattoos all over his neck, is next in the circle. He says, as if on some really good drugs, "Listen to music so you won't have to hear the voices." He kind of reminds me of the Jolly Green Giant, but not as jolly. I met Joe in my chemical dependency group. He is addicted to heroin. I know that I have seen him hanging around Dick's hamburger joint panhandling.

Frank, the man with the eye patch, walker, and round patch of skin stitched into his head, says very loudly, "It's a jungle out there." His drugs of choice are alcohol, cigarettes, and weed.

I say, "Good luck," not feeling that I truly connect or understand what life after the hospital holds. For all I know, the world has transformed into Jetson-land. It is a jungle. How does anyone get through it alive? How does anyone grow old "normally"? It isn't possible. I *need* to leave.

I'm sitting in the Five West cafeteria next to Joe. We don't talk, but we have an understanding. We sit. We stare at our overcooked chicken sandwich. The scent overwhelms the entire cafeteria. He eats his Jell-O fast and I pass him mine. He lifts his milk with a raise of the shoulders and I take it. Nenette is bowing again, this time to the nurse with the rolling food trays. She keeps stepping on her Hawaiian muumuu that she never takes off. Ann is wiping up her table. And the one next to it. And the one next to it. Her hat is off for the first time in these last two weeks. The six-foot, size-0 girl from the emergency room is no longer being fed through her IV, and the high-strung, high-fashion photographer is engaged in a loud and intense conversation with Frank about his intestinal problems.

Today I am leaving. I'm terrified and excited. I somehow don't know what to do without these people anymore. I don't know how to laugh without Frank yelling obscene things or the interplay between giggling Ann and bowing Nenette. I don't know compassion without Joe. Suddenly, Victoria's voice comes into my head, "Just remember, they are all just people." I suddenly understand the true meaning of the word "situational." I know that I will no longer judge the "bum" on the street. It is not any more his fault that he hears voices than my fault for seeking pain. These people are true. This is them. This is not an act. And it can happen to anyone.

It is right as I am thinking these things that Joe looks at me and says in his Jolly Green Giant voice, "Outside is real scary, but the voices, the voices will help you."

8. frailty

linea Well, I'm free. I am free and a completely different person. It's as if I have been in a plane crash. I have both witnessed my own death and seen who would attend my funeral. I saw that I have a lot of people that really care about me.

My memory is still very shaky because of the ECT. I want to try to journal as much as I can, but I keep feeling as if I have something really important to say or write, and then my memory escapes me and I can't think straight. To be honest, I really don't remember a lot of the whole hospital experience. But I know I need to remember that there are a lot of people who really do care about me.

I'm still in shock. I almost started crying in the video store today because I don't know what is going on in my head. This keeps happening. Anytime I have to make even the smallest decision, I freeze up and start to freak out. I can't decide. If someone asks me to pick where to eat, I just get panicked to the point that I feel like I am going to cry or my brain will explode. I have major anxiety and I am thinking in circles. I used to have a terrific memory, but now I don't even know what is going on in my head.

Today I realized how deep I had been in my depression,

when I had planned on bringing some wine, pills, and razor blades to the bath, the plan that Victoria hospitalized me for. I came across the playlist "bath songs" in my iPod and realized that it was from that night, and that I really had been going to do it. I can't believe I almost killed myself. When I think about it I am terrified.

Since the day I went to the emergency room, I feel I have aged ten years, I feel I am a completely new person. The difference between the me in the hospital waiting room and the me I am today feels like two different people. I have moved from an all-consuming feeling of terror and pain to an astounding feeling of awe. I am amazed at the beauty of the world around me, and every moment I feel as though I am taking my first breath of life. Being given the chance to live again, I feel like I know exactly who I am and yet have no idea. I have never been this confused, brave, and terrified at the same time. I feel that all I knew about myself, the layers of personality that I built around me, everything has crumbled and I am new again. I feel that I have to start all over, and it terrifies yet enthralls me. I can be whoever I want to be. I can accomplish whatever I want to accomplish. And yet through it all I know that at any moment I could go back there. I don't know what to do with myself.

I really did survive a plane crash.

cinda We were so incredibly happy to bring Linea home from the hospital. I really did believe that the worst—suicide obsession, locked in and locked down in a psychiatric unit in a major trauma hospital, ECT—was over. Curt and I were completely exhausted and just wanted to settle in and hide from the world. But as soon as we were home from Harborview, Linea wanted to go out. She had been locked in for too long and wanted to eat at a restaurant, see a movie, and see her friends. "Could we go to a movie?" Five minutes later, "Did you say we can go to a movie?" Three minutes later, "Would it be okay if we went to a movie?" Her doctors had warned us about short-term memory impairment. Her memory was indeed "impaired." Actually, her short-term memory was completely shot. Curt and I reassured each other that this was not permanent, even though she was acting frighteningly like someone with a traumatic brain injury.

The repetition of questions wasn't the only symptom. We finally took her to a movie and quickly realized it was a mistake. She couldn't follow the story line and became frustrated and exhausted just trying.

We were relieved she was home, but now we all had to learn how to take the next steps. Things were very difficult for her in the first few weeks. She didn't want to stay at home and she didn't want to "rest," which was our advice. She had been resting for too long and wanted to get on with her life. And we were trying to find the balance of helping her get well, watching over her, and also giving her the space she craved. Her dad bought her an acoustic guitar as both a token of her release from the hospital and a hopeful start to good health. Her friends came by to visit. She couldn't drive, work, or concentrate, and we tried to fill her days by taking her places, just spending time with her, and answering the same questions again and again until her memory started to lock back into place.

linea My parents drove me to the apartment so that I can pick up a few things that I left behind. Jean was supposed to show up at some point, we hadn't seen each other since I got out of the hospital. She called to say that she couldn't. She was busy with her boyfriend.

Suddenly I realized that I am not as strong as I think. I am sensitive, and Jean's rejection hurt. I started ripping my clothes out of the closet, crying, yelling, and throwing a royal tantrum. I never throw fits, but I don't care. I am hurt. I am upset. Our friendship may be over. I don't know what is going to happen, but I know that we are breaking up. We are done, and she doesn't give a shit. She doesn't care. I do. I hurt, a lot, and she can't even come by to say hello. I love her so much but am so mad at her, and now it all comes boiling out into this fit of hysterical anger.

cinda Six months since bringing Linea home from Chicago to her release from the hospital. Time was a blur. I was completely behind in my work and exhausted, mentally and physically. I had been ignoring the toll this had taken on my body and spirit. This had been much harder for Linea. She was not yet completely well but was tired of both feeling and being treated like someone who was sick. Linea wanted to go back to school as soon as she possibly could, but Curt and I couldn't imagine her returning to Chicago. She was just getting her memory back, and she was emotionally and physically fragile. I wanted to give her every opportunity to recover. Sleep, rest, good food, and as little stress as possible. But she was determined that she get her life back, and her life was in Chicago.

One day, a month after she came home, we had spent the whole day together, and I had fallen into bed exhausted. I was reading when I heard her running toward our bedroom from the other end of the house. She jumped onto the bed between us. She was crying.

My anxiety and heart rate instantly increased. What next?

"Mom, Dad, I am so sorry about using drugs." She was crying so hard that she couldn't catch her breath. She felt like she had broken our trust. She was so very sorry. She talked and talked to us about how ashamed she felt, barely stopping to breathe.

Although we had learned about her drug use while she was hospitalized, we had discussed it only briefly and around the edges. That evening, we all three talked into the night, crying together and finally laughing at the incredibly unreal situation that we found ourselves in. If someone had told us that we would lie on our bed at one A.M. in the morning and talk about Linea's near suicide and use of drugs to both self-medicate and give her courage to end her life, I would not have believed it. She was home, she no longer wanted to kill herself, but I was beginning to realize that she wasn't simply "fixed." I couldn't yet let down my guard.

linea The bed with its red comforter is warm and comfy. I feel as if I will sink right through it. The room is lit solely by the two identical bedside lamps, and underneath each lamp is a book lying facedown and open to the spot that was being read the moment before I entered. I lie between my parents, barely fitting now that I am six feet tall.

I don't quite remember why I came here in the first place, but I have never felt as happy and content as I do lying here between them. We talk about how I was completely raw in the hospital. The fact that now I said everything and anything I wanted (or didn't want to) and people still liked and even respected me. I am amazed that people have any sort of respect for me after all I've said and done.

I tell my parents that I see colors and hear sounds differently now. I tell them that I feel like things are new again. How all of a sudden the world is so beautiful because I can see it through new eyes. I enjoy listening to the space between words like a jazz lover listens to the space in a Coltrane riff. Saying this before, I would have felt this monologue cheesy and embarrassing, but I'm not embarrassed anymore. Of anything. The conversation flowed beautifully right into a new conversation I wasn't ready to have. The conversation about the night I almost killed myself.

Before we get to that night, let me first give a little background information. A little information on me and my uncle Steve. I've always had a secret preoccupation with Steve, I think because I never met him. And because Steve died at the age of twenty-three, most probably by his own hand.

Steve was that imaginary figure of older brother or uncle complete with a little friendly "bad influence." After hearing many stories of Steve's adventures, including getting busted the night he graduated from high school, I began to envision him as the counterpoint to my perfectionist ways.

In high school I would think, maybe if he were here, he would teach me to loosen up and have a good time. Maybe if he were here, I would have someone to teach me the ropes of being a rebellious teenager.

How he died was always mysterious (Steve's death was never really discussed in my family, and for most of my life, neither was Steve). I would visualize and almost fantasize about the details. There was something romantic about the car chase out to the cabin in the woods and his grand exit by crashing his Mustang. I realize that I have always had some sort of preoccupation with death (when my great-grandmother died when I was seven, I made 3-D coffins, complete with a real crayon-colored dead grandma; the story about the family that came out on the Oregon Trail and lost several children on the way was a playground game for me, I played the drowning six-year-old instead of the teenage heroine), but Steve himself was some sort of magical phenomenon. I always envisioned Steve to be a lot like me. Tall, athletic, friendly, fun. I thought I was him, a generation later. Then I slowly began to hear more about his life and wondered if I, in fact, was meant to follow in his path.

When I was fifteen, and falling into a somewhat paralyzing depression, I blamed it on Steve. I always felt him around. He was always there, a fly that just wouldn't leave my side or a crow watching down from a power line. At sixteen, when I first had real thoughts of hurting myself, they always revolved around cars hitting trees. I would fantasize about driving as fast as I could down the Lake Hills Connector and suddenly losing control until I drove straight off the steep hill into one of the many beautiful evergreens.

When I finally found out that Steve died by a shot to the heart from his own gun, while driving, I felt betrayed that I hadn't been told the full story. It was at that point that the death became something real. This part of Steve within me needed to be banished for the safety of myself and others.

For a long while after I learned the truth about Steve's death, I was able to completely banish him out of my mind. He was no longer a hero but a half second cousin by marriage twice removed. It wasn't until I moved into my own apartment, on Broadway in Seattle, that he returned. He returned one day with the flies in my kitchen and grew into an overwhelming obsession.

The night before I was hospitalized, I had had dinner with my family, and my dad drove me home. It was dark and about eleven o'clock. It was the time of night when the hip young Broadway crowd transformed into the old homeless junkies crowd. It was the time of night that I feared because the streets turned Gothic and sad.

We sat in the car outside my apartment, and I asked my dad how I was different from Steve. I asked him if, because Steve and I were related, it would be more likely for me to be addicted to drugs or alcohol. I asked him if it was likely for me to fall into the same patterns or have the same, ahem, things happen to me. I was checking, begging to find some way to see us as different, when in my mind we were one and the same. I think my dad understood my questions better than I expected or wanted.

"You and Steve are two entirely separate people. You experienced two separate lives. Steve watched three friends die in tragic accidents in less than a year. He experienced an almost paralyzing injury, one that affected his entire views on life and his career. This is something that can't be passed down. As for the suicide, it was a different time and place. People didn't know as much then as they do now. You can get help that people then could never have dreamed of."

At this point I had started crying softly, looking out the side window in hopes that he wouldn't notice how much this conversation meant to me. I was hoping that he wouldn't read too far into it, even though I knew it was too late.

"You're gonna be okay, Mi. I know you and you're a strong

girl. I trust you to take care of yourself. I know you're gonna be okay. Be safe, baby girl, I don't know what your mother or I would ever do without you. Are you going to be okay tonight?"

All I could do is nod and pretend.

"Do you need to come back and sleep at our place?"

"No, Daddy, I'm okay. I will be fine. I'm strong like you said." And with a forced smile, one to convince myself more than him, I repeated the mantra: "I'm gonna be okay."

"I'm going to trust you to be safe and not hurt yourself. I trust that you will call if you need us."

I gave him a kiss good-bye and repeatedly promised to call if I needed him. I promised to stay safe. As I got out of the car, I tried not to look back at his are-you-sure? face. He watched as I snuck past the heroin junky sleeping on the sidewalk and went up to my apartment.

This next part still will forever amaze me. I walked in the door fully planning on the end. The time between that moment and waking up, the next morning, already dressing myself, I just don't remember. Somewhere in there, approximately nine hours passed. How I managed to live through those nine hours is an utter miracle.

Anyone who has experienced severe depression realizes the strength that a wave of suicidal thoughts holds. The thing is, I love my family more than anything in this world. They mean more to me than I could ever express. The thought of doing anything that would ever hurt them would be the worst possible thing I could ever imagine doing. Killing myself could be the worst possible thing I could ever, ever do. I know what they went through with Steve. I know how a family can suffer from a suicide, and yet, that dark wave within me didn't care.

On my good days I knew these things. I knew never to hurt them, I knew how much I loved them, but the thing that I learned during my days on Broadway was that the darkness didn't care. It is not until I felt unbearable and severe pain and suffering, not until I truly felt that I was going to bleed to death from the inside out, that I could understand the power of that darkness. When I was under the control of the blood and pain, nothing mattered. In fact, there *was* nothing else, no one else in this world existed. When the darkness hit, all that mattered was making it stop. I had no control, no say over what lengths I would reach to stop it. Up until that night I had done a great job of fighting it off. I fought it off with everything I could. I first fought it with music and books and art. I quickly moved to stronger forces like alcohol and drugs, but suddenly there was nothing left. I knew that nothing was strong enough to stop it.

I had gone to dinner that night fully intending to say my final good-byes. I hugged my sister tight. I kissed my mom's cheek and gave her all of my love. I left dinner never to return. That night, when I walked into my apartment, I had planned to finish off the bottles of wine. I had planned on writing that note to Jean and retiring to the bathtub for eternity. That night was supposed to be my last, but somehow, when it hit the bewitching hour, the clock didn't stop.

The next morning I "came to" already awake and getting

dressed in my closet. All I know is I got home at night, and somehow by the grace of God, or friends, or street drugs and alcohol, or something, I was still there the next morning. I truly believe that there must have been some presence in that apartment that kept me alive. Maybe it was the trust of my parents, maybe it was Steve, but even today, when I realize that I'm still alive, I'm in shock.

At this point in our conversation on my parents' bed, I lose it. I explain between sobs that it was their trust that saved me. I explain that had I not forced myself to go to my counseling appointment the next day I would never have been here to tell them this story. I'm shaking and feel like I'm drowning in my own tears. I can't get a breath in and can't even attempt to talk any longer. My parents both hold me and tell me it's okay. They tell me how proud they are of me and, most important, how strong I am. They hold me and hold me and hold me. I am finally safe. I am finally free from that pain that held me under for so long. This is the first time that I realize what actually happened and, more important, what came very close to happening. It is now that the finality of death hits me.

All I can do is cry, "I'm sorry, thank you, I'm sorry, I'm sorry, I'm sorry." I have never loved more than I love them at this moment.

It's June, and I have just met with Victoria, my counselor. It has been a long time since we have talked, in fact, the last time I went out those doors, my dad took me to the emergency room. The last time I left her office, it was over a month ago and Harborview was expecting me. The last time I left, Victoria was terrified. She said she has been ever since.

I now feel one hundred times better. I feel like I am a new person. I am confident and brave and know that my life is worth living. I now know that I am worth saving.

She cried and I cried because we both kept repeating, "I almost killed myself. I almost did it." I almost killed myself. I can't stop thinking about the fact that I would be gone.

I would have been gone forever.

But there is hope and there is a way out. Three weeks ago, in the hospital, I would have said this is all bullshit and I wouldn't have believed any of it. In fact, I read *Prozac Nation* and thought it was a crock of shit, but now I believe. I believe that you can get through this and that it is real. I have learned that I am someone and that people do care about me. It makes me cry. Victoria cried. My dad cried.

My dad is a rock. A hero. He held me so tight when I told him that he was what made me strong. I can't get over the fact that I made it through. Even my mom was brave the last few days. She used to call me so often and worries so much I always expect her to crash, but through all this she has been strong. In fact, I have never seen my mom so happy. She is amazing. My grandparents are coming over this weekend. My grandma is a rock just like my dad. As my grandmother puts it, she has "kept the horse in the barn" for the last few weeks. This refers to my grandpa who, after losing Steve, was ready to come out to Seattle immediately. My grandpa and Jordan act strongest when they are scared. They may even act aggressive and try to hide their fear, but they care more than anyone. So does my aunt Calla; she was a rock for my mom and me. I scared a lot of people. I can't believe that I actually made it out alive. I almost killed myself.

I almost did it.

I really almost followed through.

Oh, my God.

cinda Linea saw her psychologist once weekly and her psychiatrist once a month. Linea was not driving yet the first time she saw her psychologist, so I was her chauffeur. We picked up a bouquet of flowers to give to her.

Victoria came into the waiting room to get Linea, and Linea handed her the flowers and told her thank you. I was so very proud of my daughter. I was thankful for Victoria and the connection that she made with Linea so that she could tell her the magic words "I'm not safe." I was most thankful that somehow Linea had a spark and the will to live, and even to live well. That spark kept her fighting. It was nearly extinguished many times, but Linea somehow, some way protected that tiny light and saved herself. While Linea had her appointment, I sat quietly in the waiting room and let the tears loose. I don't know why I cried in so many waiting rooms. Maybe it was because no one knew me or maybe it was because if I completely went off the deep end there was professional help nearby. I needed to keep the tears and fears locked away while fighting for my daughter's life. I was always afraid that if I let them loose, I would never be able to come back together, to be whole again, to be able to take care of Linea. By the time Linea came out of Victoria's office, I was okay.

Linea's psychiatrist had been in contact with us throughout her hospitalization, and Linea wanted me to come with her to her first appointment in case she forgot something. She told her psychiatrist that she didn't have those "feelings" anymore; in other words she was not suicidal, but she did feel "kind of flat." Not happy and not sad. The decision was still out regarding her diagnosis. Was it depression, bipolar II, or bipolar I? The label for her illness was not the issue but rather the correct medication.

"How will we know if I am bipolar?" she asked him.

His response scared both of us: "We will have to wait and see if you have any manic episodes."

We talked about what this might look and feel like to Linea. Impulsivity, racing thoughts, use of drugs or alcohol, extreme anxiety. Her doctor believed that she had at least bipolar II and wanted her to try lithium. Linea was silent, tight, and frightened. I had worked with people taking lithium and was aware of the side effects, and I was frightened as well. We left with the prescription in hand, both of us disheartened.

"I'm really sick, aren't I?" she asked when we got into the car.

I was discouraged but tried to keep up the strong mother face. Lithium. Good God, this illness had not curled up and retreated in the face of hospitalization.

"Lithium may work really well for you," I told her. She rolled her eyes. She had not been lucky with her response to pharmaceuticals; she had already been on more than ten different medications. I was so frightened. But I couldn't tell her this or let her know in any way. She would find a treatment that worked. She would be well again.

We were both hungry and we went to the very classy and beautiful restaurant in the Sorrento Hotel on Capitol Hill, the kind of place about which, as a child, Linea would cry out, "I want to live *here*!" She said nothing as we made our way to our table. Once seated, she answered my questions politely but didn't seem to be enjoying herself, as she would have in the past, eating lunch in a fancy restaurant. We sat quietly, eavesdropping on two elegantly dressed eighty-year-olds as they discussed politics and the many important Democrats they had met over their lifetimes. Linea finally smiled and let out a tiny giggle. I was happy for this small moment, a moment that felt normal, a moment that belonged to our past.

It had been two weeks since she was released from the hospital. We decided to drive the three hours to Vancouver, Canada, for the weekend, heading north after her doctor's appointment. We would get away from all of this for a while, stop talking about it and just have a fun and relaxing weekend. We desperately needed a change. We needed to shake off the minute-to-minute obsession with this insidious illness, whatever it was.

On the trip up to Vancouver, Linea was semisleeping in the backseat. She had started the lithium and said she felt high and light-headed. When we arrived in Vancouver, we checked into our hotel and headed out for dinner. Linea was tired and, by dinner's end, sleepy. She barely talked at all during dinner and fell into bed as soon as we returned to the hotel. Should we have come? I wanted everything to be the way it had been. I wanted a break for her and for us.

The next morning, she was really dragging. Halfway up the block, she sat down on the sidewalk and told us she felt weak. Curt helped her up and convinced her that food would make her feel better. As I sat across from her at breakfast, I got the full affect. She was pale, really white, and her eyes were hugely dilated.

"I feel like a zombie or a heroin addict," she said. "Not that I have ever tried heroin."

She looked like a zombie or a heroin addict. Not that I had ever seen a zombie.

I was anxious and wanted to call her doctor. Curt thought we should go home. Linea convinced us that we needed to stay and go to her favorite bookstore. She convinced us that she would feel better soon.

By the time we got back to the hotel in the late afternoon, she felt much worse. She felt as if she couldn't breathe. She was pale and sweaty, cold and clammy. The blue in her eyes was gone, all was dark pupil. Something was very wrong.

I called her psychiatrist. He said she needed to stop taking the lithium completely. If her breathing stayed shallow or she experienced any breathing difficulties, we were to get her to the emergency room immediately. He ended the conversation by telling us that she should see him first thing on Monday and he would consult with the hospital on what to do next. What magic drug could be pulled out of the hat to set her on the road to recovery?

I was more disheartened than ever. But I fought back the tears and tried to believe in the miracle of modern medicine. We spent the evening in the hotel watching a movie that Linea didn't see because she fell asleep. I got up and put my face close to her nose, listening to her breathe. I checked on her two or three times during the night, to see if she was alive. After everything she had been through, I didn't want to lose her to lithium.

linea Looking back, I can see why my parents were worried. I can see my body collapsed on the chair staring out the window. I am wearing plaid tennis shoes, jeans, and a striped sweatshirt. I am motionless and practically unconscious in this luxury hotel room in Vancouver. My body looks out the window at the Pacific and faces away from the large floral beds and mini-bar. It faces away from my anxious parents on the phone to my psychiatrist. I can't see them. To me they don't exist but for their worried voices. They are but shadows.

"We don't know what's wrong with her."

"Her pupils are the size of watermelons."

"She had to sit down after walking a block."

He told them to stop giving me the lithium immediately. Lithium is a medicine that has to be highly monitored because the only way to make it work is to use the highest level possible before it becomes toxic and deadly. The only way to make it work is to push just up to the edge of the cliff. Push up to the line but don't cross, or sudden death. As I got blood tests every week, it was supposed to be fine.

My stint with lithium lasted three days.

I live at home. Being twelve again isn't all it's cracked up to be when you're a restless twenty-year-old.

I'm trying to convince myself that living at home will be okay. I am doing yoga two times a week, trying to find a fencing class, learning the guitar, and getting in shape. I already have more confidence in myself than I ever had. There is something about saving your own life that builds an incredible amount of strength. For the first time in my life I am actually proud of myself.

Three weeks in a psych ward can really change a person. I've learned a lot about the world, and I have also realized one more thing about myself. Why waste my life on suicide? And I am so happy that I am able to see reasons for living now. My mom and I were recently driving in Port Angeles, a beautiful town on the Sound. As we were driving out here, I saw a bear through the trees. Suddenly I can see things that no one notices. Words and images are so much more meaningful. My dreams have been more vivid, too. Everything is so intense. It is exhausting, but I love it.

cinda Time went slowly, as did Linea's recovery. For about eight weeks she was not supposed to drive, as she adjusted to her medications and her brain healed from the ECT. Her friends took turns chauffeuring her to concerts and movies and barbecues. Her friend Chrisy had a summer birthday celebration on the beach in West Seattle. But Linea was still too tired to spend more than a few hours at the gathering, making it difficult for her to catch a ride with friends who were going. I volunteered to drive her. I volunteered to do anything that could possibly make her happy. I would do anything.

When we finally found the right beach and Linea found her friends, the coffee shops had closed for the evening. I didn't want to go into a bar, so I walked the sidewalk along the beach for the next two hours. It was a beautiful night, clear and warm. I looked across the water at the Seattle skyline and picked out Harborview. I was here now, on the beach, not in the psych unit with my daughter. The patients we left behind were there, behind locked doors, playing Friday night bingo.

As I walked, I watched groups of young people by their beach fires, playing night Frisbee, kicking soccer balls around, and sneaking alcohol from backpacks. They were teenagers and young twenty-somethings without a seeming care in the world. I suddenly felt deeply sad that Linea's life had changed, that it had gone in such a different direction from what we had all planned. Even if she returned to full health and never had another bout of whatever this was, she had been kicked hard when she least expected it at a time in her life when she should have been untroubled and free of worry. I felt angry. Mostly I felt so terribly sad. Why? Compared to so many others, we were lucky. The positive spin that I usually forced into running my thoughts was nowhere to be seen. Why her? And, a question I truly hadn't asked, why us? Why me? I immediately felt selfish and self-centered and even angrier. I knew we had more than many others. I knew we left people at Harborview who didn't even have a family. A deep and profound sense of grief folded over me, and the anger simmered for a loss I couldn't quite put into words.

I met Linea back at the car and we headed for home. She

had had fun but said things were different now. It was hard for her to keep up with the conversations, and she felt left out from the normal summers that all her high school friends were living. Suddenly a car switched lanes without signaling, causing me to hit the brakes and crowd the shoulder. Linea cried out in a panic.

"It's okay," I said. "I saw him in plenty of time."

She was in tears. "This is weird, Mom. Less than four weeks ago I wanted to die, yet barely out of the hospital I am terrified of getting hurt or killed. Drive really carefully, okay? I keep worrying that something will happen to me."

We meandered through the next few weeks, and just when we were starting to get on each other's nerves, Linea's friend Jamie moved in with us. She was at loose ends, having finished spring quarter at the community college, while working at Starbucks. I suggested that she stay with us while she tried to figure out what to do next.

Jamie was such a blessing for Linea. She was a new friend, but I felt they must have known each other in previous lives. They would sit and giggle over things no one else understood, they discussed ideas, from music to current events, they both cared deeply for people and were accepting of the other's quirks and needs. They were a matched set. When they announced that Jamie had decided to move to Chicago as well, I was cautiously ecstatic. Jamie and Linea could spend time together over the summer and see how they got along as quasi-roommates. I tried to take a wait-and-see attitude, but I couldn't help imagining them in an apartment together—Linea resuming her life and Jamie happy in Chicago.

linea I'm irritable. I'm angry. I'm breaking. My heart aches and I miss Chicago. I miss the snow. I miss the heat. I miss some amazing handsome guy with blondish hair in the music department whom I never met. I miss my life. I feel stranded. Stuck.

I feel awful. I am so sick of this house. Today my grandmother sent me a beautiful card and a picture of Steve as a young child. It brought tears to my eyes because it reminded me how fast innocence can give way and of the ugliness that the world pushes at you. It was hard to see him in his youth when he obliviously thought that life was still worth living. When he saw that there was still happiness behind becoming a star basketball player or a lawyer. When he still thought that life was good.

I'm sitting in yoga clearing my mind on the exhale and filling my heart chakra on the inhales when my mind just won't stop turning. In meditation you are supposed to surrender your mind to your soul, but my entire being was just buzzing with thoughts. In fact, I felt worse while I was mediating than I did before I began. I definitely feel that I have more thoughts than I can handle at this moment.

It all started three weeks ago when I felt my wrist throb with tendonitis. It sent me back to a time when I longed for a knife to stop the pain. The throbbing in my wrist comes often and I can't seem to stop it. It still reminds me of how much I once wanted to slit that throbbing vein and of how much I needed to stop feeling at all. Now it just reminds me of how sick I really was and how sick I still am because I'm still constantly reminded of knives and blood and pain.

When I think about how much I want to go back to the hospital, I start to worry. I can only stop worrying when I realize how far I am from my coke and blade needs of a month ago. Now I feel as if I am back to being that high school overachiever who desperately needs a break. What do I need a break from? What am I still running from? I need a break from trying so hard. I need to have my life back. I need to run away from home. It's true that you can't ever really go home . . .

I sit in my room, this beautiful jail cell, filling my time with things I love. I write, I paint, I read, I do all kinds of music, I do yoga, run, dance. I am free to do everything I want. I have all the time in the world and what seems like all the money. Why then do I long to be locked up again? Why do I long for a worse jail than this? What do I need? I am unable to either go forward or back. I'm stuck in this limbo that holds me between the real world and my parents' world of happiness and spoiling me.

Suddenly I realize that my yoga instructor has begun talking and that I have missed the entire first half of his speech on the joys of a clear mind.

So much for finding my center. I'm too pulled in all directions.

cinda July is my dad's birthday and he had convinced the family—two sisters, two brothers-in-law, and three grandchildren—to join him and my mother on a houseboat for a long weekend. We drove across the state and immediately headed out to purchase enough food to sustain us in case we were shipwrecked for three months.

It was a hot and sunny four days with swimming and laughs and no disagreements. As I watched Linea play board games with her cousins, I did a silent assessment of her cognitive skills. Her memory and wit seemed more intact than ever as she played Scrabble using only words heard on rap songs. She was still quiet more than not, with moments of anxiety because she said she felt "fat" and didn't want anyone to see her in her swimsuit. She wasn't fat at all, but it only made her angry when I tried to convince her of this. I wanted to make it better and I wanted to make the negative feelings go away, but I didn't know how. She told me to just stop talking about it because nothing I could possibly say would make her feel better. I knew that what she said was true, and my heart broke a little more.

But she was able to let things go more easily now than previously, and soon she was in a good mood and in her swimsuit. It was late afternoon and we had been swimming to cool off. My sister, mom, niece, Linea, and I sat together in the shade on the deck at the stern of the boat.

"So, tell me about Steve, you guys. We never talk about him. What was he like?" Linea said.

I was surprised and waited to see who would say what. The conversation started slowly, beginning with stories of his death and moving to the more important stories of his life. My sister and I shared our memories of his life, our versions separated by my position as the older sister and hers as the middle child. I vividly remembered my mother and father bringing this baby brother home from the hospital. My mother had a hysterectomy shortly after his birth, and I remembered my feeling of importance as the oldest child, the one to help. I could lift him for my mother. I could feed him his bottle and carry him for her. My next memories were reading to him and trying to teach him to read. I remembered taking him out of the town where we lived and letting him drive on the dirt roads. I was sixteen; he was ten. I remembered how he used to help sneak me in after my curfew. We laughed and shared tales and memories of Steve.

linea Got in a fight with my parents. I couldn't find my notebook of lyrics and I freaked out. They couldn't take it anymore, and for the first time since I've been home they yelled back. We fought about cleaning my room. Why? What's the point when I'm just going to leave? Why unpack when it's soon to be packed? Why pack when you're obviously still a mess? Why live when you can't even get along with people? Why live when you will never find yourself again? Why live when you will never be where you want to be? I can't be the real me when I can't tell the difference between dreams and future. Dreams of loss, being lost, and fear. Dreams of coke, sex, and addiction. You will never be free. You won't survive this.

I'm in Chicago sitting at Jake and Dean's with a small tabby cat clawing at my leg and Ultimate Fighting Championship blasting in front of me. Jake and I sit mesmerized and drunk at eleven in the morning, amazed by this new form of WWF. I watch as ten men stuck in a reality TV house discuss their big fight and then go into the ring to wrestle, street fight, and tae kwon do their enemies into unconsciousness. It's sad and disgusting but seems to be the perfect thing to do on a busy Monday afternoon while everyone else goes to school.

I am here on a visit. I am looking at apartments so I will be able to finally move back to Chicago. My doctor gave clear orders not to drink. He also told me drugs are not a good option. I take his points into consideration as I take a swig of my beer and watch Jake pack a bowl. He passes it my way, and I take hit after hit until I have a nice body high. I am now drunk, high, and hungry. I stumble through the long empty apartment to the kitchen. Plastic cups are exploding out of the sink. My eye catches a bag of whole wheat bread. I grab a dry slice and start nibbling. I then follow it by approximately six more plain pieces until Jake yells in from the living room.

"Time for the fight! Oh, shit! This guy's gonna fucking kick his ass!"

I have been drunk all week while my parents trust me with my life and the doctor's orders. We watch in awe as the large English guy beats the shit out of the American. We yell, we punch the air, we cheer.

Eight hours pass and we get ready to go to a friend's apartment party. We are tired and drained from our busy day. I drink five cups of coffee while Jake makes three lines of coke. I politely turn him down as he offers me a coolie, a cigarette laced with coke. I then turn down the line he made for me, and as much as I long for the darkness, I give in to the light. I know that at this point the only way back to Chicago is to keep myself halfway safe. I think of what the drinking, pot, and caffeine must already be doing to my system and realize that with the legal drugs in my body, I am no better off. I really think it through and almost decide coke can't be much worse at this point, but then I see my mom's face and decide to "just say no."

My eagerness to fall right back into old habits scares me. I still have an urge to be sick. I still long for pain, for numbness, for the sickness. I long to be stuck in a hospital bed being waited on hand and foot. People crying over the news. I really must be sick because anyone who knows me knows it is not in my character to want suffering for others. But now I want tears, I want to bleed and see people get weak at the sight. The difference tonight is that I stopped myself. It is the fact that I know what I am doing and I know what I want. I want to be free. I want to have my own life. I want a chance to say no in the first place and that means having my own life. My own place. My own friends. I gotta get out even if it means being good.

Back to Washington and off to Idaho. I'm driving with Jamie under the beautiful red cliffs of Challis. Butterflies whacking against the windshield of her mother's blue MG. It's my favorite car and my favorite friend, laughing, giggling. Feeling joy and safety for once in the last few weeks. I am finally feeling hope for our upcoming move to Chicago. I feel that Jamie will be the one that will truly understand. I know Jean cares and I know she tried. I know she probably didn't mean to disappear in my time of need. I know that she probably just couldn't handle it. I know that she is a person to hide her feelings and run when she thinks she'll cry. But now it doesn't matter. It's over and I have Jamie and Chicago ahead of me. Back to my old life anew. Here we go.

9. conviction

cinda We began the many tasks of preparing to move Linea back to Chicago. Were we doing the right thing? Would Linea be okay in Chicago? Her doctor wasn't convinced, nor were we, but she pushed and pushed. She would lose her scholarship if she didn't enroll fall semester. She would lose her medical insurance if she wasn't a student. She told us she would lose her very self if she had to stay in Seattle. Please, please, I prayed, let this be the right decision.

After many long discussions and decisions made and changed and changed again, we decided to drive from Seattle to Chicago, more than two thousand miles of highway along I-90. We took the southern route and pulled a U-Haul filled with Linea's and Jamie's possessions, including a full-sized keyboard that had moved home from Chicago, a small hideaway couch, the squishy green Goodwill chair that had followed her home from her apartment with Jean, and boxes of books. We were looking forward to a road trip and spending time with Linea and Jamie before leaving them in Chicago until Thanksgiving. What did we know?

We drove through a record heat wave that followed us

from Idaho to Illinois. We had to unleash the U-Haul more than once for vehicle repairs. Jamie questioned whether the difficulties getting to Chicago might be a message telling us not to go. I wondered the same.

We barely made it to Chicago in time to unload and return the U-Haul on schedule. Jamie and Linea's new apartment was two blocks from the music building, and I hoped that the convenience to her classes would help Linea stay steady and well. We set up the beds and pulled out the couch. We took the girls to dinner at Miller's Pub, full of memories from happier times. We came home and fell into an exhausted sleep with the unfamiliar sounds of the city banging at the windows and hopefulness whispering in my ears.

The next day, Linea had an appointment with a psychiatrist. Her doctor in Seattle had given us his name, and he came highly recommended by both the medical community in Seattle and my own search online. I had spent hours on the phone scheming to get our medical insurance to cover him and the psychologist working in his practice. He was outside our insurance's preferred providers, but someone within the company told me that if I could not find anyone else to take her they would consider this doctor. I called more than twenty offices until I found ten that told me they were not taking new patients or they would not take patients Linea's age. I documented this and sent off a letter to our insurance company along with a letter from Linea's Seattle psychiatrist. I somehow convinced them to make an exception for these "nonpreferred" providers to care for Linea.

Linea seemed to be stable, although given the trip that we had just been through it was hard to tell. One evening somewhere in the middle of the nation, we watched a sunset the likes of which we do not see in Seattle. Linea said, "I wish I could get excited again about a sunset." That comment stuck with me. It confirmed my belief that she was "stable" but not where she wanted to be. Her joy seemed to be gone.

We met with her new doctor, filling in her history in addition to what he had in her medical files, providing information for insurance and Visa card numbers. The psychiatrist, like Linea's doctor in Seattle, was a kind, gentle, quietly brilliant man. It had been his suggestion that Linea also see a psychologist in his practice so that they could together get to know her, manage her care, and check with each other if necessary. As I left, he said to me, "We will take care of her. Think of us as her family away from home." In that moment, I believed him, and he would soon live up to his words.

We finished everything we needed to do in Chicago, and it was time to leave Linea and Jamie. I wouldn't cry. It was time to go. I had to trust her. She said to me, "You have to believe that you can trust me. I think I have proven myself." It was true. Her fight to live was a battle and she had won the first round. And yet I wanted to stay with her, live with her, take care of her, and keep her safe. But I couldn't. I held her to me and whispered, "You will be okay. Keep safe. I love you so."

We headed west to Washington. Curt and I had thought that after leaving Linea, we would have our own time together, that we would be happy as empty nesters once again. But the worry followed us back to Seattle and the exhaustion stayed.

linea Something's wrong. I can't be happy. I will never be happy. They give me a big room. A cute apartment. A beautiful life. A good job. Friends. I don't care. I can't enjoy this. Every new addition is another thing to be sad about. A big room to mope around in. Another place to create sad memories of pain.

I have been longing to and have just started once again to cut myself. Fuck, what is wrong with me?! I'm such a freak. It feels so good, though, and everything I was just going to complain about and whine about feels slightly better. The loneliness, the sadness, the need to cry. It's gone.

I tried to puke today. I tried to get rid of the fat that is pushing out of my body, but it didn't work. I stuck my finger as far back in my throat as I could before I tried the toothbrush, and neither worked. I'm so sick.

I have forgotten to take my pills for four days in a row now. I am quite literally going mad. I have been too caught up in the fairy-tale lifestyle of an independent dweller to care. Too busy having sleepovers with boys, skinny-dipping in Lake Michigan under a full moon, playing basketball, reading books, and now it's back to kill me. I am restless. My mind is going crazy. My thoughts are racing so fast I can't function. I am going nuts.

I began reading Italo Calvino's *If on a Winter's Night a Traveler,* and I thought my brain was going to explode. There was so much going on and so many switches between thoughts, that on top of my regular crazy thoughts I started to think even faster. I had to stop and stare at the wall for ten minutes just to cool down.

Today I went to the library and read everything I could about Andy Warhol's Factory. I can't stop reading and thinking, so I went up to the roof and screamed at the top of my lungs, and by the time I got back to the apartment I still couldn't stop pacing and swaying.

I am losing my mind. I have this yearning to be part of something great. Be something great. Be in art. I can't stop thinking about it and I need it so badly I think I'll explode. I honestly think this is what I have been longing for.

I told my psychologist that I feel lonely when I go to the Art Institute and that I need something, that I'm trying to fill something and I can't be satisfied. I try to fill it with boys and drugs and booze. Sex and love won't accomplish anything. This need won't go away. I started cutting again because I needed to fill this void. Of course I can't tell anyone about that, not even my psychologist, because there is no way to truly express this. I just need something. I need to be a part of something. My own something.

I took seven painkillers. I'm going to take more because I'm only slightly numb. I just have to be careful not to take too many so I won't get sick when I drink tonight. The pills have calmed me down a bit. I stopped pacing, but now I just feel depressed that I'm not anywhere or anything.

I want to be somewhere else, or something or someone other than me. But these pills kill a bit of the need. I need something stronger. Maybe the booze will help. I have to be careful not to let anyone find out. I can't fuck up again. This all has to be secret this time. This time I will be able to keep hold of myself before I am hospitalized. I can treat myself my way without going overboard. I know I can. I have to remember to take my meds so this won't happen again. I can't get much crazier.

September—Cocaine

October—After something like ten tries at antidepressants, they have finally given me Prozac. It's amazing because already it has given me a boost of energy. I feel like I am walking on water and want to take as much as I can. I want to get rid of the outer time-release capsule and sniff all the powder inside. I hope it stays this good. They also put me on another mood stabilizer. It apparently has an appetite suppressant, and I think this could be a good way to convince myself to stop eating. Before, I could blame my eating on the antidepressant, so I ate more. Now I can just stop eating and blame it on the new pill.

We are on a train. We are both so coked up that we practically sprinted to catch it. We walked one hundred miles an hour, plowing down passersby. Pushing over old ladies, tipping cows. And once on the train we continued to run in our seats. Everything was moving. Going going going. I love the train because I felt like something was going as fast as I was. The world had finally caught up to me. Things were flying in my head and my heart. Nothing could stop. I sat with Jake. Jake in his usual attire of brown corduroys, a button-up sweater, and his hat pulled low, accentuating his nose ring. The hat always rested nicely over his glasses. His glasses that were inspired by his Rivers Cuomo phase. We were high out of our minds. I couldn't stop fidgeting. I loved the knowing looks people were giving me because I knew they weren't real. I knew they were due to my paranoia.

Jake was the only one in Chicago who knew about my coke habit. Well, Jake and the doorman who did the last couple of lines with me.

People keep coming and going. The nightly commutes of party girls and career wives makes me even more anxious. Why are they looking at me like that? Can they tell? Do they know? Don't touch your face, your nose. Don't move. I'm tense and still unmoving when the minor third of the door rings to tell us we're here.

I feel that the world that was weighing down so heavily upon my shoulders before has really only been part of my imagination. What was so important? What was I seeing, feeling, hearing before this moment? What changed this? Why do I no longer see the spaces in the words like I did when I left the hospital? Why do I feel that was nothing? But I have nothing to say. Nothing to write. Nothing to tell. Nothing but endless bouts of boredom, pain, and longing for reasons unknown. What can I say but journal entries equal to that of a twelve-year-old?

I can write of longing. I long for love. I long for the hold of someone stronger than my own demons. Someone to save me from myself. To make my heart beat fast and my tongue stutter and my speech become quick and unimportant. Someone to whom I give my life. Gives me hope once again. I long to have a reason to stop this charade of disaster.

I can write of boredom, of filling the spaces with endless banter or drugs or alcohol. I can speak of times when I pulled at my hair and screamed off of roofs out of sheer madness. Rides on trains when the train went so fast the paint chipped from the walls and the lights blurred. Rides on trains when the train went so slow I could hear the rats running beneath. I can speak of times when I walked down the street so high that I couldn't feel the people I ran over or hear the cars that honked. I can speak of boredom so strong I couldn't help but drag a blade over my flesh.

I can write of pain. I can write of the pain that develops when you hurt for no reason and have to find ways to soothe it yourself. I can write of the pain that develops out of boredom and the pain that develops out of longing when you're not strong enough to withstand the pressure.

But none of this matters. None of this gives me anything to write about. I feel more incomplete than I ever have in my life. There is no longer any way of expression worthy of this life. There is no form of art capable of expressing this madness.

Getting back to school has been difficult. I have been trying my best not to freak out. I will be playing the piano and get a sudden panic so that I can't see the notes straight and don't understand what I am reading so I have to force myself to calm down and be normal. I get close to collapsing when I think of hurting myself again, but I have been okay so far. I will make it.

Last night I dreamed of shooting myself in the head. I was calm and happy and remember thinking, why haven't I thought of this before? It is so easy! Then I pulled the trigger. I think I was in my closet. I haven't dreamed of suicide in a long time. Every once in a while it pops up like a bad dream during the day. I walk by the practice rooms and see myself curled on the floor hyperventilating and start thinking about the redness. I think about jumping into trains at times when I least expect it. But it is nothing like the old days. I know I will be okay. I will make it this year. I think I will survive. I have been contemplating buying razor blades but figured that buying razor blades is just as bad as picking up sleeping pills. I might just decide to sleep forever. One cut might not be enough. I will make it this year.

I don't know if I can do it. I don't know if I can stay out of the hospital. I am trying to be in school, trying to work hard. Trying to be safe. Trying to be good. But I can't push too hard. I am feeling lethargic again. I am getting to that point where I lie around a lot. The point where I stare a lot. The point where I can't quite function. Yesterday I bought a pack of razor blades. I decided I needed to stop using scissors and knives. I'm sick of sawing away at my flesh. I'm sick of peeling away layers; I just want to slice with ease. I used the razor blade today and it was amazing. It is so much better and it bleeds so much more. It was beautiful. I dabbed the blood with a piece of toilet paper and almost the entire piece was bright red. This was so much better than before when there were only dabs of blood. Sometimes I think I need to talk to my counselor, but I don't know if I want to go back to the hospital quite yet. I really want to make it through this time. I need to be normal for at least a little while longer.

Charlie wanted to talk. We went to dinner and he talked with nothing to say. He talked about what to do about me. He talked about what he should do because he is still in love with me. He doesn't know if he should talk to me ever again. He wants to hate me. He doesn't know how to deal with me.

He gave back the notes I wrote to him. I cried at the restaurant. I cried for the first time in months. I cried and told him they were his and that I'm sorry I fell out of love. I told him I didn't mean to or want to. He said he wanted to know why, but I can't tell him why. I can't give him answers. I can't help him feel better. I can't fix this. I feel like we broke up all over again. My heart was crushed. I went back to my room and sobbed.

Later, when I talked to Jamie, it all came out. I cried and cried. I talked of Charlie and Jean and how this depression is ruining all my relationships. I told her that I'm afraid to love again because I'm afraid I will fuck it up. I told her that I am afraid I will ruin our relationship by going crazy or being weird. I am so scared to say anything to anyone anymore because they will all just get scared away. The real me is just going to hurt everyone. The real me will scare everyone, but I can't act fake anymore.

I can't do this much longer. I'm having a hard time seeing the point in trying to have any relationships anymore. I'm having a hard time trying to see why to get out of bed or leave the house. The dishes have piled up like in the Broadway apartment. They are molding and crusting. My room is a mess. My life is a mess. I can barely force myself to go to class. This is ridiculous. I can't do homework or concentrate in class. I can't even think of ways to hurt myself.

I am really hurting here. The other night I told Jamie I thought something wrong was going to happen. I know what that means. I only say that when there is something bad about to happen. I only say that when I'm falling down again. I don't know what to do. I don't know how to hold on anymore, or who to talk to. My counselor just told me to hang in there. How am I supposed to hang in there when I can't even get up in the morning? If this gets worse, I won't be able to hang on to anything.

I don't know what to do. Charlie is gone. Jean will never call back. I can't tell my parents. Jamie tries so hard. My doctors tell me to hang on. I'm hanging on for my dear life, now what?

There's something coming down my face and I'm not sure if it's raining or I'm crying. The sky is blue. I'm sitting against a wall in a small alley off of Dearborn. It smells stale like the basement of my dad's old hardware store. A stronghold for wood, nails, and blow-up pool toys. But I'm not in that safe dark basement. I'm in an alley next to a rancid Dumpster, and for the first time in my life I truly want to run away.

I think about the teenage runaways that prowl the Seattle streets and wish I had such freedom. I wish that I had the freedom to completely drown myself in mind-killing drugs. I want a way to forget whatever this is that's happening to me.

My mind is racing. I don't know why I'm here, but I remember walking. A frantic walk toward nowhere. I remember agitation. Anxiety. I remember walking around the Loop, passing businessmen and watching their glances as they stared me down. My clothes wrinkled and falling off of me, my hair a giant rat's nest on my head.

There's something sticky on my wrist. I touch it again and it stings like hell. I'm bleeding. A small trench just above my wrist. A trench dug, I'm guessing, throughout the walk. Layer by layer taken away by agitated fingernails. What's going to happen next? I'm rocking back and forth on the cement as some man empties the garbage out the back of a restaurant.

What do I do now? I can't think straight, but I know something must be done. I know it's not normal to want to chop your fingers off with a butcher knife. I know it's not normal to walk one hundred laps around one small apartment. I know it is not me to wish I was some junkie shooting up in an alley. Something must be done.

cinda We were back in Seattle and to our lives in our empty nest, lives in which we were behind in every aspect. Linea had talked to her teachers and had her old job back as a teaching assistant in the music department. She told me that her teachers knew what happened, but I didn't believe they did. How could anyone have known how sick she really was? Or still was?

She was not doing nearly as well as we pretended, and I was not peaceful about her return to Chicago. About a month into the school year, she and her doctor decided that the medication she was on hadn't moved her out of a depression.

He wanted her to try Prozac. Once again I was on MEDLINE and researching this drug and its side effects. I thought and worried about her all the time.

A few weeks into the Prozac she had more energy. I was so hopeful that this medication would help her, that it was the answer. We still didn't have a clear diagnosis, we hadn't yet found a treatment plan that kept her stable, and I constantly questioned whether we should have supported her return to Chicago. But what if we hadn't? She was miserable in Seattle and wanted desperately to return to her music program, her friends, and Chicago. She blamed her lingering depression on her life. She was supposed to be a college student, studying on a scholarship in an exciting city. She had planned this since she was in grade school. She had worked hard to get there. She was doing so much better, but she was definitely not the way she had been prior to her return from Chicago in January. Was this enough time for her to become stable enough to live alone? She wasn't ill enough, nor could we force her to stay in Seattle even if we wanted to. I could only hope for the very best for her and try not to worry and worry and worry.

One Wednesday two months into school, she called me very excited about a ballet that she had seen. She talked on and on about the musical score, when, where, and how it was written, and how incredibly powerful it was. She eagerly told me about her plans to get a master's degree and of her idea of doing her thesis on this particular time and arena of music. I didn't know the ballet or the music, but I did know how much

Linea loves to learn. She and I share the feeling of excitement that comes with learning something new and having it resonate somewhere within. That day she was as excited as I had known her to be since before she was ill. I was not exactly worried, but as I listened to her I wondered if it was the Prozac that had allowed her to move so quickly from the flatness and distance she had struggled with just a few weeks earlier to excitement and joy. After we hung up, I thought about our call some more, and I began to worry. I convinced myself I was not thinking "mania," but maybe the Prozac was too strong a dose? Was I just pretending because I wanted so badly for her to be happy again? For her to be well, to not be getting sick again?

Saturday she called me at seven thirty in the morning and told me she had her apartment cleaned, she had done three loads of laundry, and she was practicing her piano and feeling absolutely great. She told me she finally had energy! She was thrilled. She didn't sound as hyper as she had during the call on Wednesday evening. She was just very upbeat and talking faster than normal. I hung up believing that she was okay. Maybe this medication was the one that would work for her. It had been so long since I had heard her happy or excited. I put my nagging feelings from Wednesday to rest and began to feel hopeful.

Sunday she called, again early in the morning, and told me, "My brain is racing. I feel like I can't keep up with it. I feel so jittery." She said she couldn't think straight and she was feeling very agitated and anxious. Linea said, "If I start running, I don't know where I will end up. I might not be able to stop."

At the end of her conversation she said, "I am afraid, Mom." I was so very afraid, too.

"Can you call your doctor, or do you want me to? What can I do for you?" Maybe I should go to Chicago? Linea called her doctor and got an appointment for Monday morning. I had a sleepless night as my body remembered the fear and the pain and the prayers of the last hospitalization. We had all believed that the worst was over. But I realized it was more hopefulness than belief. Both Curt and I were very disheartened. We didn't have our reserves ready for another battle, although we would do whatever it took. I knew that Linea was more frightened than we were; she didn't know what was happening to her. We spent a sleepless night, waiting and trying to reassure each other. Curt reassured me more than I reassured him. I was overwhelmed with worry.

On Monday, Linea called me after her appointment and said she was off the Prozac and now had anti-anxiety medication. She still felt her mind was racing out of control and told me that she had "felt it coming" for the last few weeks. We didn't find out the extent of what she had been through—the drugs, the reckless behavior, the sleepless nights, the dangerous outings, the cutting—until much, much later. That Monday, after her doctor's appointment, she told me a small piece of those dangerous weeks. Over the phone, she whispered,

"Mom, I have been scratching my hands. My wrists and my palms. I feel like my skin is . . . I don't know what. I can't stop doing it. I am making them bleed. I'm sorry."

I began to cry silently, keeping my tears from her. I felt I couldn't withstand this any longer. I could not bear to see her in so much pain. But I had to.

Linea did not want us to come out.

"No, I need to handle this. I have to be able to handle this," she said.

I called Curt, Curt called Linea, I called Linea, and she called us three or four times during the first part of that day. During her last call, on Monday evening, she told me that she was going to bed and hoped that she could sleep. She hadn't been able to sleep for many, many nights. I couldn't sleep, either.

linea There are four walls in this box of a room. A rather conventional setup. A bare bulb on the wall by the door. Two walls house clothing racks, shirts and dresses interrupted by standing hangers. They're pointing to the sky after their skin was violently peeled off. These skins forming a sickening pile on the floor underneath me. Most of them clean. This is where I lie. Buried in a mound of laundered clothes, wrinkled from the days of indecisive morning rituals. Clothes pulled down in anger and confusion. This closet is dark, a small stream of light pouring in from the doorway. I'm shaking uncontrollably. My brain is ready to combust or collapse. I've left my mind somewhere on the dirty Chicago streets.

This needs to stop. Something needs to happen. I need to go to the hospital. All of a sudden, like a magic spell, there is a bottle in my hand. Has it been here all along? I've opened it without knowing. There are pills in my mouth that I've swallowed without feeling. There are pills intermingled in the clothes beneath me. I'm beginning to feel much better and even a little giddy. Going backward from the number of pills in the bottle I figure I have taken around five.

It's time for me to go to the hospital. I agree and so does every other mood that swings through my brain. Six. Seven. Eight.

I'm off to the music building. Still popping pills. Nine. Ten. The bottle open in my purse. Pills like mints. Crossing the street. Fourteen. In the elevator. Twenty. In the halls. Twenty-four. Pills. Pills. Pills.

There's Carol, my voice teacher. I tell her I won't be able to make it to our lesson. I have to go to the hospital, my medicine is acting up. She's worried but wishes me luck, smiling all the while. Twenty-five. Twenty-six. I give my homework to a fellow classmate to turn in. Twenty-seven. I head to the vending machine and drop some coins as I try to insert them. After retrieving my Tart n Tinys, I leave the fallen quarters and nickels on the floor and swim upstairs. Twenty-eight. Twenty-nine. My bottle is getting awfully empty. Not many left.

Sitting outside of a classroom, I wait for Charlie. I'm getting to the point where I can't hold myself up, I'm slouching and sliding down in my chair. Thirty-two. And it's empty. The Tart n Tinys feed my need to lift small edible things to my mouth, so I eat them just as quickly as the pills. A rainbow of small candy is all around me.

And here he is. Utterly confused to see me here on a Tuesday. Confused and frightened.

Charlie. I think I need to go to the hospital.

10. chaos

linea A gurney. I think I'm on a gurney. Colors are all holographic. The world has never been so colorful. Oh, it's pretty. Things are pretty. Hi, Charlie. You look pretty in the color stream of the television. Hi, Jamie. Why are we underwater? This is funny. You guys look funny. Whoa, when I look from side to side the colors drag along like when you take a picture and leave the shutter open as you move the camera around. The light just trails along after its object. Everything's pretty and transparent. Pretty pretty.

Where am I? What's going on? Who are these people? Where the fuck am I!? What's going on!? Where am I!?

"Get away from me! Stop holding my hands. Please just leave me alone. Nonononono. Stop touching me!"

Jamie and Charlie are sitting on this bed thing with me. "Linea, it's for your own good."

I think I'm in a hospital. What is going on? I wish they would just give my hands back. They are holding them so fucking tight. We are all on this little bed thing. I'm smooshed. They're squishing me. I wish they would leave.

"Stop holding my hands. Get away. Please leave me alone. What's going on?"

Now there is some new lady that I have never met. "You're in the hospital, Linea. Your friends here brought you in because you may have overdosed. We want you to drink this. I know it's gross, but you need to drink it all."

I look and see some black liquid concoction. What the fuck is this?

"This is coal, Linea. It will help to soak up all the toxins you swallowed. It will keep you from actually overdosing. You need to drink it. I know it is hard, but it will keep you alive. We are not going to pump your stomach because this should get rid of all the poisons. This is very serious now, Linea. Drink. Drink, Linea. You need to drink it. You don't want your stomach pumped. I know you don't, it's a lot worse than drinking this."

I'm gagging and it won't go down my throat. It is so thick it feels solid. It tastes like I'm licking an ashtray. I feel like I'm eating a fireplace. My stomach hurts. Why are they force-feeding me a campfire?

"Linea. Keep drinking. We need you to drink this. It will soak up all those pills. It will get them out of your stomach. Please drink it all, Linea."

As I'm gagging, I hear, "Good job, Linea, keep drinking. Keep going. Good job. Almost done, Linea."

• • •

Where am I? What's going on? Why won't you let me sleep? I'm so tired, why won't you let me sleep! Where am I!?

I'm still on the bed and I'm still underwater. My lips are so dry. I wipe them and they are coated by something thick and black. I feel very full and very sick. I feel gross. I feel scared. I feel loopy. Something is wrong but I don't know what. Weren't Charlie and Jamie just here? Did I imagine that? What is going on? Why am I in a hospital? Why am I strapped to a gurney?

Everything was a confused state of confusion. I listened to things they told me later and tried to reconstruct that day. I remember pieces, but I can't put them together. I asked Charlie why I was missing my favorite mascara, why my best pen was gone, why I couldn't find my bracelets.

He told me he threw them away.

He threw them away. Why would he throw them away?

He told me that once he threw away the box of razor blades he found in my purse, I kept trying to hurt myself with any sharp object I could find. He said that in a time of panic he threw them all away. "That is why we held your hands. You fought us so hard. You were physically pushing us away, so we climbed on the bed and held your hands tight until you would calm down and then you would apologize. You kept going through waves of complete anxiety and anger into waves of depression where you would calm down and just stare. It was terrifying. You would calm down and then suddenly you would be back to wanting to hurt yourself. You would cycle back and forth until they finally told us we had to leave.

"Linea, you really scared us. You would say things like, well, you said things like, 'I wish I would have finished it off' or 'Maybe I should have drunk something too and then it would have worked' or 'Why couldn't I just do it?'

"You really scared us."

I don't remember all the details Charlie and Jamie tell me, but this I do know: It was never meant to be a suicide attempt. It was merely meant to stop myself *from* killing myself. It was to stop myself from using the big butcher knife in the kitchen to chop off my finger. It was to stop myself from jumping off the roof. It was to prevent myself from scratching all of my skin off. I never meant to kill myself. What is in my head? Why did this happen? Did I secretly hope deep down that I would die?

I remember lying in my closet. I remember looking at the pills. I remember counting the pills. I remember reading the drug overdose information numerous times. Over and over, in fact. I read it with every other pill I took. Because I didn't want to overdose. Because I wanted to tell them exactly how many I took so they could save me. So they could help me. I read the information so I would not overdose. So I would not die. So that I would be sure not to do the worst thing that it said in the overdose list. I never meant it to be a suicide attempt. I didn't try to kill myself. I didn't try to kill myself.

But apparently I came pretty close.

cinda Tuesday morning, Linea paged Curt and she called my cell. She didn't answer either of us when we called her back. Curt called me late morning and told me that Charlie had just called him. The flood of fear from the last time Charlie called came roaring back to me. Charlie had told me once that he would always be there for Linea. He said he wouldn't turn away, he wouldn't judge her, and he would always be there for her. Even though by this point they were no longer boyfriend and girlfriend, they had been through an intimacy of pain that few twenty-year-olds had experienced.

And now I was a ferry ride away from Seattle in a meeting with a school district, and Linea was in the emergency room at a hospital in Chicago. Curt and I concentrated on only one thing—getting to Chicago as fast as possible. I stayed in Seattle and made phone calls, coordinating with doctors and calling our medical insurance case worker once again. Curt was on the next flight to Chicago, arrived at nine thirty P.M., and took a cab directly from the airport to Northwestern Memorial Hospital and wound his way through the maze of this giant hospital to the psychiatric unit. I wanted to go, I wanted to be there. I was so incredibly frightened.

• • •

Curt and I didn't know what had happened from Monday night to Tuesday morning. While Curt was working his way from Sea-Tac to O'Hare, Charlie called me. He told me Linea had taken too much of her medication and she was so sick that he had called a cab and taken her straight to the emergency room. He said she had been moved from the ER to a bed on the psych unit. I paged her doctor and her psychologist in Chicago, hoping one of them would call me back promptly. Both called me back in minutes, and I told them what was happening.

I was so thankful that we had a team in place in Chicago who knew Linea. Her psychiatrist coordinated with the hospital, and her psychologist kept me informed while Curt flew to our daughter. Charlie told me she was too sick to talk to me but that as soon as she could talk he would let me know. The psychologist told me that her psychiatrist had talked with the hospital and that Linea had overdosed on the anti-anxiety medication. I finally called my sister and my parents and Jordan. I called Calla and I started to cry and couldn't stop. I cried in fear and desperation; she pulled me together. My sister said the right things: "Linea has good doctors. Linea has good care. Linea is incredibly tough. Linea will be okay." My parents offered to come to Seattle to stay with me, but I wasn't sure if I would be leaving for Chicago or what I would do next. I called Jordan last. I was ready and I didn't cry. I was the mom. Jordan worried and wanted to do something to help, and I convinced her that everything was going to be fine. I tried to believe it myself.

Linea's psychologist called me again and told me that Linea had taken the entire bottle of anti-anxiety medication. She was very, very sick and they were running tests on every one of Linea's systems. Charlie called me and said that it was "pretty hard" but she was doing okay. I could tell that Charlie was trying to protect me. The next time he called, he finally said, "Do you want to say hi to Linea?"

My heart was pounding. "Hi, baby. How are you doing? Your daddy is coming."

Her voice was groggy and her words were slurred. She was crying. "Mom, I didn't try to kill myself. You have to believe me. I was trying NOT to kill myself. I was doing everything I could NOT to kill myself. I want to live."

I hurt to my very core. Why was my daughter going through this pain again? Why did she have to almost kill herself to keep from killing herself? Why? Why? Why? Goddamn it. Please, God, just damn it all, damn it to hell and make her better.

I said reassuring words of some kind and mostly said I love you, I love you, I love you. She still had the phone but wasn't talking anymore when Charlie, a twenty-three-year-old boy-man, took the phone back and reassured me, "Cinda, she is going to be okay. She is sleeping."

I was incredibly low. I was alone in my house and I couldn't be brave anymore. I stumbled between rooms and ended up on Linea's bed. The photographs that she had left stared out at me from their frames, from the walls and the bookcases. She had been happy. She had a great and healthy life. She was posing in prom dresses and crazy hats and hugging cute high school boys and making silly hand signs with her girlfriends. She and Jordan were dressed up in crazy clothes with wigs and wild makeup. Where was my daughter? What happened? Where were the lives that we had planned out so carefully? I sobbed on her bed for who knows how long. I discovered that night what it means to keen. It was beyond crying. It was a sound that came out of somewhere deep inside of me and pulled me apart. I howled and wept and keened until I had nothing left. I got off the bed and shuffled around the house, waiting for Curt to call from Chicago.

Around ten o'clock Curt finally called me from the hospital. He tried to reassure me and told me she was "doing okay." Then his voice cracked when he told me about Charlie and Jamie. Charlie had been with her at the hospital since he and Linea had arrived by taxi from the music department. He stayed with her through all the paperwork, which she was unable to do, the myriad of tests, and the treatment for an overdose. Jamie came as soon as she got the message from Charlie. Both of them stayed with Linea while she cried and cried, told them to leave her alone and that she was sick of everything, and that she just wanted it all to end. At times Charlie was on one side of her bed and Jamie on the other while they held her and told her that she would be okay. They were both exhausted and drained when Curt arrived at the hospital. Linea cried again when she saw her dad and told him that it was not a suicide attempt but an attempt to save her own life, an attempt to hold the overwhelming pain at bay. I didn't know how to process this. There was a small part of me buried deep down somewhere that was crying out, *"I can't do this anymore.* This isn't fair." My mother told me once that she had been in such terrific pain in her life that she hadn't been able to go "day by day" or "hour by hour" but oftentimes only minute by minute. Perhaps that was where we were. I couldn't allow myself to think ahead at all or ask the questions that everyone else was asking: What was going to happen to her? Where would she be in five years? Would this ever get better? Would it get worse? *How could it?* What would happen to her if it did? I locked those thoughts deep away and didn't look at them again. Minute to minute, not thinking about the future.

While Curt was meeting with the doctors in Chicago and I waited in Seattle for updates, I remembered that I needed to call our insurance company again now that I had more information and get a "pre-authorization" for her hospitalization. I called Linea's case manager. Even though it was twenty-four hours later than I should have called, the caseworker put the paperwork in motion to cover the hospitalization and expressed concern about Linea. Once again I was grateful for the benefits that we had. "Grateful" was not a strong enough word. I thought about the people we met at the hospitals in Seattle and wondered how they were all doing. Was Joe back on the streets? Did Deb have a safe place to live? Did any of them have medical insurance?

Curt called me with more information after meeting with the doctors. They thought that the Prozac put her into a manic state. It had been coming on for the last month and she had desperately tried to fight it off. Her energy turned to anxiety and then to extreme agitation. I thought about the phone calls over the past few weeks and I realized that I had witnessed her losing her way. Linea is creative, and as a child she had rituals. Make a wish when the digital clock reads 11:11. Make a wish while holding your breath and keeping your feet off the floor of the car when going through tunnels. Rabbits were magical creatures to her. The last two conversations she and I had were full of rabbits and numerous symbols from operas and literature. Her creativity was on the edge of being obsessive and symbolic and was also transpiring at top speed. Had I missed something that could have kept her from becoming so sick again? Now that she had had a manic episode, her doctors seemed more certain that she had bipolar disorder.

By Friday, Linea was steady again. Most of the medication was out of her system and once again they were trying a new mixture of medications. She was exhausted and vulnerable and shaky, but she wanted out of the hospital. Curt took her home to her apartment and stayed with her over the weekend.

I was overwhelmed with a strange feeling that I could

hardly sort out or define. I was in tears because I was so proud of her—her strength and her spirit. I was in tears because I ached for her pain. All she wanted was to go to school, hang out with her friends, learn and play music; she kept getting back up and trying, again and again. I felt vulnerable and cold to my bones and tired and lonely.

I am sure it seems ludicrous to some why we supported Linea's wish to stay in Chicago. Why we didn't bring her right home, where we could watch her, take care of her, keep her close? Her overdose was one of many times we wondered if it was time to tell her we could no longer support her independence. So many times we longed to tell her she was coming home with us. But she continued to try so hard to hang on to the life she wanted. She worked so hard fighting this illness, keeping herself going. How could I take her independence from her when it was that very spirit that was her greatest ally in fighting this illness? The overdose was terrifying. But more terrifying was the thought of Linea giving up. I didn't know what to do. I wanted her safe. I wanted her to keep talking to me about her pain even if it terrified me. Don't stop talking to me. Help me keep her safe.

linea I'm fighting anger and tiredness and fear, but I have to get this all down before it escapes me. I have to get this out before my mind eats these thoughts, these feelings, this pain.

I almost killed myself, again. I took all of the pills. I took them all, and I could have lain down in my cluttered messy closet to die. But I went to find Charlie. I went to find him and save my life yet again. They say I am so strong because I find help, because I stop it before it is too late, but how am I strong when I did it in the first place?

I feel as if I have completed another milestone in my illness, whatever it is. I have finally overdosed on pills, finally had a suicide attempt. Or was it a suicide attempt? People say it was not my fault. That it can be completely blamed on the pills. These pills that alter my mind, my thoughts, my mood. Who am I anymore when I can't control myself because of the medicine that the doctors are giving me? How are they helping me when it was their pills that pushed me to this manic state of no control? Taking those pills, I lost my mind; I felt I was going to rip myself apart, the agitation was too much too bear.

Even when your doctors could be poisoning you from the inside out, you have to trust them to make the right choice, the right decision for your life. I know it isn't their fault, but how am I supposed to trust them when one pill makes me lack any personality and the other brings mood swings so large they long to kill? How am I supposed to cope, to live, to deal with these changes?

I took one pill and thought it would calm me down. I took another hoping to ease the aggression, the need to cut off my fingers or jump off the roof. I took the rest deciding I needed a reason to be locked up again. I took the rest knowing that I needed help and that this couldn't last anymore. I took the rest and went on with my daily routine. I took the rest and turned in my homework, went and talked to teachers, and waited patiently for Charlie.

What would Jamie have done if she had found me dead in the closet? What would my friends have thought, have said, if I never woke up again? I almost did it without even meaning to. I tried to kill the urge to hurt myself but instead created other ways of hurting myself. I can't do this anymore. I have to try harder. I have to find other ways to distract myself and save myself from these urges.

Today I decided not to drink anymore. No more booze, and definitely no more drugs. No more drugs. They will kill me. I will kill me. I have to be strong.

I can't do this to my family anymore. I can't do this to my friends. I can't do this to my soul. If I don't kill my body, I will kill my spirit. I have to be stronger this time. I have to take care of myself this time. I have to be willing to live for real. To live again for the third time.

cinda I wanted to be in Chicago so badly. Two weeks after Linea's overdose and hospitalization, I had a conference in Minneapolis. I went straight to Chicago after my presentation.

I took a commuter flight to Midway and rode the El from the airport to the South Loop. Linea met me in the café where Jamie worked. I walked in pulling my suitcase and spotted Linea studying at a table by the wall. Oh, my daughter. I held her and she laughed at me. "Are you crying?"

"Yes, I am." My daughter was alive.

Jamie came over for a hello and her own hug. I was so incredibly happy to be there. We had not been together for five minutes when Linea looked at me and said, "Mom, you need to know something. I used drugs. I was really, really messed up, and before I went into the hospital I was . . ." Then she was crying. I was frozen. I knew that she had used drugs prior to her hospitalization in Seattle, but I also knew how bad she felt about it, and she had promised us that since then she wasn't doing anything that would hurt her. I also knew how sick she had been and I knew that drug and alcohol abuse are very high for people with many types of mental illness, what with self-medication and . . . I knew, I knew . . . But, *what*? I was in a coffee shop, thirty minutes off the plane, and my newly reborn daughter tells me, "Mom, drugs."

Somehow I said the right things, or at least I think I did. "It is okay. We can deal with whatever we need to. We will help you. I love you."

The people at the nearby tables either ignored us or pretended they didn't hear what we were saying. Had Linea picked a public place to tell me this on purpose? "I had to tell you, Mom. I'm sorry."

Somehow we finished our coffees and went to her apartment. I felt so off balance. I couldn't think straight, but I knew that my initial feelings of joy and relief when I walked into the coffee shop were completely destroyed. What now? How could we trust her? We thought she was taking care of herself, that she was able to take care of herself, but she wasn't. Her words kept going around and around in my head. We had trusted her. She had said she DIDN'T USE DRUGS. But she did. She was hurting herself so badly. That night I lost all feelings of hope and was overwhelmed by defeat and despair. My stomach hurt and there was a hot and searing band of pain across my diaphragm. I cried and couldn't breathe. I was more frightened than I had ever been.

I think I was awake all night long. I was barely holding it together.

Sunday morning I took her out to breakfast. "Could we talk about this?" I asked her.

Linea nodded. As she spoke, I began to understand her pain at a deeper level than I ever had before. She told me about the wild moods she was having and how the medications her doctor prescribed didn't seem to help and that she was confused and afraid and wasn't sure who she even was anymore. She told me she wanted to live. She was embarrassed and frightened, and yet she was so strong. I began to understand that this illness she was dealing with was beyond anything I had ever envisioned. I began to understand that the bravest person I had ever known in my entire life was sitting in front of me. I began again to believe in her desire to live. It was one conversation, over breakfast, but it changed everything. It gave me hope, it wiped away the trauma of the night before; it gave me strength to start again.

Linea had an appointment with her psychologist (her first since her hospitalization) on Monday, and I went with her. When we got there, I asked her if I could meet Gretchen, whom I had talked to on the phone but had not met in person. "Sure," she said, and we went back to her office.

We talked for a minute and as I started to leave, Linea asked me to stay. They talked about her hospitalization and her new medication. Then Gretchen started to say something and stopped. Linea laughed and told her, "You can talk about anything you want. My mom knows everything."

Linea and Gretchen talked about what had happened prior to her hospitalization, and Gretchen pointed out that Linea had been able to recognize she needed help and to find help and get to the hospital even while she was so ill. Gretchen told her that drug and alcohol abuse are self-medications that many people with mental illnesses turn to for relief but that Linea must be vigilant about taking care of herself and learning to manage herself with exercise, nutrition, the prescribed medications, and close contact and partnership with her doctors. I wanted to force Linea to pledge to me that she wouldn't do anything again that could harm her, ever again.

But I didn't. I sat and I listened. Although I understood Linea's struggle with her illness and her attempts to stop the pain, I still had so many conflicting and unsettling feelings swirling around inside of me when we left Gretchen's office.

Two days later, when I got on a plane, leaving Linea in Chicago, I still couldn't stop thinking about our conversation and her "self-medication." An hour into the flight I started to cry. I didn't make a sound, but my tears poured down my face, as the passengers sitting next to me turned away and tried to pretend I wasn't crying.

I had always known how sick she was and how hard she had fought and how close we had come to losing her. But suddenly it had hit me that I could not fix her pain. I couldn't stop her thoughts or change what she did with those thoughts. I couldn't be with her every minute, and I couldn't get into her brain and chase this terrorizing illness away. I could be there for her and I could be with her when she needed me, but *I couldn't be in her.* This was her battle and we could only support her in that fight. We could bring her home from college, we could hospitalize her, and we could find the very best doctors in two cities more than two thousand miles apart, but I *could not keep her safe every minute of every day.* I felt panic and terror. I sat in my seat for the four-hour flight with these thoughts roaring in my head. I went around and around and finally my mind landed on my trust in her. Hadn't she proved herself a valiant fighter? Hadn't she asked for our help to hold her and be with her and stay close to her when she was near to losing the battle?

I had supported and nurtured Linea to be all that she dreamed of being with her music and her talents and her joy of performance. I wasn't a stage mom by any means, but I was proud. Her gifts on display for the world to see somehow seemed to reflect on Curt and me as parents. Besides her talents, she was so smart and kind and beautiful. As a high school student she didn't even drink, let alone use any drugs. I had two daughters who had it all, the whole package. Somewhere deep inside I thought, *I must have been a good mother.*

Linea self-medicated. She snorted Prozac. She used cocaine. She drank whiskey and used drugs. She almost jumped off the roof of her apartment building, she almost stepped in front of a train, and she overdosed to stop the pain. In the past year, I had told her over and over again, "Just *be*. That is all you ever need to do. I am so proud of you and I will love you always and forever. You need do nothing for me to be proud of you." I thought I believed this, but what if my parents found out that she had used drugs? What about the people I worked with, what about Pastor Jim, our friends and neighbors? Was this my pride or my fear of others thinking less of me and my family? Of my parenting? Somewhere deep inside of me I thought, *I must not have been good enough.*

By the time the plane landed, I had finally made sense of it. All I truly wanted was for Linea to find peace and happiness.

I wanted her sense of humor and her excitement and joy in living to surround her and us as well. I let go of my fear of her and of me and our family being judged by others and . . . I let go of my pride. I know that everyone who truly loved Linea would not judge her. I was even prouder of Linea than of all her gifts. I was humbled by her strength. I was proud of who she was, not what she did. I let go. I let go.

I still had to talk to Curt about what I had learned. We had accepted and moved on from the drug use in Seattle prior to her hospitalization at Harborview, but I worried that he would be very upset by the news of Linea's most recent drug use. In Chicago I had stayed calm when talking with Linea and had reassured her that we would work through everything and we could and would be stronger than before. I had told her how much I trusted her. After flying across the country, I had finally come to believe my own words. But I was not sure how to discuss it with Curt.

I went to work early the next morning and stayed to teach an evening class. When I got home around seven thirty, exhausted and hungry, Curt had my favorite "after-teaching" dinner ready, a baked potato and cottage cheese. We had been such a team throughout the last year of Linea's illness. We had stayed steady through a crisis that could be very hard on a marriage. We had not disagreed on treatment or support for Linea. We had taken turns doing what needed to be done, both physically and emotionally. We both kept our Scandinavian upper lips in place and hung on through the tough spots. I had even surprised both of us by not breaking down when I easily could have.

But something snapped in me that night. I told Curt that there were more issues around the Chicago hospitalization than we had previously known. I told him about Linea's drug use, and he said something about "the last time" and asked me a question that to this day I can't remember. Somehow I heard that I should have done something differently, that I could have done something better. It doesn't even make sense as I think about it now, but suddenly I was screaming, "I am doing everything I possibly can. I can't do any more. I can't, I can't, I can't." I was so nasty that instead of trying to help me, he was angry as well. We yelled at each other and then broke apart and didn't speak to each other for the rest of the evening.

Curt's and my painful pasts are part of our strong tie. Curt was with me when Steve died. He answered the phone when I got the call. He put the flight together to get us from Arizona to Washington State. He went with my dad to take care of Steve's Mustang, the car in which he died. And Curt knew about pain. His parents and other family members were killed in a horrific natural gas explosion in Iowa at what was to have been a family event. He was just a little older than Linea when he lost his mother and his father. He and I knew to value each day and each life. We also knew to be vigilant. I realized that I had left some of my fear on the plane, but there was still a place deep within me that hurt. I failed to keep Linea safe. It surged out of me when I heard, "What did you do to make it better? What did you do to keep her safe?" He never said those words, but that is what I heard. They were my own words. I failed to keep Linea safe. My stomach hurt like fire again, and I realized that I had to keep Linea safe not only for me but for Curt too.

I apologized for acting crazy. He held me and said, "We have to work together on this." I agreed. We needed all the strength we could get.

linea Charlie thought I needed a break from Chicago, so he invited me to tag along on a trip to New York with his best buddies from high school. We're in an apartment completely decorated with tropical things. They call it "the island" and it is located in the Lower East Side of Manhattan. There are thirteen boys and me.

I'm shy and afraid to make a fool of myself in front of attractive, rich NYU students. I normally wouldn't care about such labels, but for some reason they intimidate me. People keep disappearing into a room about four at a time. I know this routine. I ask Charlie what's in there because I know I want it. I want to feel more alive, to wake up, to feel like I can talk to these beautiful people. To feel beautiful myself.

Charlie won't tell me. He gets angry, but I know something's going on. I know the game. I'm not naïve. He finally says that they are only snorting caffeine pills. I laugh and say that they are ridiculous. Later they explain that it is better than blow because though they don't have the initial high, they never have a bad comedown. I don't buy it.

Charlie and I circle the subject for a lifetime, and I don't realize it but he is sitting very close and I appear to be flirting. It is unintentional and completely me not knowing how to interact with the boy that I lost my virginity to. The boy that I dated for a year. I don't know how else to talk to him. So he gives in to my "flirting," even though I don't know that I am. I seem to be working so hard to sway him into letting me do what I want.

We are sitting on the bed when he leans over to kiss me. He holds my head in his hands and I look him in the eye for a good five minutes, tears running down my face.

"I'm sorry, I can't do this. This wasn't what I wanted."

I'm crying quietly and can't tell him how sorry I am. I'm sorry. I don't know what happened. We talk forever about how he thought there was still something there. About how he thought I was hiding it. About how he thought I was convincing myself not to give in to him. He tells me to say it will never happen. He tells me to say that no matter what happens, however either of us feel, for the rest of our entire lives, we will never be together. He wants to hear that it will never happen. Ever.

I am silent.

I don't want to shut this down. I am still hanging on to the hope that I will get better, that I will love him again. I want to love him. I want everything to be like it was. He is perfect, and I don't know what happened. I want this to be better. I want to kiss him and say everything will be fine and mean it, but I can't, so I tell him. This will never happen again. We will never be together again.

I cry silently, facing the wall. He is silent. He takes big drinks of my whiskey. I go in the bathroom and search for a razor. I haven't cut myself since the hospital, but I need this. I can't find any sharp objects so I saw at my leg with my broken bracelet. No luck. No blood. No relief. I go back out.

Today is his birthday. I want to make this better, but there's nothing to do. We talk until we both are able to hold fake smiles and decide to face the party. By the time we get downstairs, it is so packed we can't even get into the room. That night Charlie got wasted. He made out with a strange girl. I flirted with strangers with no interest in a boring girl from Chicago. I didn't do any drugs.

November—Sometimes I get paralyzed. Lose consciousness while I'm still awake. Sometimes I just can't move. I stop breathing and just stare. Sometimes I have no thoughts and don't realize I'm sitting against the wall in my room on the floor just staring at the ceiling. Sometimes I just don't work. I feel broken and unable to function.

I have midterms this week and have practicing and reading and studying to do. Today someone asked me if I ever practice. Funny the impression you make on people when you're broken. I need to go back to the factory. I need to be recalled. I need to go back to the toy maker who made me so they can sew back on my arms or get rid of the tiny pieces that will choke small children. I am a hazard to all of those who play with me. I need to be restrung.

Loneliness. Silence that digs deep into your skin. Nothingness and urges all at once. Walking down the street you sense everyone. You walk against opposing traffic and feel alone. Music blaring in your headphones. There's a dead rat on the sidewalk, the blood creating a larger puddle every second. Lunch with a friend that only wants to fuck you. Am I lonely enough to give in? No. Is this loneliness affecting my vision? Is it affecting my ability to function as a normal, strong female?

The rat is decaying and there is no one to bury it. I watch couples as they pass. Think of the boys I could have had. Think of the boys I can never have. I try to initiate. Make phone calls, show up at the right moment. I send back messages, but they're either taken or uninterested.

A man in the elevator is making eyes at me, and when I would normally be disgusted, I smile. I eat up attention. I notice everyone that notices me. I long for attention when I'm not a needy girl. I am not a girl that strives to be the center of the room.

I go to a coffee shop and draw attention to myself. Hope someone will pick up my energy. I'm losing it. I'm searching for the newest haircut, the biggest change I can make to make this go away.

The good ones I push away. The impossible ones give me

what I want and then cut me off right before I get what I need. I'm rotting. I'm becoming the norm of society. There is a sad excuse for comfort in everything I do. I take what I can get and yet accept nothing.

I just want to be held. To be kept safe.

December—My horoscope reads:

> SAGITTARIUS (Nov. 22–Dec. 21): "Whether we are on the threshold of a Golden Age or on the brink of a global cataclysm that will extinguish our civilization is not only unknowable, but undecided," said Edward Cornish, President of the World Future Society. I bet that in the past year you've had comparable fantasies about the fate of your own personal destiny, Sagittarius. At times, it must have seemed as if you were teetering on the brink of a sulfurous abyss that was within shouting distance of the yellow brick road to paradise. Talk about conflicting emotions! But now that crazy-making chapter of your life story is coming to an end. No more teetering for you. No more inhaling noxious fumes from the infernal regions. I believe you have already been offered or will soon be offered an escort to the beginning of the yellow brick road. Let's hope you're not so addicted to the fascinating glamour of your pain that you turn down the escort.
>
> —ROB BRESZNY, FREE WILL ASTROLOGY

cinda We moved through the next few months without any major problems. I carefully sorted through all the medical bills and worried if we'd ever get caught up with the portion of doctors' bills not covered by our insurance. I think there were people who were wondering why we just didn't tell her she had to come home to Seattle. At what point would we have told her? Linea had struggled back from hospitalization and returned to school with a brain that was not yet recovered, first from electroconvulsive therapy and then from an overdose of the drugs that were supposed to make her better. She stayed on the president's list for her scholarship and she continued to work hard for her place in her music program. Linea was working as hard, if not harder, to stay in Chicago than we were in supporting her to be there. When would we have given up on her?

11. endurance

cinda The semester break arrived and Linea flew home with the usual maladies of a college student who had just finished finals. She was cranky at times, but like a typical college student, not like someone who was depressed or manic. In general, she was herself—fun and happy and silly and kind and loving. She and Jordan were in their characteristic funny moods over the holidays, channeling various personalities, singing, dancing, and teasing each other. It had been too long since I had witnessed them enjoying each other like this. We laughed and cooked and ate and played games and teased each other. It was a great holiday season, and too soon it was time for Linea to leave.

When she left, Curt and I were happy and at peace that she was so well.

We were thankful for Linea's life. Just be, Linea, just be.

linea I'm scared. Are things falling down again? Is my life beginning to take that spiral? I know I have no time to go out. I know that I have no time for anything but work. Piano. Piano.

Piano. I shouldn't be leaving this apartment, but somehow I can't stay. My life is completely in or out. Out flirting, drinking, smoking. Days of once again being high and drunk. Days of sleeping on couches and beds in other apartments. Days of not coming home at night. Then there is the reverse. The ins. Days inside this room on the green chair. Drinking wine and listening to eighties new wave while writing this instead of doing homework. Bauhaus, Joy Division, Siouxsie and the Banshees. Lots of talking to my fish, Axel, and my plants. Lots of wine bottles. I feel as if I should be babysat.

Jamie has a boyfriend and is never home because of work, and I feel as if my life is reverting back to the days on Broadway. I am drinking wine by myself and have honestly been drunk every night for the last ten days. And without people knowing. Drunk before I even arrive at the party. Drunk and happy. I have also started obsessing about boys again. Started wanting the warmth of arms around me.

I'm nervous it's all going to fall down again. As James Joyce wrote: "The snares of the world were its way of sin. He would fall. He had not fallen yet but he would fall silently, in an instant. Not to fall was too hard, too hard: and he felt the silent lapse of his soul, as it would be at some instant to come, falling, falling, but not yet fallen, still unfallen, but about to fall."

It's the day after Valentine's Day and I awake on a mattress on the floor shaking even though I am covered by two small blankets found in the middle of the night and my coat. A bong lies next to my head, a bottle of wine near my feet. It's eight in the morning and I have to force myself to go to work. I have woken up here before. I have woken up in the same apartment in a different bed exactly one week earlier. On that day I didn't care about being late to work. I had some strange man's arms around me, though still remaining clothed and innocent. Well, innocent if you don't count drugs and booze. Last time I didn't care if I missed the train or if it was snowing. But today I do.

Today I stand up and wonder if perhaps I have been drinking too much lately. I think about my room, littered with wine bottles of all shapes and sizes, very few shared, very many mine. I wonder if I have been smoking too much lately. My brain seems to have melted. I wonder if it's coming back. The drugs and the booze always seem to foreshadow the chaos.

So I get up. Same clothes on, I put my boots on and walk down the street in the dirty snow, my oversized sunglasses masking my raccoon eyes. I feel like a tabloid movie star the morning after, with my hair still in exactly the same shape and style as it was during my piano concert last night. My fur collar is high on my neck and my skirt short over black tights. This time it will be fine. I made it out. At home I have two glasses of wine and German chocolate cake for breakfast. I go to work by nine.

One month later—Woke up to a loud harmonica singing in my bag: "True love will find you in the end, you'll find out just who was your friend . . ." I feel as though something is in the air. It has been for about a week. It has been coming for a while. It is getting closer. Eleven has been hanging around more, and bunnies are popping out of the seams. It's everywhere.

I went to the art museum with my friend Josh, and we are watched by every guard. It was all laughs. All fun. He says he's never serious with me, he always has fun even when we get into deep discussions. Other friends say the same.

My friend Kat tells me I am the golden girl of the music department. She says at least ten men have asked about me and said I was beautiful. Neal says all of his friends are in love with me. Why are people telling me all of these things all of a sudden? I don't understand. Why don't I see it? If I'm so special, why can't I feel my self-worth? How do I see myself like they do? Why, if I am all these things, don't I get what I want? Who I want? If I am kind and fun and beautiful, then why do I always long for companionship?

I almost had a panic attack at the art museum. I met a painting and couldn't leave her. Josh and I stared for forever. It was like the monks. The monks who are still doing me in. The tantric Tibetan monks that performed last week and put me into a meditative trance so intense that I am still recovering. The silence that we shared and felt almost ate me alive.

I fell into that painting. I became her. I felt the room. I felt the red just coming but not coming now. Josh was standing there to catch me. He moved and I followed. We did tai chi in the hall, guards watching. I had to release my chi. My chest was clogged.

My chakra was enormous. I balled it up and passed it to him and he made it disappear.

It was a day of elevens. A day of rabbits. A day of recurring themes as most days have been in the last month. I have become wearier of my themes. More weary of my insides. Something's happening. It's going in circles. There is something coming.

It's Saint Paddy's Day weekend, and everyone in Chicago is drunk as all hell. Neal and I are preparing for the party. The party's going to be huge. Neal smoked a bong by himself before I got here and then proceeded to tape down everything in his kitchen. A pan duct-taped to the stove. Drawers taped shut. A spoon taped to the counter. Cabinets forever closed. If someone was to tip the entire apartment building upside down, nothing would budge.

I sit in the living room as John sets up the drum set. John and his band are the ones throwing this party, and there is a large open space intended for dancing, talking, and most likely inappropriate touching.

Neal reappears from the kitchen. Tape in one hand, a Mickey's 40 in the other. I'm trying not to drink tonight. I've been taking my pills again for the last couple weeks and they are finally working. I'm feeling better and terrified to fuck up. I'm trying to be careful these days.

"Tape meee! I'm not putting this beer down until I drink it all!" Neal screams.

"Babe, I think you should wait. I mean, people aren't even here and you're already high and drunk."

"I'm fine. Tape meee!"

"Fine, but I'm not carrying you back to my place after all of this."

"I'll be fine."

"Uh-huh . . . all right."

"Then you drink it."

"Thanks, but I'm fine."

"Take a hit."

"You're smoking again? I'm quite okay, thank you."

"All right"—holding his breath as he tries not to breathe the smoke out—"but don't complain when you're the only sober one!"

"Thanks, love, but I'll be all right."

As the hours pass, more and more people come. I'm completely aware of everyone and everything, given that I am the only sober person. I watch as people slowly become friendlier. As men slowly think I'm prettier. As women slowly befriend me. I watch the band play terribly and laugh as people bob their heads approvingly as the din enters their ears.

The hours pass and something's off. People need to leave. Something's weird. Too many. Too drunk. Too tense. I'm not the host, and I'm not the landlord, but I'm sober, and my best friend's apartment is getting trashed beyond compare. I manage to convince the roommates to clear the party out.

Chaos ensues. Noise complaints. Fistfights. Power outages. Spills. Puke. Sex. A hundred drunk and high twenty-somethings scrabbling to get out as cops flash their lights from the street. I'm sober.

I force Fighting Group A out. I help unconscious alcohol-poisoned drunk girl out. I show crazy hallucinating couple out the back passage. I calm the hyperventilating roommate. And I can do it all because I'm sober.

It is this night that I realize how much easier it is to battle chaos when you have control of your mind. Do I wish I had taken a shot, a hit, a line? In some brief flashes of panic, yes. But I didn't. For the first time in years, my medicine is working. Why fuck it up? I made it through tonight, didn't I? It was my sober state that allowed me to deal with the chaos of mania. The chaos of depression. Anxiety. In some cheesy, self-help-book kind of way I saw myself helping myself.

I remembered my mom giving me a speech when I was at a low point about "taking care of that little girl inside of you. When she cries, comfort her. Don't be mean to her. Just love her." I had practically spit at her intangible words before, but now, for the first time, they rang true. I could take care of this chaos. Perhaps I could take care of myself, sober. My moods are often incontrollable. Unpredictable. While it's easy to both cover up pain and to create joy with substance, it's hard enough to know how I will feel for more than a fleeting moment. You become numbed by the extremes. You become so used to living in a haze that you can no longer tell how you really feel outside of the party buzz around you. The worst part is that I always think I can make myself feel happy through drugs and booze. I think I can make my mind state alter to the exact assumed drug reaction, but then there is always the morning after, or evening after, or week after. The moment when you wonder: How long have I been feeling depressed? Have I been anxiously clenching my fists through this whole time without realizing it? I always think I know how I feel when I'm high. I think I'm happy, I'm dancing, I'm pretty, but then you look back the next day and remember the pain you were actually experiencing in those moments. You realize that drugs are merely a suppressant keeping down your true feelings until they can't be suppressed any longer and you become a drunken foggy mess. You come to after an epic night of fun sobbing in your room.

This night was one of the first I was able to truly see things the way they were, with perspective. I was able to cope. Was this because of my faith in prescriptions, or my fear of addictions? I have tried both prescribed help, like prescribed medication, and "self-help," better known as drug abuse. I had given up on the healthy choice many times, but that night, something within me prevailed. It reminded me that addiction was a longer, harder road than prescriptions, even if the prescriptions were at times unpredictable.

After the party, about twenty people remained. Neal and some of our friends escaped into the basement. It was bright and dirty with chipping tile and low wood ceilings. Sitting on washers and dryers, they passed around a mirror with white powder overflowing. When it was passed to me, I hesitated and with a sigh happily turned it down.

Keep pushing. Keep trusting.

cinda Second semester began and Linea was back in classes. Her music program was even more competitive, and even more practice hours were necessary to keep on top of the increased expectations. One night, not too long after the start of classes, she called and told me, "I feel afraid. I don't know why, but I just feel scared."

We were in a precarious place. Neither of us wanted to overreact, yet we also didn't want to wait too long to react. I knew she was frightened that "something is coming back." Suddenly it dawned on me that it was almost exactly a year since we brought her home from Chicago. I called her back.

"Linea, do you know what time of year it is? It was a year ago that we brought you home and you were so sick." I told her that often one's body remembers trauma or pain when the mind doesn't. I wondered if somehow her psyche was remembering. She was only now coming to terms with how close she came to killing herself. She decided to call her doctor on Sunday and made an appointment to see him Monday morning. She and her doctor decided that she was experiencing a bump of anxiety and that she would stay with the same prescribed amount of medications.

linea It has been an amazing week. For the first time in probably four years I feel as though I am finally happy. I am finally myself. I am me. The me I was under everything all along. The real me that Jamie hasn't even met yet. Today I received two compliments from two different friends. Both said that I had a glow about me. An energy and excitement. They said that they envied my excitement about life and the world and that people could see this in me. They said it was contagious. They said that they could tell I loved life and people. It is so amazing to me that one year ago I wanted to kill myself. I wanted to leave this earth. I hated life and I hated myself. I had no excitement or drive to go on.

Today I feel an exhilarating, overwhelming excitement about the future. I am ecstatic about the opportunities I have and the lives I could live. I have realized that there is more wisdom in the world than I could hope for, and yet I can still learn as much as I want by experiencing and living it. I have learned to live in the moment while still maintaining responsibility. I can now accomplish what I want without tying myself into knots. There is a way to accomplish my dreams without making a life of impossible goals.

One year ago I would have had to take Adderall or coke to feel this way. I would have had to be manic. But now I merely am happy. I am real and feel as though there is a point to the world. I feel as if I am meant to be here. I am meant to live and love and learn.

They were all right. The nurses, my family, the pastor—everyone who said I would get through it, everyone who said I would get out of it and learn from it. Everyone that I hated for telling me to hang in there. And yet I did hang in there, and I am here and more happy than I have been in years. I am myself again. The me who cries over the beauty of a sunset or a ballet. The me who is so passionate about saving the world. I am me again. I am not manic. I am not on street drugs. I am me. I sometimes question whether I am too happy and could this happiness be a symptom, but I am growing more sure that this is real.

I am extremely vigilant, and I know that I can survive anything. My next step is to find a way to inspire all of those who are struggling as I did. A way to help them know and understand that there is a way out. I have to find a way to educate without the self-help-book/cheesy-nurse feel. I have to find a way to really give people a message.

I want to tell the others who are suffering that they can be strong. I want to tell them that there are ways to get help, that there are people who care. I want to make sure that everyone does care, that everyone understands the disabling ability of this disease. I want to make sure that everyone knows the power your brain can have over you. I want peers not to judge and the sufferer not to give in. I want to tell people that if even I can find my way out of this, then they can too. I want to show people that even as sick as I was, I made it out. I want them to know that people do survive.

• • •

I am extremely scared that my optimism from two days ago was mistaken. I'm afraid that feeling of happiness was something else. I am so sick of the fact that I can't even be happy without it being something scary. The last two days I have stayed out till four in the morning. I'm barely holding myself together. I almost gave in to doing coke, but instead decided to come home. I came home angry and depressed wishing I could do it. I passed out depressed and scared.

Yesterday I went shopping and couldn't stop. I spent more money than I have ever spent in one day. I'm not even sure how much I spent. I'm feeling extremely anxious and guilty. I feel like there is something wrong and I don't want to tell my parents because just two days ago I was telling them how happy I was, how perfect and on track everything was.

I am doing really well in school and would like to think the last two days have just been some abnormal spending and nights out, but today I did something I have never done. In a rage, I threw my phone against the wall. It exploded into three separate pieces. Then I laughed and was fine and happy. I didn't care. I went and spent $100 on another phone and I'm fine.

I'm really anxious and terrified. I forgot my pills last night so I'm not sure if that is the reason I threw my phone. I'm tired, but my mind is racing. Something's up. Why can't things just be good for once? Just once in my fucking life? Why can't I just be happy and normal and good at piano and good in school? Why can't I just enjoy life and be normal?

I feel like my brain is going to explode. I feel like something bad is going to happen, but I can't stop it. It's a train wreck, but for some reason I want to see what happens. I want to see if the car will actually drive off the road or turn at the last minute. I should call my doctors right now. I should, but I would rather go out and drink and tell them tomorrow. I would rather wait this out. I have been drinking more. I have been taking my pills with wine again.

cinda Linea managed her moods until midterms, and then her phone calls became increasingly concerning as her irritation and anxiety built. She called on Thursday, Friday, and Saturday, each time telling me that she felt "crazy" and "couldn't stand it."

Just when I was almost ready to page her doctor, she calmed down and told me she was better. "I am just really stressed right now." Curt and I were both concerned and worried about where her moods were going.

Sunday she called and was talking so fast I could hardly understand her. She was seemingly happy and told me she was shopping with a friend. She hadn't spent any money on clothes for months and had found something cute that she really wanted. She told me all about it and was making jokes and laughing with her friend Rachel when she hung up.

I hated how I felt. I didn't want to interpret every up or down she had as part of bipolar. Nor did I want to ignore something before it turned on her and spun her out of control. I felt uneasy, but I knew that there was nothing I could do yet. This illness skews everything. Is she happy or is she manic? Is it "normal" anxiety, or the beginning of something much more sinister? Is she exhausted and battling a cold, or is this the onset of a mind-numbing depression? I tried my hardest to trust her but I was unable to let down my worry and my vigilance. She trusts my instincts and intuition. I asked her not long ago if she was doing okay, and she was frightened that I'd noticed something she hadn't. Do I stay quiet? How deep do I bury my fears? Learning to negotiate the first few years of this illness was like learning a dance, one in which I had no knowledge or skills. I could only stumble forward, one step at a time.

By Sunday night I was exhausted with worry. Curt and I were back to the old routine. "Do you think she is doing all right?" I asked.

"She's fine," he would say, only to ask me ten minutes later if I thought she was okay. We spent the rest of the evening reassuring each other while we both worried.

linea Today I began to get really anxious, wandering around the music building like a maniac. Staring at people like they were all insane themselves. I was irritable and high-strung. I couldn't talk without feeling extremely awkward.

I just needed a break. I needed to sit and eat lunch and relax, but instead I was late, with ten minutes to get to class with no food in my stomach. When I called my mom in a panic, it all exploded. I was hyperventilating. Sobbing on the sidewalk beneath the rusting scaffolding. Sobbing and breathless as construction workers and peers passed me by. The more I pictured me losing it on the sidewalks of Chicago, the more I panicked. There I was, on the pathway between the two most used buildings on our campus, barely holding myself up. The sidewalk used by every tourist going to the Hilton. The pathway used by everyone I knew.

I couldn't do it, I couldn't go to class. I went to my apartment and called Josh in a panic and asked him to come over. Thank God he was there within the hour. Thank God for friends. I don't know what would have happened. I don't know what I would have done. Where I would have ended up. We ate greasy pizza and colored his art project. It was grade school all over again and exactly what I needed.

Later that night I have a conversation with a friend. It triggers something, and I'm crying. My breathing becomes shallow. The tears won't stop. I don't remember the conversation, I don't remember what happened. My friend put me to bed. I must have passed out because this is all I remember.

cinda Monday morning I was back in my office and Linea called me, sobbing, and said she was sorry and she was sick and she didn't know what was wrong and she couldn't stand "this" anymore. She was crying so hard I could barely understand her.

"Mom, I'm sorry. I bought so many clothes I don't even know what I bought. I can't even take them back because I tried them all on, tore all the tags off, wore them, and most of them are on the floor of my closet. I'm so sorry. I don't even know what happened. And . . . I didn't drop my phone. I was so angry that I threw it as hard as I could and I broke it. I don't know what's wrong with me. I'm going crazy."

Neither of us could breathe. I closed the door to my office and slid down the wall in the farthest corner and sat on the floor. My voice stayed calm, but my heart was pounding and I was shaking inside.

"It's okay, honey. We can figure all this out. Can you see your doctor? Do you want your dad or me to come out? It is going to be okay." I forced myself to breathe.

She had just left her psychologist, who asked her psychiatrist to also see her. He adjusted her medication and told her to not be alone for a few days. Linea told me that I could call either of her doctors. Again I asked her if she wanted us to come to Chicago.

"I have to learn to take care of myself. I can't have you taking care of me when I am thirty. I have to do this myself," she cried. She said she had to go but agreed to call me back in thirty minutes.

I became more frightened after the next two calls. She was in the stairwell in the music building.

"I can't go to class, Mom. I can't even breathe. I am going crazy. I can't stand this," she sobbed.

"You don't need to go, honey. You can miss class for a couple of days until you feel better," I told her.

"No, no," she yelled at me. "I CAN'T miss my classes. I HAVE to go."

"Okay, why don't you go to your class and call me when it is over?" I asked her. I was trying to say the exact right things to calm her and to keep her safe.

"I can't go, I can't. I don't know what to do." She was crying very hard now. "I have to get my prescription filled."

"Linea, let me make some decisions for you. Do you have someone you can call? Why don't you have lunch with a friend? You can go to the pharmacy and then go have something to eat." I was so frightened for her as she unraveled more and more from one phone call to the next. One minute she was sobbing, the next she was yelling at me, and then she was crying again and apologizing.

She finally calmed down a little.

"I can call Josh," she told me. "Maybe he can have lunch with me. I will go to Walgreens and get my pills."

I told her to call me back as soon as she knew that Josh

could meet her. I was so thankful for her friends in Chicago who would not turn away from her.

I tried to stay calm and counsel and monitor her from across the country. Curt and I talked on the phone throughout the afternoon. Linea didn't want us to come to Chicago, but we were concerned that she was very sick. She was adamant that we couldn't always fly across the country to take care of her. I knew that as soon as she felt better we had to talk about how and when we needed to intervene when she became ill. We needed to have a plan in place that we all agreed upon so that we could help her when we thought she was too sick to make those decisions herself. But right now we had to make these decisions without a road map.

I asked her to call me every thirty minutes, and together we made plans for what she would do the next half hour. She said she was going to bed, and Curt and I worried through the night and called her first thing in the morning. She didn't answer and I tried as hard as I could not to panic. When she finally called back, she told me that she hadn't slept most of the night.

Her calls were frightening and yet reassuring because I knew that she was on the other end of the phone. For those few minutes at least, I knew where she was and also that she was falling apart.

"Mom," Linea sobbed, "I am standing on the sidewalk on Michigan Avenue crying and everyone is staring at me like

I am crazy. I *am* crazy. I can't stand this. I can't move. Everyone is staring at me. I hate this." She was almost yelling at me.

I was so frightened and not sure what to say, but I kept my voice very calm and used my I-am-your-mother-and-I-know-best voice.

"Linea, listen to me. Where is the nearest coffee shop? I want you to walk to it right now and breathe slowly while you are walking.

"Linea, are you there? Yes? Okay, go in and order something to drink. Then sit down and call a friend to meet you. Try two friends and then call me back."

She whispered, "Okay, Mom."

She called me back. "Rachel is going to have lunch with me. I'm sorry, Mom. I need to go to class but I can't. I am afraid I will just flip out in there."

We spent two more days calling back and forth while her friends spent time with her, "babysitting," as she called it. She saw her doctor again and we continuously asked her if one of us could come to Chicago. On Thursday, she was so exhausted that she couldn't fight any longer. She told me, "Maybe one of you could come."

Should we have gone earlier? For at least five days she had been highly agitated and swinging between extreme lows and high anxiety. Now I know that this was the dreaded "rapid cycling" between mania and depression that I had read about. We didn't call it that while she was battling these terrors because it seemed too horrifying to say it aloud. We simply walked—struggled—through it, one step at a time.

Once Curt had been given the green light, he pulled things together in a hurry and I took him to the airport. He got onto a flight standby and would be in Chicago by late afternoon. I called Linea to let her know when he would arrive, and she insisted on meeting him at the airport. I told her what airline and flight he was on, but she either forgot or wrote it down incorrectly, or most likely her brain simply couldn't hold any more thoughts, information, or details. Shortly after his arrival in Chicago, my phone rang. She was extremely upset and crying, "Where is he? He isn't here! Where am I supposed to go?" She was mad and scared and crying all at the same time. I asked her where she was and she told me she was in the baggage claim for the Air Alaska flights. I told her he flew United. Now she was really upset. "Why? Why didn't you tell me? That is in a whole different area from here. I will never get there in time. He will leave. I won't be able to find him, Mom!"

After numerous phone calls, he found her.

"She looks awful," he said. "I don't think she has had a shower all week and she is really a mess. She isn't doing very well." And then he added our talisman, "It will be okay." I was not sure I believed him this time.

I didn't hear from him again until Saturday morning. Linea was finally asleep when he called to update me. He was very worried that she would need to be hospitalized again. Her mood swings were terrifying, she was completely exhausted, and yet she was so agitated that she couldn't sleep.

He called me again later that day for comfort and support. They had gone to a movie to take up some time, but Linea had slept through it. After returning to the apartment, she started crying, which turned to raging. This intense anger was something we had not seen in Linea since brief episodes right before her first hospitalization. Nothing seemed to calm her. Curt convinced her to lie down on her bed. He talked to her and rubbed her back until she finally cried herself to sleep. He was exhausted and unsure of what more to do for her. I had talked to her doctor earlier in the day, and he said Linea was to keep taking her medication as prescribed, was not be left alone, and if there was any question about her safety, we should take her directly to the hospital. She had an appointment to see him first thing on Monday morning. Curt and I ended our conversation with the decision that he would take her to the hospital the next morning if she wasn't any better.

The phone rang Sunday morning at nine, eleven A.M. Chicago time. My heart was pounding as I answered.

"Good morning! Someone wants to talk to you," Curt said as he passed the phone to Linea.

"Hi, Mom! I'm better," Linea told me. "We are going for a walk in Millennium Park in a little bit. The sun is shining and we want to get outside and get some fresh air!"

Curt got back on the phone and told me that Linea got up, took a shower, and came out "looking like a million dollars." She was very tired, but her mind was calm and she wanted to take a walk and then get started on her homework. She had missed almost a week of school and wanted to be ready to return the next day. Was this a short reprieve from her illness, or something more lasting? Curt couldn't believe how well she looked and acted after the previous night's breakdown.

Linea saw her doctor Monday morning and she went to classes Monday afternoon and evening. She was up early on Tuesday, working on homework, and reassured Curt that she was stable once again and he could go home and "not worry about her."

It had been just over a week when I had the first phone call that kicked my worry into gear. It was just seven days ago that she was calling me from the stairwell in the music building telling me she was "going crazy." I was sure that this episode had been building up over a much longer period, but it still seemed to have hit her so fast. This episode was not Prozac-induced mania but happened while she was taking supposedly the right medications. I wasn't sure if she was taking the doses she was supposed to or taking her meds consistently. This episode seemed to have been precipitated by the stress of midterms. ("Episode" seems much too mild a term for what she experienced.)

She was becoming more aware and able to manage her

moods, but there seemed to be certain times of the year, particularly within the semester schedule of midterms and finals, that were more difficult for her. This time it seemed that her symptoms broke through, but once the adjustment of her medication had time to work she was stable again. My sister told me that Linea would learn to listen to her body like some people listen to their cars. She would know when it was a little off and needed a minor adjustment. Linea made it through, but it was very frightening for us on the other end of the phone, for Curt as he witnessed her agony firsthand and, most of all, for Linea as she fought her way through another crisis, trauma, heartbreak . . . these words seem more appropriate than "episode."

Linea kept fighting. She went to school, she worked in the music building, she kept up with friends, just like any college student. But the other part of her life was riding the bus from the South Loop to the Miracle Mile once a week to see her doctors and to manage her illness. She was just twenty-one years old—was this something that would be with her for the rest of her life? Secretly Curt and I hoped it was a misdiagnosis. Perhaps she would grow out of it? But slowly we were coming to terms with the diagnosis, just as Linea was. Bipolar was not going to go away, it was something we were all going to have to learn to live with and manage. This latest was a frightening attack for all of us and left us feeling anxious and unsure about Linea's future. But it also gave us more confidence in Linea's ability to know when she needs to see her doctors and when she needs to ask her family and friends for help.

The whole family had made plans to go to Mazatlán for spring break. Curt and I weren't sure if Linea would be well enough to go after her week from hell. But Linea was still feeling good and excited about meeting us in Mexico. So we decided to use the already purchased airline tickets to take our first vacation with both girls since Jordan married Cliff. We had looked forward to the trip for so long, and up until three days before we left we weren't sure if it would really happen. Even the day we were to leave, I couldn't quite believe that Linea was well enough to go, but she assured us that she was. So away we all went to Mexico.

We arrived at the airport in Mazatlán two hours after Linea's flight from Chicago. She was waiting for us, beautiful, smiling, and happy, even though her baggage hadn't arrived with her. No one seemed to have any idea where her luggage was or when or if it would arrive. We filled out all the necessary paperwork and left the airport in a shuttle to meet Jordan and Cliff at the condominium we were renting. For two days, Linea wore Jordan's and my clothes and was very excited when her suitcase showed up late in the afternoon of the third day. She handled all of this with good humor, and I felt as if things were going to be okay. I started to relax.

Linea was ecstatic to be away from school for a week. She

loved the plaza in the old part of the city and the book fair and the walks we took through the narrow residential streets in the city center. We laughed and ate and walked and swam and played and laughed some more. Curt and I were enchanted to be spending a week with our adult children. At least once a day we said to each other, "Isn't this great? Can you believe that we are actually here and everyone is healthy?" I cried watching a sunset just because it was such a simple thing and my heart was not fearful. Linea was with us and she was safe.

We were all having a wonderful time, but even though I wasn't feeling the heart-wrenching fear, I still found myself being overly sensitive to Linea's every mood. She seemed a little fragile, but I wasn't sure if it was me or her. I didn't want to worry about her all the time; when I was with her when she was happy I felt like I could finally breathe. I tried not to worry about the next thing that might go wrong. Our week was a good one, and we ended it with gratitude for this time and place spent with a healthy family. Linea returned to the last half of her semester. I prayed that Linea could finish her school year healthy and happy.

12. clarity

cinda For the month after we returned from Mexico, Linea seemed centered and happy, but she also told me that she was feeling very stressed about her music program. As the end of the semester loomed closer, Linea had more pieces to memorize and perform for increasingly critical jurors. Although she had an accommodation plan from the college, she didn't feel she could justify more than a little extra time on a paper even if she had missed a week of school due to illness. She had kept her grades above a 3.5 average with an immense amount of hard work and persistence.

Her classes in her music major were the most difficult. Performing fifteen pages of Mozart from memory demanded hours and hours of practice, the utmost concentration, and steely confidence. Linea called me one afternoon and she was crying. "If I stay in the music department I will end up in the hospital again," she told me. My heart froze and I didn't say what I wanted to: QUIT, come home, and let me keep you safe forever. Instead, I listened. I asked questions. I couldn't tell her what to do even as much as I wanted to.

Linea had known that she wanted music performance as

her life's work since she was five years old. Now she was considering changing her life, and she was frightened. We talked and talked on the phone and then she said, "Mom, I wish you could come out here and see me. I need some Momma advice." The invitation I needed.

I was so excited! I was going to visit Linea for Mother's Day. I was very happy for this opportunity. She was almost finished with her school year, and she was ready to make decisions about her future. It was a definite sign of health that she was in a place where she could make decisions. Not decisions that would please someone else, or decisions about things that were out of her control, but real decisions about her future for herself.

This time I flew to Chicago full of optimism. I was not frightened. I was so excited to spend three days with her!

The weather was wonderful and Linea looked great. She seemed more grown-up, confident, and steady. Steady as she talked about her future even though she was unsure what she wanted to do and where she wanted to go.

Then, suddenly, she said, "It seems that just when I am finally doing okay, something else happens to me." I held my breath for what was to come next.

I was not sure what she meant, but I was slowly beginning to realize that there were going to be these . . . what to call them? Symptoms, episodes, ups and downs? I finally realized that bipolar was a manageable disorder but that it was a chronic illness—sometimes mild and sometimes severe. Tentatively, I had begun to accept the ebbs and flows and crashing waves of this illness. In my mind, I was beginning to add the word "chronic" to a diagnosis that was attached to my beautiful daughter. We had weathered attacks severe enough that she couldn't be left alone, but a few weeks later she was settled again and our life had, at least on the surface, a semblance of what it had been prior to "bipolar" entering all of our lives. We had become familiar with this condition, and it didn't scare me as badly as it once did, but I was still anxious and on guard to its presence. We were slowly, slowly making peace with the new reality that bipolar is a lifelong illness that must be respected and managed, yet also accepted.

That Mother's Day weekend, Linea told me she had symptoms of a serious eating disorder. She said that she couldn't stand to have liquids in her mouth and that she felt like she wanted to spit anything remotely wet out of her mouth. She had been vomiting after meals and restricting her intake. As these symptoms became worse, she worried that she had bulimia, and—and this, for me, was the important part—she had called her doctors. Her psychiatrist wanted to see her right away, and he assured her it was likely a flare-up of anxiety that was causing her eating problems. Anxiety is very much a part of what Linea struggled with and continued to manage, and it seemed to precede the episodes of mania. Her doctor had adjusted her medication, and she had spent several miserable weeks working through the anxiety until she was able to stay steady once again.

I was not ready to hear this latest difficult news. I had no idea she was going through all of this. What next? When would she have some peace? Yes, I was close to acceptance of a lifelong illness but not prepared for new symptoms. But we had the foundation in place to move forward.

We sat and we talked, and the more we talked about all she had been through in the recent weeks, I somehow felt better. I was encouraged by her strength and her ability to manage her health while finishing the semester and taking her finals. She clearly had a great relationship with her doctors, and she was in tune with her body. She knew when she needed help to take care of herself. Even though I was frightened when she told me about her eating disorder, I was once again in awe of her honesty and thankful that we could talk freely about everything .

The next day was Mother's Day. Linea and I walked up Michigan Avenue, wandering up and down the side streets until we found the perfect restaurant. It was sunny and warm, and we sat outside on the sidewalk and ordered a beautiful brunch. As we sat together, I was close to tears. (I never cried in public as much as I have these last few years.) Just one year ago we were all in her hospital room at the University Medical Center waiting to hear when she would be moved to Harborview for electroconvulsive therapy. We were in the psychiatric unit with a full-time guard watching her so that she wouldn't try to kill herself. Just a year ago, she had told us to leave. She told me she would never be well and there was nothing we could ever, ever do to fix her. My heart had broken. One year later, Linea and I were sitting in the sun in Chicago as she told me about her new boyfriend and her life and her decision to step out of the music program.

We talked about her future. I could not find words strong enough to express my feelings. I was deeply thankful. Thankful that she was able to make decisions to have a strong relationship with a wonderful young man who loved her just exactly the way she was and saw her beauty not only on the surface but also in her soul. Thankful that she was able to make decisions to change her course in her music program, knowing what she needed to do to stay healthy. Thankful that she was able to make decisions about her life, knowing that there are few irrevocable decisions, and we can always make a better decision next time; thankful that she was not stuck on a "perfect" decision. Most of all, I was thankful she was alive.

She told me again that she thought a competitive music program would only push her toward another crisis. She talked about changing majors and transferring colleges. I knew how hard this was for her to even think about. Linea had never veered from her goal of excelling in the world of music. For her to let go of all the years of work and commitment had to be so difficult for her.

After a wonderful weekend, I headed home to Seattle. On the long ride, I thought about everything we had talked about. I didn't allow myself to make any plans for her future. She would have to make these decisions herself.

There are many people, perhaps even friends and family, who wonder how and why we "allowed" Linea to go back to Chicago after her first hospitalization and why we didn't bring her home after her second hospitalization. Linea never expected us to support her at the level we did, and I know she often felt guilty. But as hard as we worked to support her, she worked harder—to stay in her program, to manage her health, to communicate honestly with her family. It is a testament to her strength and her stubbornness that she kept going to classes, studying, reading, writing, practicing, and working to keep up with her schoolwork. Each time she was knocked down, she got back up and back to class. She struggled with her return to Chicago after the ECT. With an unreliable memory, she continued to memorize pages and pages of classical music. She managed a schedule of doctor's visits, therapy visits, medication, and drugstore runs. She kept talking to her family, with phone calls, email, and honest communication throughout. There was never a time when she wasn't working just as hard as we were to improve her health and secure her future. We were partners in this last terrible year, and we could never have taken away her desire to return to Chicago just because of our desire to keep her close. Not when she was working so hard, so well, so fiercely. Curt and I wanted the same thing—for Linea to have her life. But in the end, it was only Linea who could grasp her life. We could support her always, and get out of the way as she moved to independence, yet still be there when she asked us to.

After my Mother's Day visit, Linea worked and took classes through the hot Chicago summer and moved into an apartment with her boyfriend. There was no outcry from Curt. We wanted her safe and well, and Linea was making decisions to stay safe and well. Things were good in Chicago, and in Seattle, Jordan and Cliff gave us the exciting news that they were expecting our first grandchild in February! I couldn't believe the feelings of joy that emerged from knowing my first daughter would soon have her own child. Momma love—now Jordan would truly understand how much I loved her. Once again I was reminded that life goes on and we are offered pockets of joy, sometimes large and sometimes very small. I don't want to miss any of them!

Linea started her fall quarter still undecided about where to go and what to do next. I began mine as well. I think it is because I have been in education my entire life that fall holds such promise and excitement for the new year. Even though it is a new *academic* year, not calendar year, it still always feels like the beginning for me. I was so hopeful that this "year" would be better for all of us.

In late September, I was in Orlando, at the Disney World site, presenting a paper at a conference. At conferences, I am typically in my hotel room in the evenings, catching up on work, but this particular evening I went out into the world of

Disney. The weather was beautiful, warm, and much different from the cold rain falling in Seattle. I went on the safari ride, and just as I left the Kilimanjaro ride, my phone rang. It was Linea with news that she had finally whittled down her transfer choices to the University of San Diego and Seattle University. I held my breath. And the winner is . . . Seattle University! I was completely ecstatic and wanted to scream the news to the world. But instead, I held myself back and said, evenly, "Are you sure? This seems like a good idea, but take your time and think about it." I hung up the phone and almost fell to my knees, I was so happy and thankful. I called Curt and said, "Guess WHAT?" Linea's decision was such good news for us in so many ways, especially in that it was *her* decision, not one forced upon her by her illness.

It is hard to parent from the middle, but the middle is the only place you can parent an adult child. Adult child—what a contradiction for both the adult child and the parent. Let go. Help. Give advice. Don't. We struggle to figure out the dance in a way that will leave us both intact. Me, confident that she will be okay. Assured that she won't fall off the edge of whatever dangerous thing is lurking. Taking every precaution not to lose her again. Letting go, trusting, stepping away. Her, confident that she will be okay. Not wanting to fall off the edge again. Needing so much to trust herself. Needing her family to trust her to do so. We are getting there, but it is hard.

At the end of fall quarter and in the middle of a Chicago

snowstorm, Linea moved back to Seattle, and she brought her boyfriend with her. They packed their things and shipped them across the country: Linea's books and instruments and music and life along with Josh's books and instruments and music and life. They moved into her bedroom in our house until they could find an apartment, and her dad said not a word against the cohabitation. He was welcoming and gracious and hopeful. Josh is kind and caring, and he and Linea were so very happy together. We celebrated the holidays together while they looked for an apartment. They found one and moved in on New Year's Day. I am cautiously optimistic. I breathe easier. I sleep better at night.

linea We are sitting in a bar in Seattle, Jean and I. Sitting, just the two of us, for the first time since I moved back. We are sitting with our false facades of happiness and okayness. Sitting secretly with our suffocating fears of remembrance, pain, and guilt. We are trying to remember forgiveness. We are trying to find the past, the time before my fall when we were still okay, still really happy. We sit here silently, scared smiles on our faces, fearing the inevitable talk of this book. What it means to us, what it means for us, for our future. I am terrified—the anger, the sadness, the loneliness, and the betrayal that I felt when she left me alone at my worst are still suffocating me.

When finally I speak, I timidly tell her that we have to talk about the book. I explain that I was angry and that passages in the book are unflattering and were written through my hurt perceptions at the time, making the story line skewed. I tell her that there is no reflecting on what she might have thought but merely angry words and hurt feelings. I tell her that I need to know that she is okay with me publishing these passages. I remind her that we were both scared and confused, two kids who didn't know anything about mental illness or how to live with and around it. I tell her that I was devastated when she disappeared with her boyfriend, leaving me with my pain when I thought she was the only person I could count on.

When I'm done speaking, I sit in terror, still not knowing how to talk to her anymore. Slowly she takes a breath and speaks. She tells me that she was terrified. That she didn't understand how bad it was. She tells me how scared she was for me. That she tried so hard to be there for me, but that I was difficult, angry, and vacant. In the end she didn't know what else to do. She then tells me that she was most terrified of my mom. Having grown up as part of our family, she thinks of my mom as her second mom, and she was terrified of the anger that my mom might have at her for abandoning me.

I continue to tell her that when she disappeared, I didn't understand and that I began to take the fear out on her and her boyfriend. That I didn't think about her feelings or the fact that she had never experienced this before. I tell her that I didn't realize then that we were so young and unprepared. I was so angry.

I can't even begin to explain to her how sorry I was for my anger. For my misunderstanding and frustration with her and

Eric. It wasn't their fault. My depression skewed my logic. Our inexperience affected our actions in every way. It was not ourselves who blocked each other out but our fear and lack of education and experience.

Every time she takes a breath to speak, I panic, but I know this is for the best. I tell her that I love her with all my heart. That she is my sister and always will be. I know that she didn't mean to do the things she did. I know that now. I know that she and Eric did all they could at the time. We were so young.

And now we sit. We feel that great rift between us begin to close, and our fears and anger begin to heal.

We sit, and an hour is merely a few minutes. Jean breaks the silence. "Mi, I want you to tell the story. I want you to use it all. People have to understand how relationships are affected. How kids react when they don't know what is happening. I want you to tell our story. It is important. It will help so many. I love you."

And I sit and cry. And Jean sits and cries. And I think about how years afterward I still carried the pain and anger, of being sick and alone, of being misunderstood. The years when I returned to Chicago and had short, awkward, fearful conversations with Jean over the phone and wondered if we would ever survive. If it was worth it. I sat and cried for ever doubting her. For ever doubting us.

True friendships last. They take work and forgiveness and more talking than some people can give. But in the end, friends care. It's just that sometimes they don't know how to deal with it.

In the narrative of mental illness, the friend's story is more important than we can ever know. It is the story we often don't understand. It's the story we fail to reflect upon because pain and anger build walls between those who suffer and those who love us.

She is my best friend now. She is my sister. And whether I like it or not, we will never part. Even if our relationship changes, in the end we will continue to be connected. These experiences of pain solidify relationships, if you can hold on long enough.

It is possible to love again.

cinda In late February, my phone rang at six in the morning. Jordan and Cliff were on their way to the hospital less than two miles from our home. She told me I didn't have to come right away and that it was likely a false alarm. I canceled my meetings anyway, called Curt, who had just left for work, and Linea, and I headed to the hospital. This would be the first time I had been in a hospital since Linea was sick. I was terrified. I forced myself to imagine the best, not the worst-case scenario. My heart was pounding, and I had a major case of anxiety for my daughter and soon-to-be grandchild.

I was in the waiting room for only about thirty minutes when Cliff called me from his cell phone. He was less than thirty feet away, but he wouldn't leave Jordan's side to tell me, "We're having a baby!" Curt and Linea arrived ten minutes later, expecting to spend the day waiting for this first grandchild to arrive. In less time than I ever could have imagined, Cliff came out to the waiting room and asked if we want to meet "his son."

Jordan was holding her son. All the emotions I had felt with the birth of my own two daughters came flowing back to me, but this time without the exhaustion. My daughter is a mother! A new life in our family!

Feelings surrounding the birth of this incredibly beautiful baby were overwhelming. It was a miracle and utmost joy and a huge burst of indescribable love all in one amazing package. Baby boy Thomas, I love you so and so look forward to knowing you! What wonderful parents you have! What a wonderful family to hold you and love you and keep you in our hearts forever!

Jordan, the one who doesn't like to show her emotions, who doesn't like to cry, couldn't stop crying as she held baby Thomas close. We were all in the throes of happiness and overwhelming and achingly sweet wonder. Linea was crying and laughing and amazed at the tiny bundle that was her nephew. Slowly, slowly we settled down. Curt and Cliff talked and laughed. Linea and I left to find food to bring back. We made our way through the sprawling hospital, and as we crossed through the largest of the waiting areas, Linea stopped and began to cry. Her cries turned to sobs, and she was in my arms, crying and gasping for air. I thought of the airport the day we brought her home from Chicago, when she sobbed her tears into my skin where they have remained for these last years. Once again people were walking cautiously by us, wondering about our tragedy, not wanting to stare but unable to look away. She struggled to say, "I almost wasn't here. I almost missed this."

linea I'm standing in the hospital in Bellevue sobbing uncontrollably. People passing by don't even look. I scare them with my tears. My mom is standing beside me. I can't stop. I don't want anyone to see me.

When we got the call, there was so much excitement. My sister was having a baby! When we finally got there, we were starving but didn't dare leave until we met him. Soon Cliff was calling. It was time. He was born. We were invited to see him and hear him and hold him. I had a nephew!

When I saw him, I couldn't help but cry. He was the most beautiful baby I had ever seen. He was the youngest baby I had ever seen. His toes, his eyes, his hair were perfect. Everything was perfect. When I finally got to hold him, it was like everything in the world was right. It was as if the world was okay again.

Holding him, I remembered when Jordan's best friend, Carman, came with her new baby boy to visit when I was in the hospital for the first time. Holding Carman's sweet Ashton made me okay. Even when I was suicidal and in so much pain. For that second, everything was right. That was when I first realized the power that a child had. That a new life had. Everything starts anew with a life.

Thomas is pure beauty and joy. He makes life right. He makes everything better, even though I am happy and my life is right.

And Jordan was so beautiful. Tired and exhausted, but so strong and powerful. She was glowing. Cliff was wonderful too. I could feel his pride and love and excitement flowing throughout the room. This family was so happy, so bonded, and this baby boy brought our tight family closer.

After a while we remembered our hunger. We walked to the lunchroom beaming, giddy. And then, as we walked down the hall, it hit me. Steve hit me. I almost didn't make it. I almost missed the birth of this child. I almost missed seeing my family's pride and elation. I almost killed myself.

Now I am sobbing. I can't stop crying because the more I try to stop (I don't want Jordan to see me), the more I think about Thomas and the more I think about Steve. I think about how I never got to meet Steve. How I never had an uncle, just a ghost. I wonder if Thomas would have been as affected by my death as I was by Steve's. I think about my family. I think about the pain I put them through. But now we are all right. Everything is right. I am here and I got to hold this sweet child in my arms.

And I know now that I will make it. I will make it because I want to be here for him. I will make it because he is hope and love. He is everything that is right in the world. I will make it for Jordan because she is the best friend I could ever have. And the most beautiful woman I have ever met. I will make it for the strong yet gentle men in my life. The hilarious men that sneak Coronas into the hospital room after the birth of the first son and grandchild. I will make it because I have the strongest and most loving mom in the world. Because though she feels all my pain twofold, she courageously brings me forward.

epilogue

cinda I didn't know how this story would end, and it seemed that there were times we both thought, "Good, it is now finished. Stability at last." And yet, that was not the case. As I read through it for the hundredth time, I realized that we are all richer for our experiences. I still feel an overwhelming sense of fear and sadness when I reread portions of this memoir. I have realized that we all have some posttraumatic stress hovering around us from almost losing our daughter. Most of the time I can let loose the anxiety that accompanies worrying about the future, but sometimes I cannot. I do know that I could never have predicted where the telling of our story would take us.

When we first spoke with our wonderful agent, Stacey Glick at Dystel & Goderich Literary Management, she asked us why we wanted to share this intimate journey with the public. During those years, as we struggled to find the right treatment, care, understanding, and support, we became very aware of the stigma attached to mental illness and the fear people have of the mentally ill. In conversations with patients, family, and friends, the outpouring of cries for assistance and for understanding and support compelled us to step out and share our own experiences. Stacey told us to do whatever we wanted to accomplish, whether the book was ever published. What wise advice. As we spoke at more and more conferences and to larger and larger audiences, the response was the same. There were so many people and families who struggled with the challenges of mental illness but were afraid or unable to seek help or find their own voice. Linea found her own voice, and I was privileged to watch it happen. She found power in her voice, and she wanted to share that power.

I am still learning every single day how to live with an illness that causes a person's mind to unravel and sometimes makes it impossible for that person to care for herself. My heart aches as mothers from across the country reach out to me with their own stories full of pain and worry about children struggling with a severe mental illness. I hear from people who have been wounded by the pain of growing up with a parent with a mental illness, feeling alone and not having anyone to talk to about what was going on in their home. I teach my classes differently now than I did when I experienced children and young people with mental-health conditions only during the school hours. I know what it feels like to be unable to let go of the worry throughout long weeks and months and sleepless nights when your child, your heart, is sick.

Linea once told an audience that she wouldn't change anything that she has been through. I didn't agree at the time, and

I am not sure I agree completely now. I never want my daughters or grandchildren to go through this amount of pain. My internal prayer has always been, I will always remember those terrible days, but I also know that I am a stronger and braver and perhaps a better person for having experienced them. And I know so much more now about depression and bipolar disorder. These lifelong illnesses go into remissions and have flare-ups, just as do many physical illnesses. It can be overwhelming to think about that prognosis in the same sentence as "my daughter." But, like chronic diseases, Linea's partnering with her doctors to treat her bipolar disorder through management of medications, counseling, and therapy will lessen the likelihood of flare-ups and if any do occur, they will be less often and less severe. She is learning how to manage this, and I am learning how to support her.

In this journey I am reminded to relish each moment of peace and joy and believe that more such moments are coming. Life goes on with all of its unpredictable pain, and also with joyous surprises. My work is to let go of the fear and agony of the past few years and to trust in the future. I don't know what is next, but I do know that Linea is living her own life—slowly, one step at a time, sometimes taking a step backward but, always, steadily moving forward. She has proved how much she wants to be well, how much she wants to live.

Her commitment to others and her articulate and brilliant voice have opened the door for people to understand and embrace an illness that is common to so many families and not one to be hidden away in fear and embarrassment.

Although our story is now public and there are a few nights when I lie awake wondering if it was the right thing to do, I am ready to take the next step. Ultimately, my family is okay. More than okay. We have not turned away from one hard conversation, from one honest yet painful discussion, from one heartbreaking episode of an illness called "bipolar disorder." Yet it doesn't define us. It has challenged us and, in so many ways, enriched our lives. We have not turned away from loving each other.

linea It has been five years from my first episode with bipolar and two years since its most recent chapters. As I think about how to sum up all that I experienced, learned, and felt, I wonder how to end something that never really ends. How do you end a memoir? How do you sum up this illness in one book? I don't know if I can ever fully express the difficulty—hours upon hours, years upon years trying to figure out how to conclude something so large.

All I can hope to do now is try.

I think about all that has happened since I started this journey and where it has taken me. I would have never dreamed of being where I am today, pursuing this career of a mental-health advocate. I would have never thought I could survive without a life fully immersed in music. But things change. And I am happy with the change. Music will always be my great love. My best friend. My secret. But my illness and, more accurately, my personality could not live a happy and healthy life with only music. At least not at the moment.

It is amazing where this world has taken me. Though I am not religious, it seems as though some strange forces are pulling me in directions I would have never gone. I can hardly grasp the fact that I have become a national public speaker and that people might actually know my name, not because of music but because of my work as a mental-health advocate.

I get teary at the thought that five years after I was hospitalized for suicidal ideation, feeling so alone and so embarrassed at my sickness, I am sitting at a table with Glenn Close and Rosalynn Carter discussing the importance of speaking out. Sitting with people I never thought would talk about something as terrible as what I went through, let alone talk about it publicly.

And I could never have expected the change my experience with this illness has made in my relationships. I could never have expected how close my family would become. How honest we all became. Five years ago, I would never have expected we would become so much closer and learn so much from one another. I would never have imagined that I could love again without the fear that I would ruin the relationship. I could never have expected that I would let someone get as close to me as Josh has. I never would have envisioned that my relationships with the two former romantic interests in my life would turn into lasting friendships and love.

All of this amazes me. I realize now that suicide is not

something selfish. It is not something you choose. It comes at you, a force of its own that you may be able to ward off, but that can take hold of you, stealing your power to fight it off. It is so strong that you have to fight with your entire self to keep it at bay. It is something that many cannot fight when their illness takes control. Suicide is a symptom of illnesses that may be preventable with treatment. My relationship with bipolar has evolved. When I was first diagnosed, I was fighting. I didn't want it. I wouldn't admit to myself that it was something bigger than me, something that was part of me. I couldn't understand the word "acceptance." Once I did, I let the illness define me. I was nothing but the illness. It took control of my life and I didn't think there was any semblance of a "me" left. Bipolar was all I knew.

And then I realized that I was not my bipolar. I realized the power of words. I realized that by saying "I *have* bipolar" instead of "I *am* bipolar," I was myself with an illness, not myself defined by my illness. My illness is part of me, it is something that affects my life, but it is something, not all. It is not my life; my life is merely affected by it. It does not define me if I don't let it.

The last thing I have learned is complete honesty. Honesty with my family and myself. Honesty with the public. When I started speaking out publicly, I thought I was supposed to be the poster child of wellness. I thought that if I told people that I still had bad times, they would think there is no hope. I thought they would think all was lost. But perfection is not part of life. Things are never perfectly stable. That is the nature of the illness. It is cyclical. It changes from day to day, month to month, year to year. I have learned that honesty helps more people because they know that even if someone is still having "dips," he or she can come out of it. It is possible to recover and find stability.

With honesty it is important to admit that I am in a dip right now. I am once again struggling, somewhere near the depths of anorexia, anxiety, and depression. I am in a dip bigger than some of my recent ones. And I think it is important to share, in this story without an ending, that I do still struggle, but it is bearable and manageable. I struggle sometimes, though not often.

My episodes are different now; they are shorter, not as deep. These feel completely different if I make myself step away from the posttraumatic fears of "it" coming back. "It" has never come back. I have not been suicidal again. I have not been hospitalized again. I have not been full-on manic again. And aside from a short relationship with anorexia, I have not been self-destructive again. But I think it is important for people, me especially, to realize that this is something that will not go away. It can be treated and managed, but it is part of me. Something that I wouldn't want to live without.

My levels of acceptance come and go. I still get angry and fight and kick and throw temper tantrums over the fact that I will have to go through these ups and downs from time to time. I still get sad about the fact that any of it happened in the first place. But I know that it has taken me to places I had never expected. It has taught me things I never imagined I would learn.

It is important to be honest with yourself and your life. It is important to share your truth so that we can all learn from one another. It is important for those newly diagnosed nineteen-year-olds to know they are not alone. It is important for those undiagnosed fifty-year-olds to hear that others share similar symptoms and that a diagnosis can lead to stability. It is important for our youth to know what this illness is so that they can create a world free of stigma. A world where people can share their feelings and worries. Where an illness of the brain is as important as an illness of the body. We must share our truths.

acknowledgments

To all of our amazing family, for supporting us and pulling us forward.

To Dad and dear husband, Curt, you are our rock. Thank you for keeping our family safe and always supporting our dreams.

To Jordan, you can bring a smile on the worst of days.

To Josh, for loving Linea as she is, even when she was afraid to love again.

To Lois, Jerry, and Calla, for taking this journey with us.

To our incredible friends, who were brave enough and strong enough to be there in the worst of times, and special gratitude for those who allowed us to share their stories.

To Charlie, for loving Linea so deeply and always making her feel safe.

To Jean, for letting Linea expose her deepest anger, confusion, and insecurities and for always loving her.

To Eric, for always supporting Jean when Linea made life difficult and for trying so hard to support Linea when she pushed away.

To Jamie, for standing strong through the storm and

always showing Linea she had a hand to hold when she was so far away.

To Charlie "One," for always bringing joy to Linea.

To Renee, for teaching Linea she could be a writer and that she always had a voice.

To our amazing agent, Stacey Glick, who told us to follow our passion no matter the results. We wouldn't be where we are without you. Thank you for pushing us for what seemed like forever to finish the perfect proposal. Thank you for selling it overnight once it was!

To our wonderful editor, Nichole Argyres, for helping us shape our story into *Perfect Chaos*, while never losing the heart part. Thank you for allowing us to change things at the last minute and helping us make the hard decisions. Thank you for the "around-the-world" and midnight phone calls. Thank you for understanding our story so intimately.

To Laura Chasen at St. Martin's Press, for the support and constant attention she provided as she patiently helped us navigate the world of publishing.

To Rachel Ekstrom and Tanya Farrell, our publicists, for believing in us and sharing our story with a wider audience.

To Jennifer McCord, for being our constant guide and starting this great process moving forward. To Sheryl Stebbins, who did a very first read, giving us confidence with her wise and experienced words.